MY
MILLION-DOLLAR
DONKEY

The Price I Paid for

Wanting to Live Simply

MY
MILLION-DOLLAR
DONKEY

The Price I Paid for

Wanting to Live Simply

GINNY EAST

HEARTWOOD PRESS

HEARTWOOD PRESS
17507 Waterline Road
Bradenton FL 34212
www.HeartwoodRetreatCenter.com

ISBN-13: 978-0-9971460-0-4
LCCN: 2016903705

Distributed by Itasca Books

Cover Design by Biz Cook
Typeset by C. Tramell

Printed in the United States of America

To Kathy—my student, my teacher, my friend.

A portion of the proceeds from this book will be donated to the World Literacy Foundation. http://worldliteracyfoundation.org.

Humble thanks to my husband, David Shaddock, whose love and support has inspired me to bring this manuscript out from hidden under my bed to a place where it may find an audience. No one has, or probably ever will, read this book as many times or with as much sincere attention to both the content and the deeper themes within. His honest feedback and diligent line editing demonstrate not just his devotion to this project, but his devotion to me. I am indeed lucky, lucky, lucky.

CONTENTS

"Most of the luxuries, and many of the so-called comforts of life, are not only not indispensable, but positive hindrances to the elevation of mankind. Cultivate poverty like a garden herb, like sage. Do not trouble yourself much to get new things, whether clothes or friends. Turn the old; return to them. Things do not change; we change."

—Henry David Thoreau

NO SHADOW

When some people go through a midlife crisis, they buy themselves a Porsche. Me? I bought a donkey. That probably says something about my personality, but I'd be afraid to find out exactly what. In some ways, buying a donkey was the best thing I've ever done in my life. In other ways, not so much. I suppose a girl should expect a touch of disillusionment if she's foolish enough to choose an ass as her life mascot.

Perhaps I should point out that I didn't buy a donkey because I lived in a remote Mexican village where four-legged animals are the normal mode of transportation. I didn't go the donkey route because I couldn't afford a Porsche, either. Actually, I had just deposited a million dollars into my bank account. I didn't win the lottery or rob a bank, and I did not pass GO 5000 times in a Monopoly game. My knee-jerk reaction to the stress and inconvenience of a busy life was to give up, cash in, and start over. Starting over isn't all that uncommon if you believe all the articles and books published on the subject of life reinvention. Our boomer generation is famous for creating a world of disposable products. No wonder we consider our very lifestyles disposable when they aren't working just so.

Now you're probably thinking, *so you cashed in your life, got a million dollars, and went out and bought a donkey? Get real.*

Getting real was exactly what my husband and I had in mind. For years, we worked at building a local dance school business, knowing our choice to make a living in the arts meant we'd always live a humble sort of existence, the kind of life where bouncing a check wasn't all that unfamiliar a mortification. We were the sort of people who hemmed and hawed over whether or not we could afford a car with a sunroof, and we always ended up skipping that small luxury. We drove around with a shadow over our heads, and I mean that both literally and figuratively.

Then, one day, exhausted by how much upkeep our modest lifestyle took, we sat down and figured out just what we would have to work with if we cashed in our life and started over. Thanks to America's real estate bubble and years of paying a mortgage on the two buildings that housed our little dance school business, our real estate net worth alone came to somewhere in the neighborhood of two million dollars.

Like most people who clip coupons, we had a lot of experience playing the "If I had a million dollars" game.

I'd see an expensive designer gown hanging in a boutique with a thousand dollar price tag and I'd comment, "If I had a million dollars, I'd sure buy that dress."

My kids would whine, "All my friends have a [*fill in the blank*]." And I'd quip, "Well, if I had a million dollars, you'd have one, too."

Standing in line once at AAA for discount tickets to Disney, my husband Mark once stared at a brochure for a trip to Paris and said, "If I had a million dollars, I'd take you there." And an hour later, sitting at a red light, we both looked at a Porsche pulled up alongside our sensible Dodge Caravan. "If we had a million dollars, I'd buy one of those in blue." I said.

"Red would be better," Mark corrected.

Buying a donkey just never made an appearance in our "if I had a million" fantasies—unless you count a very brief encounter I had once on the way to our annual family vacation. Every fall we tried to slip away to the Georgia Mountains to observe the colorful foliage and feel the crisp air of autumn. One year, we stopped at a quaint roadside stand to purchase boiled peanuts from a place oozing country charm. A donkey stood at the fence.

My kids couldn't resist pausing to look at the beast. I had no clue whether or not donkeys are biters. Luckily, the animal stood docilely by.

"Isn't he the cutest thing?" Neva, my youngest daughter, said.

The donkey's soulful brown eyes looked at me through long lashes fringing eyes that welled with understanding and compassion. I know a donkey is an ass, a synonym for foolish and stubborn behavior, but 'cute' was not the word I'd use to describe him. As far as I was concerned, the answers to all the world's problems rested in his calm gaze.

I urged the kids to go back to the car, reminding them that boiled peanuts and a bag of homemade peanut brittle were all we had stopped for, but first, I reached out to scratch the animal behind his ears. "We have to go," I said, fighting some unexplained instinct telling me to stay awhile.

The kids ran back to the car, but I stood a moment longer staring at the beast with a nagging sense of longing.

"See ya later," I said.

The animal winked. I *swear* he did. And as I turned away, he brayed. The echo of that thunderous call resonated inside me long after we drove on. The vibration from his call is with me still.

In retrospect, coming face to face with that gentle, unassuming animal was probably the catalytic moment that sparked the paradigm shift in my worldview.

At nightfall, we checked in to a rustic little cabin in the woods for the weekend. I unpacked my laptop and a pile of dance industry catalogues, thinking that while the kids played in the creek by the cabin, I might catch up on some costume ordering. My husband unpacked his briefcase and set up an impromptu office on the kitchen table to call in payroll the next morning. This, you see, was our version of taking a few days off. We never stopped working, really; just made a stab at changing the scenery now and again so we could *pretend* we were taking time off.

As dancers and artists, we loved our work, but that didn't mean we didn't wrestle with secret wishes to simply walk off into the shadows, leaving the glittering, sequined world behind. We longed for a life with less stress, less financial struggle, and mostly, a life with less foolish drama, the sort of ridiculous behavior revealed on the hit show "Dance Moms," which was reality TV that proved a little too real for us.

A vacation, no matter how small, seemed to stoke our quiet desperation, awakening that small measure of dissatisfaction that is universal and yet so many of us feel is uniquely ours. The crunch of fall leaves under our feet and the numbness of our chilled noses made us feel a longing for more of the same, but just as the feeling of peace settled around the corners of our hearts and minds, we had to return home. We left the quaint cabin craving more. More mountains. More time for the family. More freedom. More.

A few years later when we received our first noteworthy tax return check ever, we visited the mountains again and put a down payment on a dilapidated old cabin in the woods, hoping the sacrifice we made each month to make the payment might 'guilt' us into taking time off for family. The tumbledown shack was quaint and had a two story bunkhouse off to the side that we imagined, if we added plumbing, would give us room for hobbies or more expansive living.

Not many city suckers (oops, I mean slickers) would see potential in a cabin with no insulation. The plumbing in the cabin itself was shot and the roof was caving in, but the little fixer-upper had a lovely mountain view. We adored the place for the potential we saw—not just for the home, but for us.

On the day we closed that cabin purchase, we took a walk through the town's historic village. Feelings of an impending adventure made us giddy with good humor. In the same way a catchy song gets stuck in your head, we couldn't stop the chorus and verse of imagining what an alternate life might be like, now that we owned property plopped right in the middle of a world we associated to peace and right living.

That conversation urged us to consider options. With little trust that our frustrating, hard working life would be worth anything other than a kick in the pants to someone else, we visited a business broker just to verify what we believed would be the case: that no one would want to embrace our misery, and they certainly wouldn't pay for our life of drudgery. Shockingly, the broker informed us that our little family dance school business was worth more to a potential buyer than the sum of all we'd earned in the past eight years.

We could barely imagine an identity unconnected to dance, but how could we not be curious about what lay beneath our leotards if we really did have a shot at reinventing our world?

Bravely, we threw the gauntlet at fate's feet and put our specialized business up for sale at the price recommended by the broker (*a million dollars!*), and proceeded with what could only be described as tongue-in-cheek optimism. Five days later we were called into the broker's office to meet a nice couple I'll call the Smiths.

"Do you believe good business people without a dance background can run your school successfully?" Mr. Smith asked.

Mark glanced at the floor thoughtfully. We had discussed this very thing and both agreed that the school might prosper best with experienced management at the helm. "My wife and I spend far too much time and energy on the creative end, and don't always attend to the business side as carefully as a school that has grown to this size requires," Mark said. "The school might even do better without us putting artistic considerations above practical business decisions. But if a buyer really didn't know anything about dance, they would have to allow us to stay involved for a while."

"We were thinking the same thing." Mr. Smith exchanged a knowing look with his wife, turned to face us, and then said the three little words that dropped freedom at our feet like a pigeon shot from the sky.

"We'll take it."

Mark and I both sat forward in our seats.

"Pardon me?" I said.

"We'll take it."

No offer/counter offer bargaining period to heighten the drama of the moment? No demand of time served on our part to help in the transition?

Mark swallowed and forced his eyebrows down from the top of his forehead, and gravely shook Mr. Smith's hand. "You've got yourself a deal."

Naturally, everyone's eyes turned to me, and of course, I reacted as any sophisticated CEO and founder of a small business would. After all, I had 20 years of entrepreneurial experience and a BA in business management backing up my professional demeanor. My chin quivered, my nose started to run, and I burst into tears. I folded over like a soft-shelled taco, buried my wet face in my hands, and bawled.

"You do want to sell the school, don't you?" the broker whispered.

I sat up, trying to recover some small semblance of dignity. "Of course, but for the record, I love my school."

A truer statement couldn't be made, but for some reason that donkey's lovely bray was still resounding through my spirit long after he called out to me. I was ready to heed that call, so an hour later we were drawing up contracts and I was trying to wrap my brain about a new reality—the business that demanded almost all of our waking thought and effort for the past eighteen years would now belong to someone else.

We were going to have to drop the news to the kids. I made a big Sunday breakfast, careful to include everyone's favorites: pigs in blankets, breakfast casserole, pancakes, homemade cinnamon rolls, and fruit salad. I set the table on our cedar porch, decorated to look like a cabin in Georgia (a testament to our long-time longing for a cabin of our own), and summoned the troops.

My kids had no clue this day would be different from any other. I was always trying to squeeze as much togetherness into the corners of our life as possible, and sitting down to break bread together seemed to me a path to deeper connections. My family often woke on a Sunday to grandiose meals made by a mother who dragged herself out of bed hours before anyone else to create a picture perfect family morning.

After eating, laughing, and sharing news of friends and school, we sat down for the proposed family meeting. Only two of our children were still living at home and I felt the weight of the empty seat where my oldest daughter would have been sitting had she not left for college a few months prior. Mark and I began with small talk, slowly merging into the subject of how tired we were and how guilty we felt about working so much. We talked about our goals as a family and how we wished we had time and energy to devote to life beyond dance.

"We put the studio up for sale, thinking a semi-retirement would provide a chance for us to spend more time with family. We never dreamed someone would come along wanting to buy it so soon, but they did."

The kids stared blankly, as if they couldn't quite process what we were saying.

"The people who want the studio are willing to pay us a million bucks. Do you know how much money that is? We won't ever have to work again unless we want to. So . . . we are moving to Georgia. We have a chance to do whatever we want with our lives. It's gonna be amazing!"

We expected the kids to be surprised, awestruck at the thought of our having money, maybe a bit disappointed at the thought of leaving friends behind, but at the same time, delighted to embrace a life with full-time parents. But rather than voicing a question, our thirteen year old son's face screwed up and his eyes turned bloodshot red.

"You've destroyed my life!" he shouted. "I hate you." Then he ran to his room, sobbing.

Our daughter, Neva, reacted with her typical eight year old wisdom. "I hate the dance school anyway. But why do we have to move?"

"If we move to Georgia, you can have your own horse."

"I'd rather have a bunny," she said, hopping off the couch and coming over to curl into my lap. She was wearing one of my nighties, the straps tied up around her neck to keep her tiny frame primly covered. She held the sides up delicately and the satin trailed to the ground, floating behind her like a bride's train. I noticed a dash of flour on the hem, remnants of the mess she made helping me cut out the biscuits an hour prior. We could cook together every day if we did indeed make this life shift.

"Kent is upset," she said.

"He'll be OK after he gets over the shock." I tried to sound confident, but the first flicker of seller's remorse had sparked in my gut. My parents had mentioned more than once that when we were older we'd look back and see these busy, stressed times as the best years of our lives. Selling a business at the height of success was madness in my dad's opinion, and he had no compunction against telling us so. *What if Dad's right?* I now wondered.

Later, we called our eldest, Denver, to give her the news. She was a freshman at the University of Central Florida, so we didn't anticipate much of a reaction other than perhaps amazement that the parents who always seemed stressed about money would suddenly become financially well off. When we dropped the news, the line seemed to go dead.

"You're going to move to Georgia?" she eventually said. "And leave me here in Orlando? That means I won't be able to come home on weekends."

"You can't really care that we are selling the studio now that you've graduated and left. You never come home on weekends anyway. And you can still visit as much as you want, but you'll be coming to Georgia, which will feel like a wonderful vacation. "

"That studio was my life! Even if I don't live at home, I want to know I can visit. Kent must be devastated. Everyone must be devastated."

"Everyone will get over it," Mark said. "Um… You might try to be happy for us. This is a dream come true for your mother and me."

"Since when? Mom, do *you* really want to do this?"

"It was her idea," Mark said, rolling his eyes as if Denver's question was silly.

My gaze shifted to the floor. True, I was ready for change, but perhaps we should consider taking occasional vacations rather than undertake a huge life overhaul. The idea of setting off on an adventure with the family was beyond exciting in theory, but actually walking away from our livelihood while we still had kids to raise and educate was scary as hell.

"I love the studio, as you know, but I've always wanted to be a mom more than a dancer or a business owner. Working as much as I do has been an unfortunate necessity, something I did because I had to make money to help care for the family. The idea that I can lay down the burden is pretty amazing. And I have to admit, I'd appreciate more time for writing. Yesterday I was accepted to one of the low residency MFA programs I applied to, as if everything happening is meant to be. So yes, honey, I really want to do this."

She hung up, but not before making a few tongue-in-cheek comments that left me feeling judged and somewhat guilty for daring to follow my own aspirations rather than to continue a life of servitude and sacrifice for my children. *Am I making this choice for me, or for them?* I started to wonder. *Just what are we running to, or away from, really?*

As respected business owners, we were icons in the community and treated as local heroes. My children enjoyed a small level of notoriety themselves as members of the renowned dance family. Mark and I had worked with over six thousand families over the years. True, we were busy parents due to the demands of running a business, but my kids weren't latchkey kids nor did they spend after school hours in childcare with strangers. I took them to school each day, picked them up, and stopped for a snack as we headed back to the studio.

Each season I planned my teaching schedule around my children's interests. No matter how busy I was, I carved out the time to be a Girl Scout leader or classroom helper. I did everyone's laundry and the dishes so no one other than me would feel burdened with mundane chores. I cleaned their rooms and left little gifts of a favored magazine or treat on their pillows. I took the kids to music lessons, camps, and parties, and liberally hired substitute teachers anytime my children had an open house or school event. And when I couldn't be there, parents of students would take my kids under their wing, offering rides, snacks, gifts, and praise. If it takes a village to raise a child, I certainly had a dance village to help me do the job. My children had it pretty good.

In fact, the more I thought about our life, I could see our kids probably spent more quality time with their parents than most every other kid we knew, the ones who had full time mothers at home and a father who went to work in an office each day. My kids didn't have a dad who spent Sundays golfing, or a Mom who spent each evening grading papers or working long shifts as a nurse or real estate agent. Instead they had parents who were always nearby and accessible; parents who were deeply involved in their lives. We even had great relationships with their friends since we taught them all dance too.

Mark and I took our children to Disney, bought tickets to concerts or shows, organized family art projects for fun, and spent numerous days at the mall buying clothes or school supplies. We made a huge deal out of holidays with the planning, cooking, decorating, and entertaining a significant family affair garnished with laughter and poignant family traditions. We were connected to extended family too, spending time with both sets of grandparents. Mark's sister was a significant presence in daily activities. She worked for us by day, and spent weekends joining us at movies or just hanging out at home. I never made plans for the family that didn't include her, always paying the cost of the ticket or the experience for her so nothing would stand in the way of her joining us.

Life had been satisfactory for everyone *except* Mark and me. Our customers adored us and appreciated the quality of our school. Our employees enjoyed good, steady jobs doing the work they enjoyed. Our kids felt safe and loved and their needs were provided for. Our families were involved in our lives. We had pre-paid college plans, a car for each member of the family who drove, and we made enough to take humble vacations now and again.

The problem was, as parents and owners, we were burned out, tired, and our marriage was stressed to the point of breaking. Selfishly, we wanted to change things to put our dreams and wishes at the forefront of choices, because deep down, we believed everyone's life was easier than ours. Everyone's. And we were envious.

"Maybe what we need to do is to realign our priorities, not change our lives completely," I said, feeling guilty about everyone's hysterical disappointment regarding our decision.

"Realigning my priorities is why I'm ready for a new life," Mark said.

"We could stop micro-managing and travel as we always said we someday would. Maybe we should buy a different house, a bigger one; with a workshop so you can make art in your free time. We can buy a boat and spend some weekends involved in recreation that isn't dance related. God, I'd love that. I'll get my master's degree and write something noteworthy. You can go to school to study interior design. You've always said you wanted to have a career in design."

I was straying from our initial enthusiasm and he wasn't pleased, but I kept on. "I'm thinking we may be premature to retire while we still have a family to raise. Not like we can run off to Europe or live in the wilderness and do whatever we want while we still have kids who must attend school. "

"The kids deserve a better life and they won't get one here," Mark said. "I hate Florida. It's too hot and flat and there's nothing here but malls and restaurants. Mostly, I hate the studio. I hate the people. I hate the dance profession." Mark said. "And my body can't take this work anymore. You know how bad my hips are."

Mark had been diagnosed with arthritis and his hips had caused him discomfort for years. Despite my frequent suggestions that he get hip replacements so we could both live a full and more active life, he refused. He didn't believe in formal medicine, or so he said, and frankly, he wasn't all that bothered that his physical limitations were the death knell to my yearning for active recreation.

"If nothing else, you have to be proud of all we've accomplished over the years. We've created a fantastic school. We've trained great dancers and built an amazing facility. We've changed young people's lives and contributed a great deal to our community."

He pulled away from me, the distance a reminder that if I didn't give him what he wanted, I'd be treated to a painful dose of alienation, Mark's usual weapon of choice. "Dance was never my thing the way it has been yours. I just went along for the ride, because I wanted to marry you."

In the beginning, Mark had been obsessed with dance, so his comment now felt like nothing but an excuse to get what he wanted. I knew he wasn't happy. Mark was the kind of man who would quickly propose romantic and exciting ideas, regardless of the fact that they were totally impractical for a couple with kids and loans nailing their feet to the floor. I took on the role of the responsible one, always working ceaselessly hard - not because I was ambitious, but to alleviate his need to shoulder the full burden of raising a family. From the beginning, I always wanted to give him everything he ever wanted; I just wasn't in a position to do so, and being made to feel guilty for his lot in life now stung.

What Mark had wanted all along was freedom from work and responsibilities. And who could blame him? After years of focusing on his happiness, my children's needs, and the burden of keeping life all together to protect my parents' investment in our business, I was more than ready to enjoy some freedom and self-indulgence myself.

The problem was everything just seemed to be happening so fast and my practical side couldn't resist mulling over "what if."

Mark and I had a history of taking risks that paid off. But we also had a history of poor financial management which unraveled our success more often than not. We were great at making excuses and justifications to explain our folly, and logic led me to believe we might be doing that again. We liked telling ourselves that our innovation and talent had manifested our financial stability, but we both knew deep down that talent was only half the equation.

Considering all this, I felt honor bound to voice a few important considerations. "What if we lose it all? I've never done anything but teach dance, and I'm so tired, Mark. I just can't start over and do all this again at my age. I'd love freedom and retirement as much as anyone. But if I'm ever going to be expected to work to support the family again, we have to keep this school."

Mark smiled in his endearing way. "Do you know how much money we will have when we sell the business and the buildings, too?

Three million dollars. It's impossible even for *me* to lose *that* much money. And even if I did, I would take care of you. For the last 15 years you've been the driving force of our finances and our life. You started working years before I ever got my first job. I promise I'll take care of you and the kids whatever happens."

All my life I had wondered how those women married to men who took responsibility for their wife and kids felt. The promise that Mark would assume that role was exactly what I needed to feel safe, loved, and cared for in a legitimate way. But though he was voicing the words I longed to hear, I had some doubts.

"I'm not the only one of us who has only taught dance for a living. How would you take care of us if we ever needed income?"

"How hard could paying for the basics be? We'll have a house paid off. No debt. Worst case scenario is I'll have to earn enough for our food. I could do that as a window washer. Trust me. We'll be fine."

He looked so earnest. So hopeful. So filled with conviction.

"I'm deathly tired of your dad having a say in how we live." He added. "He treats me as if I'm that same kid who drove us off the financial cliff years ago. I need and deserve to have control of my own life, my own decisions, my own family, and my own money. I'm not the young kid I was when we first got married. I've learned so much by working with your father all these years."

Mark was 39 years old. Didn't every man deserve independence by that grown-up age? My handsome, charismatic husband was talented, unhappy, and begging me to let him off the leash. I prided myself on being a woman who loved and supported her husband in every way. For years I had devoted the lion's share of our expendable resources to his ever-evolving interests. Now, we could invest in his dreams, however romanticized they might be, without the financial fallout being my problem to solve.

"Okay. Let's move to Georgia," I said.

Putting voice to the words felt empowering—a validation that all the work and frustration and sacrifice we'd made for years had been part of a grander scheme, bringing us to this opportunity, this moment, this chance to live a free, creative life.

The next day the Smiths notified us that they wanted to waive the due diligence period. They didn't want us to participate in any transitional period and would prefer if we would leave immediately. We signed the papers and, overnight, we had a million dollars in the bank and total freedom.

What did we do? Well, I didn't rush out and buy expensive clothes. My husband didn't zip out to buy us tickets for a whirlwind Paris vacation, and we certainly didn't purchase a red or blue Porsche. Mark left me in Florida to pack up the house and handle our affairs while he headed off to Georgia to begin remodeling our little vacation cabin so we'd have a place to live in. His giddy delight spilled from him by way of animated speech, bright smile, and happy eyes.

I was happy because he was happy.

Within the week, Mark spied a "For Sale by Owner" sign on 50 acres of beautiful, undeveloped land, primarily forest, with about eight acres of pastureland. Instantly, that surreal million dollars parked in our bank account caused an itch in his pocket you could liken to poison oak on his butt. He wanted that property. Bad.

He drove all night on an adrenaline high to get back to Florida. "You're going to flip when I tell you what I've found." He sat on the bed to share his new, brilliant life plan which involved our buying this huge tract of land with most of our cash on hand. He would build a cabin each year for us to sell. When he was done building to his heart's content, we could sell the final home (ours), and we would have made so much money we could move to Italy or someplace equally exotic for our next adventure. We'd be rich(er), thanks to him.

"Fifty acres?" I asked in disbelief. "We agreed we wanted a simple cabin on a mountainside, like the ones we've been renting for years. We said we were going to live a smaller life, not a larger one. You gripe every week about mowing the half acre of suburban lawn we have title to now. What will we do with fifty acres? And why are you suddenly talking about a construction business? I thought we were going to spend some time relaxing and enjoying time with the family. You don't know anything about the construction business."

"We will still live a simple life, only now we'll be putting that little cabin on 50 acres," he said. "No more nosy neighbors, no more customers infringing on our private life. No more *people*. Just us."

"You want us to become hermits?"

"I'll build us a simple log cabin out of the very trees gracing the property," he said, his eyes as bright as a child on Christmas morning. "Thoreau did it."

Seventeen years of marriage can make a man a master of pushing a woman's "romantic ideal" button. He well knew I was enthralled with writers, primarily the transcendentalists, and my deepest dream was to emulate them.

"We can stay in our vacation cabin in the interim and have an adventure. I've been promising you a trip for our twentieth wedding anniversary. If you let me do this, I'll take you anywhere in the world you want to go. Anywhere."

The promise that the two of us would take the romantic trip that I'd been pining for forever, and live like my hero Thoreau, meant I certainly wasn't going to refuse him anything he wanted in the bargain. Residing in a rural area would be a huge shift for people like us, but living where the closest Starbucks was over an hour away and a trip to the mall practically demands you pack an overnight bag was bound to realign our focus to the things that matter most.

So we made the decision. The Hendrys would leave consumerism and the American middle class obsession with accumulating wealth behind. We would walk away from security and abundance in the spirit of realigned values. We had no clue what in God's name we'd do to support ourselves if this adventure proved to be folly, but despite our reservations, we felt a pull to that 50 acres and the idea that our family story could unfold in a new way. If our life had been a piece of origami, the time had come to create a new animal from the same flimsy piece of paper.

So, we started spending the cash that represented our lifetime of hard work and sacrifice, fueled by the idea that we weren't spending our nest egg irresponsibly—just investing in a different sort of future.

Mark absolutely loved remodeling, decorating, and interior design in any form, and for the first time ever, he had money to burn at Home Depot and Lowe's. He began buying tools, wood, and fixtures.

Me? Still vibrating from the echo of that one encounter long ago with a beast of nature that somehow tapped into my deepest longings, I embraced the concept of country living and as soon as I had the chance, I bought a donkey.

The donkey was two hundred and fifty dollars. A new halter to make him look dapper was eleven. The land we purchased to house my midlife crisis pet and to appease Mark's latest fascination for building cost half a million, leaving us with enough cash to build a reasonable cabin home and take a sabbatical from a traditional job long enough to reinvent our lives. Meanwhile, we still owned the buildings that housed our business, and when the new owners of our school eventually bought them, we could sock the cash away to provide income for life.

With such ample resources and a common agenda to embrace the simple life, what could go wrong?

"This spending of the best part of one's life earning money in order to enjoy a questionable liberty during the least valuable part of it reminds me of the Englishman who went to India to make a fortune first, in order that he might return to England and live the life of a poet. He should have gone up garret at once."

—*Henry David Thoreau*

ONE TWO-STEP FORWARD

The Smiths didn't simply forego our offer to help them learn about the dance business; they ostracized us and made us feel unwelcome to give advice or in any way be involved with the transition. Customers called us to complain, begging us to intervene, furious that we had sold the school to people who were now making drastic, unnecessary changes. Our staff turned on us too as if we'd selfishly and purposefully left them in inept hands. We made numerous attempts to help, but our words and actions were twisted to make us out the enemy. On the day we were physically thrown out of the building by our former, dearest employee, we had no choice but to accept that we were powerless to affect what was happening.

I was hurt by the way people I once cared deeply about were now behaving. Worse, I'd spent so much of the last twenty years trying to please my staff and customers that it was almost impossible to let go of the feeling that I was responsible for everyone's satisfaction and welfare still. In an attempt to make our former friends and students see things with more perspective, I had heart to hearts, blogged, and even drove back to Florida a few times to intervene when trouble stirred. But as every well-intentioned action was enthusiastically misinterpreted, I eventually had to admit defeat.

I felt like a dog with her tail between her legs and no understanding of why she had been beaten. Everything I once loved and felt reverence for seemed superficial now. I grieved over lost relationships and soiled memories.

Mark's attitude was, if twenty years of teaching, caring, and sacrificing for students hadn't earned us even the dignity of respect, the hell with them all. Overnight, my ballerina husband turned into a tree hugger, and I'm not talking about the kind saving the world one tree at a time. He caressed the trees as if they were wooden mistresses, basking in the feel and smell of virgin oak or poplar. Mark was hugging trees to determine their girth, staring at them as if he was imagining their trunks supporting a roof or stairway. My husband wanted to build a new life, and he decided the place to start was in building a home. The fact that he'd never built anything before didn't seem a big obstacle. If a pioneer could forge a homestead without even the use of power tools, certainly a dancing boy with a million in cash at his disposal could figure things out.

I suggested we hire a construction company to slap up a quick, affordable home on our big tract of land, thinking that would allow us the time and money to take that promised trip to Paris. I wanted us to immediately start making up for years of servitude to everyone and everything except each other. Mark, unfortunately, had other plans. He wanted to be in control of everything connected to our new home, from designing the floor plan to sanding down the individual logs that would become the foundation for the earthy decor. Building a dream house was a millionaire's right, in his opinion, and since we'd never been in a financial position to create a home that reflected our tastes and ideals before, he was obsessed with his ability to do so now.

"But we agreed we'd take a trip to celebrate our good fortune and focus on our love," I whined.

I was still reeling from the sting of our old acquaintances' disrespect. What better medicine for hurt than to run away to some far-off place with my husband so I could curl into his arms for warmth, self-worth, and comfort? I wanted to travel not so much because we needed a vacation, but because I wanted to be exposed to new sights, sounds, textures, and experiences. I had a romantic notion that venturing hand in hand into the unknown with the love of my life would set us on a path where we approached each day as a banquet of experiences to be savored. I was starving for that kind of existence and believed our moving was a part of a new spiritual journey we were ready to take.

"We *will* travel. Later. I'm going to build a home for far less than what the local construction company wants to charge us, which means after I'm done, we'll have extra money for travel," Mark said, too busy leafing through building magazines to look me in the eye with understanding, love, or any other fond emotion. His obsession with leaping into his solitary desires now that he had money to burn was more than a little disappointing to me, because I was attached to this ideal of the two of us celebrating together.

I attempted to write my way out of my funk by composing a book about the emotional trauma a dancer faced when retiring, using it as my MFA thesis. I begged Mark to read the manuscript to give me feedback. Mostly, I think I wanted him to recognize my grief and show interest in my new art and recognize that I needed a friend – no, a lover, at this time of emotional turmoil.

"I hate that you're writing this," he told me, putting the work aside after half-heartedly reading a few chapters. "Move on. I am."

Nothing I said or did could get Mark to focus in any direction other than towards his building aspirations. Eventually it became obvious that my new main squeeze (the donkey) and I would just have to create our own entertainment until my raw wounds started to scab over a bit.

So I hunkered down with books to investigate just what kind of adventure a gal could have alone on a big chunk of undeveloped land. I subscribed to *Mother Earth News, Hobby Farms,* and *Grit Magazine*. I devoured country lifestyle memoirs and how-to books on homesteading. I even re-read *Walden*.

Meanwhile, I blogged. I journaled, ruminated, and cried. I wrote and wrote, telling myself the avalanche of words was necessary as part of my MFA studies when, in reality, I wrote because that was my process to hold it all together. I wrote my way into viewing my new life as happy, fulfilling, and steeped in deeper connections. Life was good, on paper if nowhere else.

Each day we drove from the decrepit vacation cabin where we were temporarily camped out to our beautiful fifty acres to visualize our future. Looking at 50 untamed acres of trees and woodland debris was daunting with spring heads and a creek swallowed by underbrush. Where should we begin? Everything takes time. And money. We thought we had a windfall to work with, but our stash quickly dwindled on items we didn't anticipate, such as several tons of lime for the pasture and gravel for half a mile of driveway. When we cleared a site for the house, we hit a mountainside of solid rock that had to be dynamited away. So, too, did we chip away at our recently flooded bank balance.

Mark hired some men to help him tear our cabin apart and prepare for remodeling. As we peeled back layers of the cabin, we found a multitude of shocking construction sins. The ceiling joists had been cut, thus the sagging roof. A second story had been added over the living room, but the floor creaked awfully so we removed the carpet and discovered the floor supports were attached to drywall rather than studs. It was a scientific marvel that the entire place hadn't collapsed in on itself. There was dry rot and water damage everywhere, and to my children's ultimate fascination, a huge dead snake was found shriveled up under the stairway like a dread omen.

As warped paneling, old furniture, and broken stair rails turned to ash in the fire pit, the ghost of the former cabin disappeared into the air in a puff of smoke and our old identities seemed to be hitching a ride.

One day, as Mark removed the bathroom toilet to lay new tile, the commode fell right through the rotting floor. One eyebrow raised, he watched the toilet bowl rolling down the mountainside.

"I could have been sitting on that!" he said.

Grumbling, he crawled underneath the house to inspect the damage and discovered a jack propping up the sagging foundation.

"What do you think will happen if I remove this?" he said, clearing the bushes aside to get a better look.

"I'll collect a big life insurance check," I said.

I watched him write *new extra jack to help hold up cabin* on his shopping list. "I was taught never to crawl under a car that was held up by a jack because it might be unsteady. Now I'm supposed to eat, sleep, and make merry with nothing but a jack keeping my entire home from rolling down the mountain?"

"People do it all the time around here," he insisted.

Apparently old timers in Georgia country towns had a do it yourself mentality. Unfortunately, they just didn't always have do it yourself capabilities. Farmers are not big fans of shows like *Extreme Makeover* and *Trading Spaces*. But Mark was, and he believed his love for interior design and reading lots and lots of home building magazines was all the educational foundation he needed to be a big time builder.

He began frantically running back and forth from the cabin to our land three times a day preparing for his next project before the old one was half finished. We hadn't adjusted to "country time" yet (picture a clock running in a vat of molasses) so taking on two projects at once didn't seem all that big a deal to either of us. The problem was the workers on country time didn't harbor our same sense of urgency. They showed up late, stayed a few hours, and then disappeared for days on end. When they returned, Mark would demand an explanation for why they left the job site.

"It's huntin' season, don't ya know? Can't expect a man to work while the deer is runnin.'"

"Got myself throwed in jail for fightin' and Larry here had to pawn my tools to get me out. Couldn't come to work with no tools, don't ya know, so I had to take a job balin' hay to make some cash to reclaim the tools. I'm here now. Wouldn't let you down, buddy."

But of course, they did let him down. Over and over again. Now, we had two expensive building projects going, and neither stayed on budget, nor did they take shape within our expected time frame.

"Could you at least call when you aren't going to show up?" Mark asked, sensing that pressuring these boys to be more responsible would only give them an excuse to walk off the job altogether.

"You want to sit around jabberin' all day, or you want me to fix this porch?"

"By all means, fix the porch."

Mark started talking to the boys in a southern drawl, leaning against the porch rail and casually joining in the talk about plantin' peas or shootin' possums in some desperate attempt to keep them on task. I, too, found myself using colorful country metaphors, revising my vocabulary so I fit in. We were treated to stories of mountain treks and wildlife encounters, each tale concluding with an insightful moral or memorable life lesson. Thanks to the easy conversation inspired by a country porch, we learned never to try to ride down the raging Ocoee River on a raft held up by bicycle tires, and never to try to outrun the sheriff at a roadblock, because dang if the town sheriff wasn't a stock car racer on weekends. We became privy to intimate details of the boys' lives, such as how old they were when they got a lickin' for stealin' some of their grandpa's moonshine, how old they were when they got a lickin' for aimin' at squirrels but accidently shot their aunt's cat instead, how old they were when they got a lickin' for talkin' back, for skipping school, for stealin' apples from a neighbors tree, or for failin' to milk the cow. In light of all the "got a lickin'" tales, it was a wonder these boys had any skin left on their hides at all.

The remodeling eventually progressed enough that we could move from our temporary camping quarters in the unfurnished, unheated bunkhouse to the cabin's upstairs bedrooms. We finally had a few luxuries, like a working toilet and a stove, yet I still worried that we were wasting the best years of our children's lives, making them live like squatters. We were in a position to buy, outright, a nice home and devote our time to family togetherness, but Mark considered that kind of thing a waste of resources, all of which he wanted to allocate to his new passion for building.

"We won't live like this forever. I'm gonna build us a dream house soon," Mark promised. "As soon as I find a builder I can trust."

"And then, we'll take a trip?"

"Of course,"

Mark kissed the top of my head and since that was the most intimate contact we'd shared in months, I all but swooned.

He sat on the bed and took off his work boots. They landed on the floor with a heavy, dull thump, a thick sound so unlike the dance shoes I used to watch him cast aside that I smiled.

"Can't we just pay a company to build us a house quickly, or hire the guys working here on the cabin to do it? Let's celebrate our good fortune. Let's take the kids on a trip overseas and broaden their understanding of the world."

"Are you kidding me? I can't leave now. I have to pay for everything twice as it is. These country builders make so many mistakes that if I don't watch these guys every minute they will ruin the entire project."

Since I didn't know anything about building and Mark seemed so confident, I couldn't argue. Just that week, the workers had installed the plumbing in the bunkhouse upside down. Oops. I was told I could now have a shower or a bath. Not both. Of course, they wouldn't mind fixing the plumbing, but the carpenter had finished off the wall, so repairing their mistake meant paying for demolition and re-plumbing and building another wall, since they didn't guarantee their work. And who had time for all that anyway after they dropped a hammer in the newly installed bathtub, causing not only an obvious mar of the surface, but a hairline crack that leaked water through the new ceiling to the floor below? With the best of intentions, they set about to repair the tub, but cut into the freshly installed air conditioning vents and severed several electrical wires in the process. We'd already paid to have the electricity rewired twice and several outlets still didn't work, and now, when I turned the water on, it came gushing out from the fuse box.

Continuing to pay for every job two and three times stung, knowing the general attitude was that "rich city folk" like us could afford whatever they charged. With every repair I felt the coveted trip I imagined as a launching pad for our new spiritual journey drift farther and farther away.

I started to question the intentions of the men working for us, too. Obviously, no matter how friendly we became on one level, we were outsiders to be taken advantage of on another. Were these men really this incompetent, or milking the job for every cent they could get?

"You told me you could do this remodel for thirty thousand dollars and we've already spent three times that. What happened?" I asked Mark one night as he was going over a bank statement on the computer. I tried looking over his shoulder to see where our finances stood, but he closed out the screen as if I was prying into his personal diary.

"This cabin became a way bigger project than I expected once I got into it. Trust me, we'll make our investment all back and more when we sell. Don't you like what I'm doing with the place?"

Who wouldn't appreciate the rustic charm of wood siding, extra fireplaces, and laurel walkways? I blindly accepted his explanation that a builder commonly spent three times what was budgeted for a project of this scale. As the work unfolded, Mark's artistic eye urged him to add even more special details like wooden beams and a glorious additional deck to display the long-range mountain views. His remodeling project now escalated to four times what we agreed to spend. I accepted the shocking number as a part of the learning curve for a man new to building. But I started to worry.

"Do we really need to add so much detail in a cheap vacation cabin that you say is made so poorly that it isn't worth keeping as a rental property?" I asked.

"I hate when you do that."

"Do what?"

"Question me. Obviously you don't trust my judgment."

"I just want to know where our money is going and what you plan to do next. You know me, I write a business plan for everything, and it seems to me our life would be more successful if we treated the financial end like a business and we followed the plan we made together."

Mark sighed. "You've held the reins of our life for years, and now it's my turn. Relax. Be a mom. And trust me to do my thing. I'm better at this than you realize. "

His dismissive air made me ashamed, as if my questions made me an unloving or unsupportive wife. I swallowed back a whole slew of concerns regarding impractical decisions and unnecessary risk on his part. One night Mark and I rented *The Money Pit*, a comedy about a couple who bought a dream home that ended up a daunting remodeling project which nearly destroyed their marriage. Sadly, the film felt like reality TV.

Fearing our funds would run out long before we had a place to live, I finally convinced Mark to visit an established firm known for building affordable homes on any lot you owned. He seemed interested at first, looking at tile samples and house plans, taking pleasure in the shopping process. An agent joined us and we spent three hours planning the design of a new cookie cutter country home, carefully choosing pretty kitchen counters and cabinets, light fixtures and roof tiles. Mark added tons of extras to the package, such as recessed lighting and extra footage in bedrooms. He upgraded materials and appliances, which of course ratcheted up the cost, but still the final product was right in line with what we agreed to spend on our new home. I was delighted until, at the final moment, Mark couldn't bring himself to sign the contract.

"I don't want any house built by some generic company."

"What difference does it make what kind of house we live in? We decided to move to Blue Ridge so you could do wood turning and I could write, and we both agreed that the first priority was to spend more time with family."

"You'll never get a house with decent closets if you don't let me build," Mark insisted.

Threatened by the close call of what he perceived as my almost robbing him of the fun of building his dream house, Mark redoubled his efforts to find a builder after that. A few days later he found Ronnie, a builder by trade and God-fearing preacher on the side. Ronnie epitomized the salt-of-the-earth country stereotype. He described himself as "country as cornbread," prefacing every conversation with, *"Now, I'm not claiming to know everything, 'cause I only have 'bout a sixth grade education, but it seems to me ..."* Then, he followed this disclaimer with some nugget of wisdom that always rang true and right.

Ronnie's corporation consisted of just himself and his two sons; not a big crew, but a diligent and trustworthy one. Three men building our home would take much longer than an established company, but Mark would serve as additional labor and project manager, so the house would eventually manifest. The men shook hands and the project began.

Mark began devoting 60 hours a week to his building project. My days were filled with driving the kids to school, going to the laundromat to wash clothes, and running errands to keep our makeshift life afloat. We were busy, stressed, estranged from each other physically once again, and too distracted to enjoy the beautiful mountain view just outside our door. All I could think of was that we had set off on a grand life journey, but darned if we didn't take ourselves along. If I had any hope of sustaining sanity during this life transition, I would have to find something more meaningful than laundry and country lifestyle magazines to focus on, and quickly.

"I have always been regretting that I was not as wise as the day I was born."
—Henry David Thoreau

THE ABC'S OF STARTING OVER

For years I dreamt of a life where work wasn't the central focus of my days, but doing nothing of consequence was not the vacation I imagined. I constantly had a feeling that I was supposed to be somewhere, doing something more important than washing clothes, cooking meals, or walking in the woods. I missed feeling necessary and productive. I missed working. I missed training dancers. I missed our former friends. I missed my husband being an interactive part of my life.

The very work you long to escape shapes your life in ways you never understand until your purpose is gone. Homemade fried chicken dinners served under the canopy of an elm tree are nice in a romantic Martha Stewart sort of way, but personal pleasure doesn't replace the sense of accomplishment gained from meaningful employment when your work affects the lives of others.

Needing to apply my energy to something positive and life affirming, I dug into writing and my MFA studies. If I didn't *have* to work, I could at least work *at* something. With my focus now on reading, writing, and the power of words, I stumbled upon an article about the ongoing problem of illiteracy in the Appalachian region. Inspired, I called the Georgia Literacy Commission and volunteered. Perhaps teaching a new reading student might help fill the emptiness created by the twelve hundred dance students we'd left behind. The effort would be my offering to the writing gods, which I felt would establish good karma and perhaps help me find success somehow.

The director of the program, Donna, called to welcome me aboard. She explained that learning to read is a daunting process, and as such, few illiterate individuals have the courage to step forward to tackle the task. Interestingly, a forty-year-old woman had come in just two days prior, so my timing was perfect.

Her name was Kathy, and her assessment test revealed she could recognize all of the letters in the alphabet and could sound out most of them, with the exception of a few vowels. The problem was she didn't recognize any full words—not even a simple "it," "me," or "cat." This information should have intimidated me, I suppose, but I was delighted. Kathy would be my very own Eliza Doolittle makeover project. My mind spun with images of the two of us sharing great literature, like *Moby Dick* and *A Farewell to Arms*...after I'd exposed her to the rest of the alphabet, of course.

I agreed to meet my potential student at the nearby literacy center to determine whether or not we were compatible, like blind dates meeting for a quick cup of coffee before daring to commit to dinner. On the day of the meeting, I dressed in casual jeans and a sweater, trying not to look too eager or too square. I even wore my glasses, a small tribute to intellectualism that I hoped might gain my student's confidence.

I heard Kathy's steps long before she entered the room. She had long, silky, blonde hair pulled neatly up into a perfect ponytail, and the kind of delicate bone structure I've always envied, accented by well-applied, understated make-up in the pink tones that are so lovely on blondes. A nice pair of jeans and a stylish top made it obvious she'd made an effort to look nice.

I don't know what I expected a non-reader to look like, but for some reason, I was taken aback by how normal she seemed. Then she smiled, and instantly things were put into perspective. Kathy had only three front teeth on the upper bridge of her mouth and none on the lower. When comedians blacked out their teeth in skits on television shows, I had laughed at the silly portrayal of "hicks from the sticks" like everyone else. But now, sitting across from this beautiful woman whom, despite all the good aspects, looked older than she should because her cheeks were sunken in and her lips were curling inward made the romance of teaching someone to read slip away as the reality of her situation crashed over me.

Who was I kidding? This woman was so disadvantaged that basic dental hygiene was beyond her resources. I would never tweak this woman's mind with grand literary masterpieces. I'd probably never even get to expose her to the commercial novels I sometimes read for fun. With luck, I might just help her to function in the world with a modicum of competency. Was I really up for that kind of project?

"What's made you want to learn to read?" I asked, knowing it was a pretty lame question, but I had to say something to break the ice.

"I have a son with A.D.D. I was hoping someday I might help him with his homework. I'm also awfully tired of being dependent on others. I just want to be able to do things for myself."

"Such as?"

She picked at the nail polish on her short nails and shrugged. "You know, everyday things. I feel stupid in the grocery store because I always have to ask for help. I try looking at the pictures on boxes or cans to guess what things are, but then I go home and open a can thinking I got tuna, but something else is inside. Sometimes I get nervous and throw whatever is in there away. Don't want to feed something to my family that might not be good for them."

I listened as she gave more examples of life as a non-reader, nodding as if I understood, even though I couldn't put myself in her place any more than I could relate to a man's experience as a linebacker for the Green Bay Packers.

"Did you ever attend school?"

"Sure. I went to school up to ninth grade. I never even learned the alphabet, but my teacher was very kind."

I could make a case that kindness wasn't served when Kathy was passed from level to level without mastering basic skills, but I kept that opinion to myself.

"Do you have a driver's license?"

"Yes."

"How is that possible?"

"There's a law that says the test questions have to be read to anyone who can't read 'em themselves. I studied the rules with my husband and passed that part, but failed the sign test three times. I memorized the shape and colors, but couldn't seem to remember the words. At last, on the third try, I guessed good enough to pass. Been driving ever since."

Kathy's lack of teeth made her pronunciation peculiar. As unkind as it sounds, she sounded like a 6 year old with a lisp and an old woman with a mouthful of mashed potatoes at the same time. I could follow most of what she said but was distracted by her overall persona as I tried to sum up what I was feeling about her.

"So your husband can read?"

"Only enough to get by. Not as well as he'd like."

Kathy spoke of her husband with true tenderness, telling me he drained septic tanks for a living, and she was constantly worried about his having to go into them with only the Dollar Store masks she bought him as protection from the fumes. Nevertheless, she insisted he made great money—ten dollars an hour. Unfortunately, the other men working at the company were getting fifteen, but her husband knew better than to ask for a raise because…She leaned over to whisper the rest of the sentence as if the confession was a secret just between us, "He doesn't have other skills to rely on if the company ever chooses to let him go."

I fought the urge to explain equal opportunity and fair play, and instead, nodded supportively, admiring her tenderness, her trust, and her positive attitude despite what I considered dire circumstances.

"I don't know if I can, but I'd sure like to learn to read. I worked with a tutor once before, but after two months, she quit. I figured if the teacher didn't care, maybe it was because I wasn't worth the effort so I didn't want to try again after that."

I stared directly into her eyes. "I won't quit."

She sat up straighter. "Then neither will I." Leaning forward, she put her chin in her hands. "So, why are *you* doing this?"

I decided there was no reason not to be honest. "I didn't go to college until I was 35, and now at 46, I'm finally tackling my dream of graduate school. It got me to thinking a lot about reading and writing and I started thinking that teaching someone else to read might help me learn some important things too."

"Doesn't seem like a woman like you would have anything left to learn," she said.

"You'd be surprised."

"If you already have a college degree, you probably know an awful lot."

"Believe it or not, I often feel just plain stupid."

"Stupid is going to school for nine years and not being able to read," she said.

"You don't seem stupid to me. The problem is you have 40 years of thinking of yourself as a non-reader muddying your perception of what you can be now. It's the same way with me. For years I taught dance for a living. Now, I feel like a dancer inside, no matter what else I do. Maybe we can both change the way we think and feel about ourselves and discover that we're more than we realize."

She smiled then, covering her mouth with her hand in a subtle gesture that revealed her self-consciousness. Every instinct in me screamed to just write her a check. Our cash flow was tight once again, but still, I could afford to offer help in a case like this. The problem was I knew what this woman needed most were the tools to open doors of opportunity. To tackle the task at hand, I needed this woman to relate to me so I could become her teacher and the friend I sensed she needed. I needed to be more like her than unlike her, and if she knew I had just come into a million dollars, even if I now felt financially stressed, I doubted she'd feel a common bond. I simply asked, "When shall we start?"

"I can meet you anytime, except when I am busy doing community service."

"No problem. I admire people who commit time to community service, church, and helping others."

She cleared her throat. "I'm not a do-gooder or anything. Three years ago I started hanging out with a bad crowd of people and got into trouble. Meth... When they caught me, I was given the option to go back to school or do a month of prison time and community service. Since I couldn't read, school wasn't an option. That's when they took my son away and I knew I just had to try to learn to read again. I still have to volunteer 100 service hours and report to a pa-role officer." Her eyes were downcast. "I just want you to know the truth, before you find out later and quit because you decide I'm not worth your time."

I understood her now. Motherhood was the hand guiding Kathy to the altar of reading rather than a desire to enter the world of phi-losophy and great works. Motherhood would be our common bond. I would do anything for my kids too and, instantly, I wanted nothing more than to help her be a better mother as well as a more functional female in general.

"Are you clean now?"

"Absolutely, and I plan to stay that way."

That was good enough for me. We made plans to begin the fol-lowing week.

Driving home, I couldn't help ruminating over how normal Kathy seemed and yet so different. I stared at my neighbors going about their business. That man closing the gate on his pasture of cows: did he know how to read? How about that woman picking beans in her garden? She looked Kathy's age. If she grew up here, she probably went to the same school during the same years. Was she capable of reading? On the other hand, I'd met more than a few lifelong Blue Ridge residents with accents as thick as Dolly Parton's who were not only literate, but had even gone to college. Was Kathy the exception or the rule?

I felt a small itch of worry. Had I moved my children to a place where education and intellectual stimulus from peers was less than it should be? Mark and I had chosen to simplify life, and if that includ-ed simple acquaintances, so what? A fair number of the intellectual people in the city I left behind seemed pompous bores anyway. I could probably learn more from Kathy than I could from any one of them.

That night I told Mark about Kathy's past, explaining that, in my opinion, a person who volunteered to be a tutor and then quit, leav-ing the poor non-reader with worse self-esteem than when she start-ed, had to be pretty irresponsible.

"But I can see how that happens. After all, this is going to be at least a year commitment, don't you think?"

For the first time I considered the time frame of my little project. The entire point of our life reinvention was to spend more time together as a family and I'd been looking forward to celebrating my leisure hours as a mother, and when not in service to the family, contemplating lofty, intellectual thoughts. I wanted to be free for that trip to Paris when Mark got over his obsession with building. Teaching a person to read would undoubtedly involve a tedious hike up a mountain of words. Was I up for that? I had no training for this sort of thing and I was going to be awfully busy with my MFA studies. So why was I taking on an unnecessary pet project that didn't support our new life mission statement?

I came up with a dozen selfish reasons why I shouldn't take on this project but there was a name and a face on my cause now. I no longer wanted to help with literacy; I wanted to help *Kathy* with literacy.

I spent the rest of the weekend studying the different techniques used to teach reading and phonetics, trying to understand how the human mind processes words, connects sounds, and associates meaning to them. I wasn't a trained academic teacher, but certainly I could figure this out.

Mark came home to find me poring over reading books, taking notes. "You're not ready? I thought we were going to drive over to our land and pick the perfect location for our dream home. Ronnie and I are ready to apply for a permit."

I shoved the papers aside. "I'm sorry. I was so busy I lost track of the time. The English language is more complicated then you'd ever guess. I'm not qualified to be a reading tutor, you know."

"You know how to read. Kathy doesn't. That makes you qualified enough. I think it's great. Teaching someone to read will keep you busy while I work on the house. Come on, let's go pick a site."

I followed, sighing under my breath. More and more, I felt like I was trying to run with shoelaces knotted together while Mark was marching along, confident and inspired by our changing world. I just kept tripping along behind him, wishing he would turn around and offer an arm so I could keep up. Had he paused to notice how alone or lost I felt, he might have, but a man busy building a house doesn't have time to pause. Besides, his arms were filled with tools and house plans, and there was no room for anything else, least of which would be my hand.

"But men labor under a mistake. The better part of the man is soon ploughed into the soil for compost. By a seeming fate, commonly called necessity, they are employed, laying up treasures which moth and rust will corrupt and thieves break through and steal."

— *Henry David Thoreau*

THE TRANSFORMER

A month later, I stood on the porch of our cabin holding an empty Diet Coke can, deep in contemplation.

"What's up?" Mark said, leaning on the rail beside me. "You look troubled."

The bottoms of his jeans were covered in mud, which meant he'd been crawling around inspecting the underside of the cabin again. I sighed, thinking about wasting yet another afternoon at the laundromat.

"I don't know what to do with this," I said, waving the can in front of his face.

"It might make a nice planter, or perhaps a Christmas ornament."

"Very funny. But really, what am I supposed to do with it?" I threw the can into a bag at the corner of the porch that was already brimming with other empty soda cans.

Deep in the heart of rural living, they don't provide residents with recycle bins. They don't even provide local trash pick-up. You have to bury or haul your trash to the dump and *pay* for the disposal. All that lovely yard art, the rusted cars, and the stacks of broken household items that we saw stacked on, around, and under porches wasn't there because farm folk are lazy, you see. Country people are just economizing. Without free trash removal or the convenience of having a Wal-Mart a stone's throw away, people make do with what's on hand. Items with any potential utility are not dumped in the country, but stored…usually where they can be seen and not forgotten, like in your front yard.

So, given that we were not in Oz, or even Kansas, anymore, I accepted that in order to consider myself "planet-friendly," I had to find a way to live in harmony with the land without having to rely on tax-supported county services doing most of the work.

I located a recycling center and started saving recyclables, purposely avoiding any acknowledgment that the greenhouse gasses I'd emit driving the twenty minutes to get to the recycling center defeated the purpose. Mark explained that we were expected to dig a huge hole on our fifty acres for a burn pit and whatever I didn't want to recycle, we would simply burn.

"We're going to need a tractor to dig a hole," he announced.

"How much is a tractor going to cost us?"

"About fifty grand."

"Well, by all means, let's purchase a 50 thousand dollar machine to dig a hole so we can save 15 dollars a month on trash pickup fees."

Mark did not look amused. "You know I'm going to need a tractor to lift the heavy logs I'm using to build the house. I also will need to bush hog the fields, dig holes for fence poles, uproot the garden when we get around to planting one, and all kinds of other tasks connected to maintaining such a large piece of property."

So we went tractor shopping. Our previous budget-driven life had conditioned us to buy used big-ticket items whenever possible, but in this case we had no clue about how to repair, maintain, or even drive a tractor, so we decided to purchase a spanking new one with a solid warranty and an operator's manual. Thankfully, tractors don't come with sunroofs, so we didn't have to wrestle with issues of "extras," except, of course, the slew of attachments available. Mark claimed he needed a hole-digger, bucket excavating attachment, fork prong, bush hog mower, and a few other extensions that made the machine a very pricey big boy's Transformer toy.

A few days later, Mark's fully loaded tractor was delivered. We stared at that alien monster of a machine as if someone had dropped a helicopter in our driveway.

Mark gave me a nervous smile and climbed into the cab. "How hard can driving this thing be?"

I've seen my husband drive many vehicles in our eighteen years together. He had always been a truck man, claiming he needed a pickup for toting supplies to and from our dance school, and for carting stage props to the recitals. We rented U-Hauls on occasion and even owned a used RV one summer. He ran the dang thing into an overpass only once. But for all that my husband was fairly adept at maneuvering big vehicles, nothing prepared me for seeing my boy ballerina behind the wheel of his spanking new orange Kubota, scratching his head as he stared at the variety of levers, knobs, and buttons from his swivel seat.

Mark fumbled to maneuver the huge claw-like bucket attachment into the air. The wheels spun backward instead of forward and he ran over a clump of daffodils. "Don't worry. I'll figure this out. I've seen fourteen-year-old kids driving tractors all over town."

Fourteen-year-old kids were more adept than him at working a computer, a cellphone, and an iPod too, but I kept the comment to myself. A tractor was BIG—a man's undertaking. After years of wearing tights and choreographing ballet, my husband deserved an all-man toy if that was what he wanted. I was just glad he hadn't lusted for something more dangerous, like a crossbow.

The tractor had feet that dug into the earth for traction and arms that were interchangeable. One end of the machine was used for digging, the other for hoisting, so Mark simply had to spin in the seat to shift from one chore to the next by changing the direction from which he operated the two-headed monster.

"You're doing great, babe," I called over his mumbled swearing, thinking he reminded me of Ripley in *Aliens* when she strapped the loading dock machine to her body so woman and machine could become one finely-tuned weapon of efficiency.

Watching his arms tug at levers as he tried to steer at the same time, his body swiveling to and fro in the cab, was like witnessing my former dance man in a silent tango with frustration rather than the graceful duet that our neighbor farmers seemed to pull off.

He'll get it, and I'll never see the old boy in tights again, I thought to myself.

Not that I was bothered by the idea. I thought Mark looked just as good in overalls as he once had in tights. I even liked the way the sun was bringing out the gray in his new mountain-man beard.

Eighteen years with the man had taught me never to be shocked by my husband's ever-changing looks, life ambitions, or attitudes. Inside his wedding ring were words I'd engraved when we first fell in love: *You are all men,* a romantic tribute to his diversity and constantly changing persona. I believed his eclectic interests, multiple talents, and morphing personas meant I'd never need or want any other man. Here was a partner who embraced the talent, excitement, and charm of every man.

Only later did I realize his varied talents and interests were a result of hopes and dreams that swung like a pendulum, dissatisfaction seeping into the seams of whatever he did once his initial obsession with a project waned. I loved him fiercely, but I never knew which husband I'd have from year to year. His weight escalated or dropped a hundred pounds or more at least three times during our marriage. Sometimes he stopped eating all together, becoming so slight that the veins stuck out along his neck and his hips disappeared. Other times his obsession with working out and taking protein supplements made him look like a puffed-up cartoon superhero. Most years, excess soft flesh hung over his belt, making him hide behind the kids in every family photo. But no matter how his exterior changed, I only saw Mark, the man I loved.

He'd had his hair shaved, as well as grown long enough for a ponytail, which he liked to pull up into a little fountain on top of his head like a sumo wrestler. His hairstyle changed from straightened to curly, dyed, shaved, shaped... I'd seen him with every manner of facial hair, too, from full beards and goatees to the sexy George Clooney three-days-growth of hair I favored. His constant desire to get just the right "look" led to braces on his teeth, Lasik surgery, monthly facials, weekly colon cleansing treatments, and every sort of vitamin, mineral, herb, or muscle supplement money could buy. I watched him go through periods of wearing nothing but overalls and torn work clothes to teen-inspired fad clothes few men his age would dare attempt to pull off. Some phases had him wearing

tight t-shirts, dark glasses, and gold chains like a GQ model. Later,
it would be sporty baseball hats, followed by floppy brimmed hats.
Next it was cowboy hats, and the year he went "ghetto" it was ski
caps and grunge all the way.

I watched my husband follow a variety of diets, too. He became
a vegetarian, a raw foodie and juicer, a candy- and junk-food-crazed
binger, and a consummate carnivore and protein-obsessed eater, all
in the course of a few years. He variously gave up sugar, carbs, wheat
gluten, alcohol, soda, and meat in a never-ending cycle of experimentation, passionately insisting he had one or another physical af-
fliction that made it necessary to follow a special diet. He was going
to write a book about whatever health regimen he embraced in the
moment, but before he ever wrote a page, he'd be binging on those
very things he had blacklisted only a week prior.

His ever-shifting moods affected me personally in ways outsiders
would never understand. I'd experienced months where he was a
sensuous, extraordinary lover, followed by years where he would go
to any length to avoid touching me in any intimate way, his excuses
so thin and the periods of abstinence dragging on so long I was
left questioning his sexual orientation and the authenticity of our
married life together. At times like these, I was convinced marriage
to him was just an excuse to play house. I desperately craved a lover
rather than a glorified roommate, but loved him too much to do anything other than share my heartache in endless heart-to-hearts with
him as I begged him to visit his issues so we could both be emotionally and physically satisfied. There were always plenty of excuses and
reasons for his abstinence, so when nothing improved, I just prayed
for the next period of change in hopes his veil-thin excuses for why
he was disinterested in a physical relationship would eventually be
expended. Sometimes I'd get lucky and we'd have short periods of
intimacy. They just never lasted long and always left me more deeply
feeling the poignancy of loss.

I patiently endured periods where my husband claimed all he wanted in life was to become a dancer, a potter, a landscape designer, an
interior decorator, a singer, a business manager, a playwright, a wood

artist, a graphic designer, a realtor, an architect, and a Tony Robbins
life coach. I watched him enroll in college but never finish, discuss
business ideas that were promising yet never went beyond the talking
stage, and listened to him type out the first chapter (only) of several
books or a play he planned to write. I was always encouraging and
supportive, but over the years had learned to never get too excited or
drawn into his enthusiasm because as soon as we devoted the lion's
share of our resources to his proclaimed passion, and the time came
for him to dig in and face the drudgery of hard work, he'd announce,
"Never mind, I'm over that now."

Yes, I was supportive, but at the same time I had to do whatever
was necessary to keep his feet nailed to the ground to keep our life
from imploding. There simply wasn't room in one family for two
artists indulging their every whim, so I buried my natural instinct to
approach the world in my own romantic, dreamy way, and became
the voice of logic and practicality.

I was always amazed that despite my husband's flighty changes
of heart, the one and only thing he had remained committed to in
life had been me. His loyalty may have been more a matter of convenience than anything else, but I clung to his disinterest in other
women as validation that he did indeed love me, despite any evidence to the contrary. Deep down, I always feared that one day, if
ever I demanded any kind of true sacrifice from him, he would turn
away from me just as easily as he turned away from our business or
any one of his other passions *du jour*. Proclamations of love were in
abundance but I longed for sincere acts that showed love.

I was determined to believe things would be different this time. At
long last, I had released my constant grip on practicality and said yes
to one of Mark's idealistic dreams. I said yes to fifty acres because
not only did I want change as much as he did, but I thought this plan
we had hatched to simplify life could work, thanks to the wealth
of resources we had at hand. I had, without reservation, given him
exactly what he wanted, which I trusted would earn me the love I so
desperately craved. Maybe I'd earn the life I craved too. The idea that
I could pursue my own dream to write and parent my children with

full attention and awareness and not worry about money was almost too exciting to bear.

I had purchased Mark a bright orange hardhat on eBay, a symbolic gift of support and encouragement. Now seemed a fine time to present him with my thoughtful gift.

"You expect me to wear this?" he said, laughing at the plastic hat when I held it out to him.

"Just in case a tree falls on your head, city boy."

"If a tree falls on me, a plastic hat isn't going to help. I'll be nothing but an orange speed bump."

"The man in the tractor brochure wore one. I even picked one out in orange to match your nifty new Kubota. You'll be a vision."

"I'll look like a Village People impersonator."

I placed the hat on his head, pausing to kiss his cheek. "Humor me."

He took the hat off. "I'll tell you what, the day you can point out one farmer wearing a hard hat in these here parts, I'll put it on."

I suppose I should point out now that Mark never did wear the hat. I instead inherited a nice orange hard hat planter, good for nothing more than sporting a few pansies. I suppose a man finds it far more appropriate for the hat to wear a pansy than the man to look like some kind of pansy wearing a hat.

Within days, Mark had figured out enough tractor basics to go roaring along our gravel road or across our field, hoisting a tree stump or digging in the mud to clear weeds out of the creek. One day, he announced he was taking our son Kent out to cut firewood. Twenty minutes later I watched the tractor roll by with our boy lounging in the bucket, his hands behind his head as if he were relaxing in a hammock. The two of them waved merrily.

I quelled my kneejerk reaction to shout a reprimand. Other moms in America were fretting because their sons were bumming a ride to hang out at the mall. If my biggest worry was my kid bumming a ride in the jaws of a tractor careening across a meadow filled with poppies, I really had no worries. Both of my beloved boys—husband and son—were at long last immersed in a world that supported and integrated their masculinity. Life here was raw, dirty, and filled with boyish adventure. I couldn't help but be happy for them.

As the weeks rolled by, Mark grew ever more adept as a tractor pilot. I'd walk down to wherever he was working and wait until I could catch his eye so I could hand him a mega-sized lemonade. As Mark lifted heavy logs the back tires would lift right off the ground and the cab would tip. I'd catch my breath, certain the vehicle would land out of kilter, but eventually everything would level out and return with a thud back to a centered position and my heart would start beating again. This was the same feeling I had about our entire life now, a feeling that I was holding my breath, waiting fearfully for things to even out and settle rather than topple.

When Mark wasn't on the tractor, he was stalking trees with his chainsaw, or chainsaws plural, I should say. Every day new tools, wood, and machines were added to Mark's stack of man-toys in our temporary garage. Our old all-purpose chainsaw stood abandoned in the corner now that several new chainsaws had arrived. He'd bought one for debarking trees, as well as one for cutting small limbs. He'd gotten a Paul Bunyan-sized contraption for big jobs, the size and weight of the machine taxing even before it came in contact with wood. The heavy-duty chainsaw seemed his favorite because he could take down trees as easily as I would weed a garden now, which, to be honest, is a fair comparison because I consider weeding rather hard.

Out with the beetle-infested pines that were as quick to drop at your feet as a fainting goat when you yelled "Boo!" Out with the pesky, spindly trees that took sunlight and nourishment from the hardwoods. Out with the deadwood that made our forest look as ominous as Sleeping Beauty's castle, engulfed with a hundred years of ignored undergrowth. Out, especially, with those select beautiful wood specimens possessing character and interest because they were destined to be a part of our dream home.

Most of the time, Mark's calculations were fine, but occasionally he'd emit a low whistle as a trunk came crashing to the earth in the wrong way. "Um…I guess I cut that one at the wrong angle. You didn't really want that azalea bush, did you?"

"No," I'd whisper, my breath catching in my throat, but as I watched him sidestep catastrophe, I felt compelled to learn at least the basics of driving a tractor just in case I might discover my mate with a tree lodged on his chest someday. If I didn't, I imagined myself pushing the wrong buttons, squashing him into that messy little speed bump I was so worried about him becoming.

"I want to learn how to drive the tractor," I announced, thinking that explaining my request would be too gruesome.

"Why?" he said with that same wary tone a little boy uses when he suspects someone untrustworthy wants to play with his favorite new toy.

"For safety purposes."

"For safety purposes? Get real. You have trouble backing up the truck."

"I'll only go forward, I promise. Besides, I don't want to drive the tractor; just learn how all those levers work."

"Is this because my hard hat is now a pansy planter?"

I kicked at the dirt with my toe. "I'm afraid something will happen to you. All these falling trees. The tools. Hillsides. A few months ago, you were gluing sequins to headpieces. Everywhere I look now, I see something that could snuff out the life of my loved ones. I'm uneasy."

"And I have to worry about a donkey kicking you in the head."

I glanced over at Donkey, standing docilely at the fence, blinking in slow motion. He was too lazy to shake the flies off his nose. Big threat.

Another tree careened to the earth, causing even the donkey to take a step back.

Mark slid the brim of his new cowboy hat to the back so he could better see debris filtering through the air, and swatted at a sweat bee with an overly dramatic swoop of his hand.

"I *hate* bees," he said, overreacting in my opinion, considering the bee was the size of a speck and Mark was looking rather Viking-manly-like in his tractor seat.

The bee flew off, allowing Mark to continue carving away at the land as if he was working on the Thanksgiving turkey. I stood there, the roar of our new, quiet life drowning out my plea for his assurance that all would be well.

"In any weather, at any hour of the day or night, I have been anxious to improve the nick of time, and notch it on my stick too; to stand on the meeting of two eternities, the past and future, which is precisely the present moment; to toe that line."

—Henry David Thoreau

FRIEND FOR DONKEY

As months slipped by, I grew more adept at country ways, though I felt more like I was on vacation than permanently encased in a new life. I longed to feel as at home in our new world as Mark seemed to be, but my old persona clung like a deeply embedded tick. Certainly there must have been a time when dance didn't define me, but for the life of me, I couldn't remember when.

I did recollect spending one summer riding horseback as a child. That was a glorious, carefree summer filled with great non-dancing memories, and perhaps the origin of why I found a donkey so appealing now. My new life mascot was like an old dream that went blurry around the edges, turning the great steed of my deep youthful desires into a plodding ass, a fair match for my middle-aged self.

I was only eleven on that dance-free summer. My sister, ten years my senior, had gotten her first job and bought herself a high-strung palomino. Inspired, my father "rented" the family a second horse so we could all ride together. We devoted that entire summer to horseback riding, experiencing what you could call "limited-liability horse ownership." Whoever paid the monthly rental fee was responsible to ride and groom the beast, so my summer responsibility was to provide exercise and care for the horse, and ride as much as I could to validate the rental fee.

I still had vivid memories of riding through the mountains, pausing to pick blackberries or swim in the lake while my horse, Chiquita, grazed nearby. I was a fearless pre-teen, standing up in the saddle in an attempt to master tricks, urging the horse to run every time the land opened up, and when I wasn't in the mood to hoist the heavy saddle I'd ride bareback, even though the horse's sweat made the skin between my thighs itch for hours afterwards.

Every day, I toted a quarter to the stables to buy a bottle of orange soda from the vending machine. I'd pour the pop into my hand and share with my chestnut mare, her warm tongue lapping at my palm as her trusting and appreciative eyes gazed into mine. I gave her baths, soaping her up like a car, both of us ending up squeaky clean as the water cooled our mid-summer flush. If I held up the hose just so, the water cascaded over my wrist to form a fountain. We took turns drinking, both the horse and I, sucking water through pursed lips, nudging each other aside to assert our right to the next gulp.

Occasionally, all thousand pounds of Chiquita would accidentally step on my boot and I'd yell and punch her, but I followed the reprimand with sugar cubes, two for her and one for me. I'd suck the sweet sugar slowly, running my hands through Chiquita's mane and whispering that she had to watch where she stepped. It never occurred to me that I should take my own advice.

I don't remember when or why we gave up that horse. I don't recall saying good-bye, or pining for her months later. Most likely, school started, so Dad simply stopped the rental program and I went back to the dance studio, my horse affair becoming nothing more than a summer fling once I returned to my true love, dance.

Thinking about horses now felt like rewinding my life to that specific point when I decided to choose dance over all other interests. No one ever told me I had to make a choice, yet make one I had, and suddenly the idea that my narrow youthful mindset might have stopped me from exploring the world beyond dance seemed a correctable mistake. Where better to rediscover the love of a horse than on 50 acres?

"Donkey needs a companion," I told Mark while running a curry comb over his coat (the donkey's, not my husband's). We were the only family in Fannin County with a donkey groomed as finely as a prize show dog. "Donkeys are herd animals, and without a herd to hang out with, he's unhappy; I can tell."

Mark looked at the donkey, now blinking calmly and munching on the M&Ms he found in my pocket. (Again, the donkey, not my husband).

"He looks perfectly content to me."

"He's not. Trust me. He needs a horse."

Mark was cleaning up fallen wood around the pasture. He stepped over a tree trunk and put his chainsaw on a stump. "*He* needs a horse?"

"*We* need a horse. What's the purpose of having 50 acres if you don't use it for something?"

"We *are* using it. We're building a house here. What do we know about taking care of horses?"

"What do we know about building log cabins? Nothing, but some things you just rely on instinct to accomplish. For your information, I had a horse when I was young. I was quite the rider. If we get a horse, I can teach Neva all the basics. I thought we were moving here to spend more time together as a family. So far, you have been doing your thing alone, and the kids spend their time in school and soccer. If we had a few horses, perhaps the kids will ride with me. We need to do things as a family to forge togetherness."

"Your sister was the horse woman. You danced. Besides which, horses are expensive to keep, aren't they?"

I gestured to the pasture. "Not like you have to have a million bucks to own a horse. They eat grass. Everyone living around here has a couple of horses, and none of them are millionaires. You promised that if I agreed to sell our business we would devote some of our money to recreational toys and trips, but you don't want to buy a boat, or take a trip."

I was beginning to suspect that if I didn't convince him to allocate some of our money to play now, there wouldn't be anything left when he was finished building. Mark seemed blind to any notion of proportion or conservation, so my chance for enjoying just a small portion of our windfall was now or never. Animals, while a small concession to what I really felt we needed, were at least "fun". I let my eyes slip to the chainsaw next to him, a subtle insinuation that all the tools he had purchased and the snazzy new workshop he was building were a much greater investment than a measly little horse could ever be. Donkey let out a loud bellow as if to add his pro-horse vote to the conversation.

The mention of travel always made Mark's eyes go blank, as if my reminders of his travel promises made me the greatest bore on the planet. "If a horse will make you happy, and you believe the kids will be into riding, get one," he said, turning his back on me once again.

I should have been delighted, but his acquiescence seemed obligatory rather than enthusiastic.

The next week, a man named Eric came out to fence in another section of pasture.

"Awful nice pasture for just a donkey," he said.

"I'm getting a horse to keep him company," I proudly boasted.

Eric nodded in that slow, country way common to those born in Appalachia. "What kinda horse didja buy?"

"I haven't bought one yet. Mark just decided we could get one recently."

"It just so happens I'm sellin' a horse, if 'n you want to come have a look-see."

Here I was, wanting to buy a horse, and the first person in the country I mentioned this to just happened to be selling one. I marveled at the coincidence.

That evening we went over to Eric's farm—just to look, of course. Doghouses were plopped around like plastic houses set up on a hard dirt Monopoly board. Several dozen oversized, collie-type dogs wandered about, but I didn't see any horses.

We parked in front of an old barn with graying boards and rusty hinges and were immediately greeted by three carefree children with sunburned faces and dirty jeans. Each child held a puppy, the youngest one's dog dangling like a stuffed animal with paws sprawled over his forearms and the animal's head flopping to and fro like a rag doll.

"Come see our pups," the boy said, wiping his nose with the back of his hand and wiping the hand on the dog. My son lifted his eyebrows as the kid grabbed his hand and pulled him into the barn.

"How many dogs do you have?" I asked, losing count because the animals wouldn't stop moving.

"Twenty-three or so...not counting the puppies."

Blue Ridge had an epidemic problem of strays, despite the efforts of several grass roots organizations trying to make neutering afford-able. Country residents considered drowning an unwanted litter or dumping strays on the side of the road more practical and cost-ef-fective than paying for neutering. Eric obviously was an exception to the rule. I liked him for that.

"Must be hard to find homes for all these puppies," I mumbled, petting one dog's matted head as I followed Eric into the barn.

"That's why I've got twenty-three dogs."

Inside, eight adorable puppies nestled around a nervous border collie mother. My son, a dog aficionado, fell to his knees before the snuggly, whimpering pups and was instantly lost in the bliss of pup-py heaven.

"Why don't you take one home?" Eric said, ruffling my son's hair. "They're ready."

My son turned hopeful eyes up to his dad, and to my utter sur-prise, Mark nodded. "Go ahead. You've been asking for a dog."

This, from the man who'd been complaining for years about our little schnauzer, griping that the dog smelled, dug up the yard, and farted every time we gathered to watch TV?

"Is he kidding?" my son whispered as Mark stepped outside to talk to Eric.

"Just pick yourself a dog and say no more," I advised, deciding I would employ the same tactic when we got around to looking at the horse. I watched my son bend down to tenderly pick over the pup-pies feeling a powerful sense of rightness. It was such a small thing, allowing a child to pick his own dog, but the moment felt symbolic, as if we were offering our son not just a dog, but a chance to expe-rience a world of new, expanded choices.

Eric led us across the barnyard to a stable that looked in even worse shape than the barn. Half the wall boards were missing and those still in service were held up by two-by-fours wedged against a nearby tree. Two miniature horses, a dozen chickens, and a few donkeys watched me with curious eyes as I gazed at an animal I considered the most unappealing horse to ever set hoof on the planet.

"Hope that's not the animal he's selling. That has to be the ugliest horse I've ever seen," I whispered to Mark.

Eric flashed an amused grin. "Probably because that's a mule."

I blushed as I realized he had heard me. "I knew that," I lied.

"I'll take a mule over a horse any day. Mules are smart, good-natured, and stronger than any horse."

I paused to take a good look. The beast had a big head, long ears, and a scraggly coat, but otherwise resembled a horse in every way, as if a mule was a horse with the beauty gene removed, leaving only muscle, buck teeth, and the barest hint of equestrian finesse behind.

"Is that one pregnant?" I asked, pointing to a rather portly mule farther back in the corral.

A small dimple appeared in Eric's cheek. "Nope. She's just fat. Mules themselves are sterile. You can only get a mule by breeding a horse with a donkey."

"I knew that."

Eric, no doubt, could guess I didn't really know the reproductive cycle of a mule. Heck, I didn't know the difference between mules, ugly horses, donkeys, or probably unicorns for that matter. But kindness in the country was offered up as freely as a flick of the middle finger in suburbia, so he was warmly tolerant of my naïveté.

He led us to a riding ring where a lovely bay mare named Dixie was standing. I don't know if it was luck or fate that this horse happened to be the exact replica of my childhood horse, Chiquita, but the moment I saw her there was no question whether or not I'd be taking her home. I took a two minute ride around the ring, pulled out my checkbook, and wrote the price quoted me. It didn't occur to me to bargain. How was I supposed to know the price of a horse was a starting point, like when buying a car?

Eric acted surprised, guilty even, at how easily the transaction occurred, so he threw in some tack, a saddle, and offered to deliver the horse for free.

"You're getting a good bargain considering this mare is pregnant and all," he said, leading Dixie to the trailer.

Mark's eyes doubled in size. "Pregnant?"

"I bred this horse to my best stallion a few months ago."

"We'll have a baby horse in the spring, honey. We're getting a great deal, two horses for the price of one."

"I don't know..."

Eric waved his hand as if we were being silly. "You'll have a mule of your own next season if you keep this mare with your jack after she drops this colt. At least by buying a pregnant mare, you won't end up with a mule this season."

"Our donkey's name isn't Jack."

"Every male donkey is called a jack. A female is a ginny," he explained patiently.

"I knew that." I not only didn't know that, but until that moment, I had no clue I'd been named after a female ass. I was, however, feeling like one more and more nowadays.

We got into our car and followed Eric's trailer towards our land. Kent cradled his new puppy with more reverence than he ever afforded his X-box or Legos. I listened to him gush forth lofty plans to train his dog to be so perfect Lassie would seem like a slacker by comparison. I wanted to throw my arms around Mark and kiss him for saying yes to our son, to me, and to life in general.

I leaned over in the car to offer the kiss, but he shrugged me away. "Are you sure you're ready to deal with a baby horse?" he said, as we watched Dixie's tail swish at flies a few car lengths before us. "You have the donkey to take care of already. A horse and a donkey is enough to make our property feel like a farm, don't you think?"

"I suppose."

I craned my neck to get a closer look at a bunch of chickens pecking in the dirt at the side of the road. "Gee, but chickens are interesting! The kids would have fun raising chickens, don't you think? "

"I don't want chickens. I want a puppy like Kent's. Can I have a puppy too, Dad?" Neva said.

"One pet at a time," Mark said as he craned his neck in the same direction as I. The difference was he wasn't looking at chickens.

"See that tree they are cutting down back there? I wonder if I could nab a section of the trunk. I could make something nice out of that."

"Chickens can't be hard to raise. I see them everywhere. And they lay eggs, you know."

I smiled at the variety of birds I spied scratching in the yards we passed.

"Maybe I'll come back later with Kent and toss a piece of that tree into my pickup. Whaddayasay, want to thank me for the dog by helping me with that log?"

Kent and Neva were so engrossed with the new puppy that they couldn't care less about chickens, logs, or anything else their parents found interesting.

"Are you even listening to what I say?" I said to Mark.

"Are *you* listening to what *I* say?"

In that moment, Mark and I were together, both gazing in the same direction, both wanting to create a new, country life, yet we were seeing totally different things in the same landscape. For a couple who had always shared a common vision, this difference was as if we were going blind.

"Let us first be as simple and well as Nature ourselves, dispel the clouds which hang over our brows, and take up a little life into our pores. Do not stay to be an overseer of the poor, but endeavor to become one of the worthies of the world."

—*Henry David Thoreau*

SIXTY FIVE PERCENT REAL

My Eliza Doolittle project was set to begin and I was armed with information.

Sixty-five percent of all written literature is composed of 300 "instant" words. Beyond that, reading is simply a matter of building vocabulary. If a person can read only the 300 primary words, they can get by, but there are an additional 600 important instant words that a beginning reader must learn in order to function well. Thanks to the Internet and a book on literacy, I was ready for my first reading lesson.

I arrived bearing flashcards:

and, a, to, in, is, you, that, this, the, and *it*

The words seemed easy, although I imagined memorizing random words without subject matter to string them together would be difficult. So I wrote Kathy a story, trying to use as many of the above instant words as I could.

"Kathy wants to learn to read. Reading is not hard, but when you first begin, it feels as if you are facing a big mountain that you cannot imagine climbing. But, if you take it one step at a time, and keep your eyes on the top, you make progress and before you know it, you are up there in the sky, enjoying the amazing view. Sometimes, Kathy will not be in the mood to read... Sometimes she will enjoy the work. She must keep at it when it feels good or when it feels bad, because the top of the mountain is a very wonderful place to be. Once Kathy can read, she will be able to see far and wide and all the words and sentences and paragraphs will have been worth the effort."

I knew Kathy wouldn't be able to read all the other words in the paragraph, but that wasn't important at this early stage. I had used as many of the little words on the 300 list as I could, and I planned to read the story aloud then let her take the paper home to scout out and circle the instant words as her first homework assignment. I also created an "interest inventory" questionnaire to help me pick material she'd be inspired to read. If she liked cooking, I could bring in cooking magazines. If she liked movies, I could bring in pulp magazines about the stars. I had no shame, plotting ways to conquer her handicap. Once I found out the vacation destination of her dreams, I could find books about that place. I'd use the information to write short stories for her, too, so we wouldn't be limited to reading preschool children's books, which I feared would seem condescending to an adult student. Yep, I had this reading thing all figured out, or so I thought.

I arrived for the lesson early and sat on the reception couch filled with a mixture of anticipation and confidence. The clock ticked away, first for seconds, then for minutes. Eventually an hour had passed and Kathy hadn't shown up.

After waiting yet another thirty minutes, I had to accept that my reading student had blown me off. I cried. Left. Cried more on the way home.

There was a garbled message from Kathy on my answering machine when I got home, explaining that something had come up and would I meet her on Wednesday instead? I was leery of devoting further time to someone whom I now feared was less committed to enriching her life than I was. But I'd said I wouldn't quit, and here I was with all these nifty flashcards all ready to go, so I agreed to try again.

"Why are you so upset that she didn't show up?" Neva asked putting aside her copy of Harry Potter's newest adventure. At only eight, her nose was buried in a book more often than not.

"I feel it is important I help this woman so she can read books like you."

"Reading is not very hard," Neva pointed out. "I'd be happy to help you teach her."

"Maybe someday," I said, imagining how self-conscious an adult reader might feel if an eight-year-old showed up to give her instruction. Still, I was moved to imagine my child wanting to help, and pleased to think I was setting a good example for my kids by volunteering time to someone less fortunate. This was a benefit I had not considered before, and now I was more anxious than ever that my new student show up.

When I pulled up to the college on Wednesday, Kathy was leaning against her rusty truck, smoking. She flashed a happy smile and called out a confident, "I'm here!"

She didn't look at all concerned about whether or not I'd show up after our miscommunication before, but when I approached, I noticed the cigarette trembling in her hands. Any notion I had that she was casually abusing my time dissipated instantly.

We settled into a conference room and discussed the weather, our kids, and the price of gas. Then I began easing into the task at hand.

I explained that just as she was a beginning reader, I was a beginning teacher. I told her I had spent the weekend studying how I should go about helping her and had some good ideas and pointed out that her going to school for ten years and never learning to read may mean she had a learning disability. We would have to explore that possibility.

"I ain't got no disability. I was tested. They just kept passing me," she said.

"Well, then, the problem must have been with the teachers and not with you."

She lifted one eyebrow skeptically.

"Hey, teachers fail, too. A person can go through the motions of teaching, but if they aren't really reaching their audience, the effort is pointless. That's why you have to talk to me and let me know when you're confused or frustrated. We'll take tests, but when we do, we won't be testing you. We'll be testing me."

She laughed at the possibility. "You don't need a test. You already know how to read."

"Yes, but we have to test whether or not I'm doing my job well. If you answer questions incorrectly, we will discover I didn't convey the material in a strong enough way. Some people learn better when they see things; others when they hear them. I'll have to try different ways of explaining the same thing until I figure out just how to anchor the material best in your mind. My just showing up is not enough, and I hate to tell you, but you just showing up won't be enough to get the job done either."

She smiled shyly and sat taller.

"Do you cook?"

"Yes."

"What's your best meal?"

"Hamburger Helper."

I've made Hamburger Helper once or twice, and as I recall, I figured out how to go about making the meal by reading the back of the box. "How do you follow the recipe?"

"I look at the picture and just guess. Sometimes what I make comes out watery, but usually it's pretty good."

"So, you know enough math to use a measuring cup and all."

"What's a measuring cup?"

"Never mind."

Practical application assignments would hopefully be motivating as they impressed upon her that reading enhances day-to-day living. I made a mental note that as soon as she was able, I would bring her a recipe and all the fixings for a meal. She could follow the recipe and bring the leftovers to me the next day as homework.

I pulled out the flashcards and spread the first ten instant words on the table. She stared at the word "the" for a few moments and then correctly guessed what it was.

"How did you know?"

"I just sort of know "the" from seeing it all the time. Lots of sentences start with "the"."

Perhaps this isn't going to be as hard as I imagined, I thought, as Kathy revealed a familiarity with the words "a", "and", "to", "it", "is", "the", and "or".

I plunked down another flashcard and said, "What is 'THAT' word?"

She shook her head.

I tapped the cards patiently. "What is 'THIS' word?"

She shook her head again.

I waited until realization dawned on her.

"You told me the words as you set them down, didn't you? Those words are 'this' and 'that'. Gosh, I'm dumb."

"Not dumb, Kathy. Never dumb. You just don't know certain words yet. I bet you know a lot of stuff that has nothing to do with reading."

"Like what?"

"Like how to raise chickens."

"Well, anyone can do that."

"Not me."

She chuckled.

We worked more on the first ten flashcards, and then added ten more. Watching her wrinkled brow, the way her lips moved silently as she stared at the words, made me want to cry—for joy, for shame, for pity, for pride.

Donna had mentioned that many people tackle illiteracy because they want to read the Bible, so I thought I should explore whether that would motivate her. I'm not involved with organized religion personally, and frankly, I think the Bible is difficult reading even for advanced readers, but that didn't mean I couldn't find a way to bring faith-based assignments to the table if they'd inspire my student. I asked Kathy about her faith, and she admitted that reading the Bible had recently become important to her.

We hung out for two hours, our student-teacher relationship curving in at the corners to establish a foundation for friendship. But as the lesson unfolded I had to accept that cooking homework was months away, and Kathy sitting down to read the Bible would be as big a miracle as any described within the good book's covers. If she became competent enough to fill out a job application at the end of a year, I'd be amazed.

That night, I slogged through my MFA homework reading Faulkner. The literary finesse of this great author seemed somehow secondary to my awareness that his story was nothing but words, sixty-five percent of which are simply those 300 "instant" simple words, the kind of words Kathy would know by summer if I kept working with her. I was humbled to realize the most complex literature is really nothing more than good down-to-earth basics woven together in a lyrical manner.

The same could be said about life. Mark and I had left a world of clutter and confused priorities to live in a place where, hopefully, a good life story was just the basics woven together in a lyrical way. The conveniences that I once considered an important part of easy living were really nothing but excess verbiage mucking up the storyline.

"I ain't never had homework before," Kathy said as we wrapped up the lesson.

"Be patient. Learning new things takes time and trust," I said.

But for all that I could teach the concept, adopting the principle was much harder.

> *"A man is rich in proportion to the number of things which he can afford to let alone."*
>
> *—Henry David Thoreau*

MY BRAVE BRAYER

Imagine, if you will, a horror movie. The director wants to insinuate something so gruesome and revolting that instead of using special effects to demonstrate the alleged atrocity, he chooses instead to show you the face of someone watching the action. That face is contorted in such spine-chilling, harrowing disbelief that your imagination goes wild, conjuring up something much more horrific than the reality could possibly be.

That happened to be the exact look on my husband's face as he stood by and watched the veterinarian neuter our donkey.

The animal slept through the operation. Mark wouldn't sleep for a week afterwards.

"That neutering process was the most vile thing I've ever witnessed," he said.

"You watched me give birth to two children," I reminded him.

"Yeah, but this looked like something that really hurt."

"Oh, that's right. The six-hour childbirth thing I suffered was gravy compared to a donkey that slept through his ten-minute ordeal."

I turned my attention to the vet, now working on our horse, Dixie.

Dixie, he explained, was 14 1/2 hands high and weighed 800 pounds. She was not seven as we were told, but closer to 11. Beyond this, most of what we were told proved true. She was indeed pregnant and in superior health. Our donkey weighed 300 pounds and would probably live over 30 years. That meant he could be with us another 29 years, much longer than any of our kids. At least we wouldn't have to send *him* to college and he didn't talk back.

The donkey's anesthesia had begun to wear off and he came to, staggering to his feet like a drunk.

"Is this little fellow going to be a guard animal or something?" the vet asked, taking the pet's bridle and helping him stand. "You don't seem to have anything for him to guard."

What could I say? *Does guarding against boredom count? Because this donkey is a symbol of everything I've failed to experience in life. He's my new mid-life mascot, helping me to break out of the worn-out groove I've created over the years. He's my rebellion from all things suburban, traditional, and familiar. And he's my pal, keeping me company while my husband is engaged in his own endeavors.*

"Just a pet," I said, not up for explaining how Donkey broke the barriers of what did and did not define me. Just a week prior, I received a catalogue from a local folk arts school that offered dozens of crafts, hobbies, skills, and studies that interested me. I jotted down the classes that sounded interesting: chair caning, cloth doll sculpture, soap making, storytelling, basketry, pottery, hand spinning, winemaking, and even beekeeping. I was ready to explore all manner of country crafts and hobbies and in time, I actually would take courses for every one of those subjects. But for some reason, my first instinct was to enjoy our acreage and continue circling round to animals over and over again. I don't know if the animals were surrogates for my dance students, or if I just felt more comfortable with creatures who didn't judge me or turn away from my outstretched hand at this precarious time in my identity shift, but the only time I wasn't battling loneliness or confusion was when I was fussing with the donkey. There is an entire science of using animals for healing. Perhaps that's what was happening for me because my animal exploits seemed deeply poignant and offered me the calm and connection I dearly craved.

The vet certified that Dixie was healthy and could be ridden pregnant for many months to come. He packed up his truck and drove away while I stood there staring at my new horse, working up the nerve to rekindle my childhood joy. I was able to go riding for the first time in thirty-five years.

I put Dixie's bridle on easily enough, but when I tried to saddle up,

I stood there, fumbling with the girth strap, unable to remember just how to secure the leather. I pulled the straps through the metal loop and cinched everything up tightly, but creating a neat knot to hold the tack in place made me feel like a child trying to tie her father's tie with no clue of how to accomplish the deed. I vaguely remembered a back strap that was fastened loosely around the horse's midsection, but the saddle I had been given with the horse didn't come with any straps other than the girth. When I tightened that, the saddle started lifting up in the back. Obviously, I was going to need a refresher course on the ins and outs of horse tack.

Mark flashed a bemused grin while I removed the saddle and hung the contraption back on the fence. "Memory lapse?"

"Saddles are for sissies," I said, motioning him to lace his fingers together to give me a boost.

As a newly retired dancer, I still had enough flexibility to effort-lessly swing my leg over the animal. I gave my husband a smug nod as the horse trotted away and I managed to hang on for about thirty seconds, my butt bouncing around in disgrace before I slid to the right. How did I manage to hang on a bareback horse when I was a younger and smaller person and my legs were both shorter and less developed than the gams I had now? I'd been a dancer and a runner for years, but despite all the fitness training, obviously I was in no shape to sit on a horse without a saddle. I pulled the horse up to a stop and slid down to the ground as quickly as I could.

"I think I'll wait until I can use the saddle," I said, hoping my voice wasn't shaking as much as my confidence.

"We can call Eric and ask him to give you a refresher."

"Nonsense. I'll remember," I said, thinking I'd hit the Internet and YouTube as soon as I was alone. I patted Dixie on the nose and picked up the currycomb. "She needs grooming anyway."

That night I ordered half a dozen horseback riding books from Amazon. I subscribed to *Horse and Rider*, *Equus*, and *Horse Illustrated* magazines. I surfed the web to read articles on horse care. As I gathered information, my heart sank. There was way more to horse ownership than I remembered.

"I'm going to need to worm the donkey and Dixie every six weeks," I said.

Mark didn't bother to look up from his log cabin building magazine.

"I'm supposed to stick a wand filled with paste in their mouths. Do you think that will be easy? Worming must be easy."

He continued reading.

My eyes stayed glued to the computer screen. "I'll also need a farrier to shoe Dixie every six weeks or so. And Donkey's hooves will need to be trimmed occasionally."

He glanced my way. "What's all that going to cost?"

"Well, I doubt as much as buying a pair of shoes for one of us," I said. (Later I'd discover I could buy myself several pairs of shoes for the cost of the average farrier's visit.)

"You did have horses as a kid, so you knew all this stuff would be important, right?"

"Well, we actually just *rented* a horse. I didn't have to feed or be in charge of the animal's health care or anything. I just rode, but lots of people around here have horses and most of them don't have much money. How expensive can taking care of a horse be when you own the place where you can keep livestock?"

"I suppose that depends on whether you are a cowboy or a dancer."

"I happen to be both ..." I leaned in to study my computer screen. "Feeding them isn't going to be a problem...we have half a million dollars' worth of grass. But I might need to give the animals a supplemental grain ration once in a while, especially since Dixie is pregnant and all. And vitamins."

I had his attention now. "Anything else?"

"No, that should be all. Once I get organized, having a horse won't be a big deal."

He ripped a picture of a huge oak front door from his log home designer magazine and put the page in his ever growing "ideas" file.

The next day, I took a trip to the local feed store and asked some questions. I returned home with several fifty-pound bags of high-caliber feed especially suited for an expectant horse, a new bridle and lead rope, several feed buckets, a new saddle blanket, a second strap for the saddle, horse wormer, horse vitamins, equestrian shampoo, various grooming brushes, fly spray, horse treats, equestrian medicine for cuts and scratches, a salt block, leather saddle cleaner, fly mask, and a book of barn designs.

I hid the barn book under the seat of my car and owned up to the rest, not because I was feeling particularly inspired to confess my shopping sins, but because I had no clue where to keep all this loot and needed Mark's suggestions for storing horse paraphernalia somewhere.

He offered me a corner of his workshop where I could stuff my saddle between his rusty tools and stacks of wood. If I wanted to ride, all I had to do was drive up to the workshop, haul the heavy tack into the back of my car, drive back to the pasture, and unload everything without letting the blanket or saddle fall into the dirt. Riding would be quite an undertaking since there was no place else to put the tack but on the ground, and after I enjoyed time in the saddle, I would have to haul everything back up to the workshop in my car and lug the heavy items through his tools again to the dusty corner.

"Mighty inconvenient, having to go all the way up to the workshop and carry this heavy saddle through your minefield of tools every time I want to ride," I commented. "Not to mention that I'll have to buy feed in small quantities, because storing grain in a trunk sitting out in the sun and rain will cause the feed to go bad pretty quickly."

"What other choice do you have? Not like we have a barn."

"Yeah. Most people with 50 acres and animals *do* have a barn. If we had bought a turnkey homestead…or let that company build us a less expensive house…"

He gave me a sideways glance. "You'd have a house without big closets."

Again with the closets. My husband truly associated happiness with closet space. Or did he associate his happiness to building, and my need for a big closet gave him an excuse to follow his heart's desire?

"I never realized living the simple country life would require so much *stuff,*" I said. "But at least once we get everything we need for farm life, we'll be set up to live more conservatively."

Mark nodded, understanding the twisted logic as only a fellow baby boomer of the disposable consumer generation would. "A barn is a little out of our budget now."

"I was thinking a small storage shed would be enough. Just something to store feed and some tack so I don't have to climb over stuff in your workshop."

"I can't afford to spend money on something like that," Mark said firmly.

"I could use money from my student loan, and we could pay that back later."

His head bobbed back and forth as if weighing the option, and he surprised me by saying, "I'd be OK with that."

I perked up immediately. "That would be perfect. All I need."

In my own defense, I really believed a shed would alleviate my need for an actual barn, but at the same time, a voice in the back of my mind questioned whether a shed was more or less than the cost of a trip to Paris. Not that the comparison made a difference, considering my wanderlust was going to have to be satisfied right in Blue Ridge until my husband was finished building. If I wanted to see the world, right now I had no choice but to do so from a saddle.

"You must live in the present, launch yourself on every wave, find your eternity in each moment. Fools stand on their island of opportunities and look toward another land. There is no other land; there is no other life but this."

—Henry David Thoreau

HORSE OF A DIFFERENT COLOR

Each day, I'd drive 30 minutes from our cabin to the land to feed the animals. Rain, sleet, snow, or a runny nose was no excuse; the horse and her donkey sidekick had to eat. I had planned on grass being the main course, but the pasture turned to mud overnight, which meant we had to start buying hay as well as grain. A few simple farm animals cost us more to keep than eating dinner out in a trendy restaurant, but since we now lived in a place without trendy restaurants, I chalked the feed bills up to a fair tradeoff for our entertainment dollars.

Caring for animals was more work than I expected. I tried to get Mark to help, but he insisted he couldn't lift feed bags or shovel manure because his hips were so sore. All the ladders and tools he was dealing with were aggravating his infirmity. He began limping upstairs, explaining that bad hips were why he couldn't do his share of everyday chores, like taking out garbage or driving the car when we went places. Just as I had done when we were dancing for a living, I begged him to get hip replacements.

"We can afford to take care of ourselves, you know, and it's not like you can't take the time off to attend to your health. Your hips are one more reason we should let someone else build us a house. Let's take some time for ourselves, get your operation done, and enjoy having some fun without being encumbered by pain." I didn't want to admit I was growing weary of the extra burdens I had to embrace because my husband chose to remain an invalid rather than take initiative to make himself whole. Even if he didn't want to become a fit, active person for himself, shouldn't he do something about the problem for my quality of life?

"Let it lie. I don't believe in operations and I'll never get one. Besides, I am needed to take care of this family and provide a home. I'm working on that very thing, and can't afford the time off. "

I had imagined that retirement would include us hiking, canoeing, exploring nature, and making love in the Georgia mountains. Mark professed he couldn't do any of the above because his hips hurt. I sighed, feeling like a child who had been given the doll she wanted most in the world, yet watching the adults put the coveted item on a tall shelf for posterity to protect the doll from childish play.

I couldn't make him get an operation that he insisted he didn't need or want, so I kept to the only "play" I could engage in without feeling lonely. I groomed the animals daily, each time running my hands along Dixie's belly hoping to feel the baby kick. Rarely did I ride. Even though everyone assured me riding a pregnant horse would not be a problem, I worried about her carrying extra weight at this delicate time. Then there was the issue of the tack storage being too inconvenient. Most of all, riding alone wasn't nearly as appealing as my Hallmark card memories of riding with friends when I was a kid. So, I ended up spending my time caring for the animals and reading about equestrian good times rather than living them.

"I thought you wanted a horse for riding," Mark commented one day after yet another morning had been devoted to hauling feed to the land. "You're working awfully hard considering you don't really ride your horse."

"I really *do* want to ride more, but going out alone isn't much fun. What we need is another horse so two members of the family can ride together. That's what my family did when I was young," I said. "I want the kids involved, and a second horse would make riding a family affair."

"I'd like to ride myself," Mark said.

"Can your hips take that?" I asked, surprised.

"Of course. I'll be sitting, so my hips won't be a problem."

Thus began my case for buying a second horse, preferably a larger mount to support Mark's 6'2" frame, but gentle enough for Neva to ride as well. I imagined romantic afternoons with my husband, us riding side by side, followed by idealistic images of a mother and daughter bonding on horseback. The dream would take a small investment up front, but buying another horse would set us up for years of low-cost, family-friendly entertainment. Mark agreed we should add another horse to our tiny herd, but this time, since the horse was for him, he wanted to pick the animal.

The next time the farrier stopped by I mentioned that we were thinking about purchasing another horse, perhaps something bigger in stature than Dixie.

"As a matter of fact, I just happen to know a guy with a few good horses for sale, if'n you want to have a look-see," he said.

Another coincidence? Hmmm... So that night we stopped by another farm to look at more horses. The seller, Tom, had a John Wayne swagger and a curt way of talking that made me feel as if every question I asked made my naïveté more obvious. His equestrian facility seemed quite professional, so I trusted the horses were of quality. That is, until he led us to a stall with a huge monster of a horse pawing the ground. The animal had to be 19 hands high with feet the size of steering wheels and fur as thick as a bear's.

"Eric told me you wanted a big horse. This one's a gentle giant, and I believe he's just what you're looking for," Tom said.

The horse looked like an animal that could breathe fire from his nostrils if he had a mind to.

"I thought only Clydesdales came that large."

Mark eyes glistened. He liked the idea of towering over everyone else while riding. "You have to admit, he looks pretty cool."

"Yeah, for Paul Bunyan."

"I'm gonna try him out."

I grabbed his arm. "A horse this size isn't for beginners and you've never had any real riding experience."

"I thought we were shopping for a horse for *me*," he said, his expression making clear I had to be open to what he liked or we'd be going home empty-handed.

I stepped back and let him climb up that mountain of a horse, all the while biting my tongue to keep from voicing predictions of doom and destruction. The horse bucked slightly and pranced around the ring like an overexcited dog, then started snorting and rolling his eyes.

"I'm OK," Mark said, more to himself than as a statement to anyone else. He clicked his tongue, a bare hint of sound. The horse took that whispered click as an order to spring backward and sideways like an erratic silver ball shooting around in a pinball game. Mark held on like a cowboy at the rodeo. Tom quickly grabbed the horse's bridle so Mark could scramble down, the color draining out of both men's cheeks. The horse kicked the air and tried to take a bite out of Tom, just to be sure we all knew his stance on welcoming a rider onto his back.

Tom said, swatting the horse's head. "Sorry. I bought this horse at an auction last night and the guy selling him said he was good. You can bet I'll take him back to the auction, or the glue factory, next week."

"Are you telling me you don't really know anything about the horses you're trying to sell us?"

Tom held up his hands. "Just this one. I picked 'im up because I heard you wanted a large horse. Don't worry. I've got others. Great horses. Not so big. Come on, let me show you the beauty I have in the back."

Mark and I exchanged a look of mutual distrust while Tom brought out a beautiful, black Tennessee gelding, statuesque, but a little less high-strung than the last animal.

"He's not what we're looking for either," I said, unnerved by the powerful build of the animal.

"I like him," Mark insisted. "He looks like Black Beauty."

"He's pretty, but we need a calm horse. One the kids can ride, too."

"No reason to decide right away," Tom said, tying the horse up under a bright light so his healthy, coal-colored coat gleamed. He brought out a twelve-year-old dapple-gray quarter horse gelding next. This animal stood a respectable fifteen hands high, and though he was plainer looking, he had gentle eyes and a smooth gait. He was also registered, which validated his age and genetic background, hardcore information I considered a plus since we obviously were apt to believe anything we were told by horse traders.

"His name is Peppy and he has lots of experience in the show ring. The owner only gave him up because she's trading up to a higher-end animal."

"Let me guess, she only rode him to church on Sundays," I said.

"How did you know?" Tom said with a grin, moving to saddle both horses before either of us could voice an opinion for or against.

We took a sample ride on both of the horses. The black horse required a heavy hand but was majestic and energetic. The gray horse was less showy, but wonderfully well trained. My gut was convinced that the calmer grey was indeed the horse for us, but Mark was leaning towards the showy Tennessee Walker.

"I think the bigger horse is better," Mark said, slouching in the saddle like an imitation of an urban cowboy, which he really couldn't pull off.

"But anyone can ride the grey horse," I said, patting Peppy on the neck. "The black horse isn't as user friendly."

"Why don't you just buy both?" Tom said, "I'll make you a deal."

"We don't need three horses. Besides which, we have one on the way. My mare is pregnant," I said. "And we have a donkey, too."

"So, get rid of the donkey," Tom said, patting the gray gelding on the shoulder. I decided I really didn't like Tom much.

"Anyone who knows a good horse wouldn't let a fine animal like this one go." He said, smiling at Mark. I thought of the story of the emperor's new clothes.

Sure enough, we came home with two more horses that day. Tom unloaded the animals just as dusk was setting in.

"Don't they look sweet together," I said, watching the donkey and new horses stand nose to nose, getting acquainted like shy friends. "I'll need to feed them tonight, but I'm afraid I don't have buckets for four animals.

"Just dump the grain in piles on the ground. That's what I do," Tom said backing out of the gravel drive.

Donkey brayed, causing Tom to pause his car a moment. "What's the donkey for?"

"Perspective," I muttered .

After waving goodbye to the horse trader, I poured a ration of food on the ground for each horse in neat, separate piles as I was told. Tom's empty trailer rattled in the distance, tossing dust up on the gravel road. Meanwhile, the horses turned their attention to the food with such ravenous passion you'd think they hadn't eaten in a month. Suddenly, one of the new horses pressed his ears back. I scurried to get beyond the gate just as Dixie looked up and flicked her nose at the newcomers. Then, as if deciding her grain pile was not only sacred, but rather smaller than she'd like, she backed up to Peppy's grain and fired off a hind kick. Unwilling to give up his territory, Peppy kicked back. A kicking duel began; loud, violent, and scary as hell.

"Whoa! What am I supposed to do?" I shouted, panicking at the sight of the formerly gentle animals now in a full-out fight.

"Why the hell are you asking me?" Mark said, waving his arms and shouting "Shoo!" as if the horses would see this gesture and respectfully stop with an "aw shucks, we didn't mean it" attitude.

Donkey looked up, his eyes watching the battle like someone following a ping-pong game. He kept chewing, slowly.

The fight only lasted about thirty seconds, barely enough time for a person to crack his knuckles, but enough time for a gush of red to start pouring down the quarter horse's foreleg. He limped aside, humbled like a dog with his tail between his legs.

I stared on in disbelief and looked imploringly at my husband. "Now what?"

"I'll call Tom. He can't have gone far." Mark stepped over to the only three-foot area of our 50 acres that actually got a cell phone connection, made the call, and came back a few moments later looking uncomfortable. "Tom said our mare is just showing the newcomers who the boss is. This behavior is perfectly normal. By tomorrow, the horses will be getting along fine."

"Did you explain that Peppy has a hurt leg?"

"He said we city folk worry too much. The injury is probably nothing, but if the horse still isn't walking normal tomorrow, he'll stop by and take a look."

"Isn't there a ten-minute warranty on new livestock or something? When you buy a car you get three days to return the dang thing, you know."

"Not if you crash into a wall while driving off the lot. I did fish a bit and mentioned something to that effect. Tom told me in no uncertain terms that Peppy became our horse the minute we wrote the check. If he is wounded, he's our problem now."

"How can he say not to worry when he hasn't seen the wound?"

"He's a horse guy; he has a sense about these things. Told me we had to just wait and see."

I pulled out my cell phone. "He also said I should feed the horses in piles on the ground, but that was a wrong choice. I'm calling the vet."

"Don't you think we should just trust the horse guy?"

"Trusting anyone in the country is getting harder for me each day," I said as I moved to the cell reception point on our land.

The problem with being ignorant of any subject is that you're at the mercy of those who *allegedly* have more knowledge than you. Who's to say Tom did or didn't know what to do regarding an injured horse? As city folk, we were trying to learn our way around the world of tractors, livestock, and mountain living, and our innocence forced us to turn to the natives for guidance on lots of matters. We wanted to trust those with experience, but lately the information we were given just led us deeper into the land of green mistakes.

The vet at the clinic down the road was a general practitioner, mostly experienced with dogs and cats, but at least he was a trained animal doctor. I described the accident, and made an appointment for the next morning. We'd have to pay for a costly home visit, but I couldn't put my horse in a carrier in my back seat and bring him to the office myself.

"I'll call and cancel if the horse looks better tomorrow," I mumbled guiltily to Mark. The next day, the horse was standing alone under the trees, his leg swollen and covered in dried blood. His head hung low, and even his tail looked droopy. He had no interest in food and seemed so lackluster that even Mark admitted he was glad the doctor was coming.

The vet showed up on schedule in a mobile unit van packed with medicines, syringes, and medical gadgets. He filled out paperwork and had me sign releases, then gave Peppy a shot for pain, an antibiotic, and wrapped the leg in miles of gauze.

"I recommend we x-ray the leg. You can never be too careful with a horse injury in the ankle area. You have no electricity here, but we can run an extension from the neighbor's house. If this injury is as bad as it looks, we might have to operate," the vet said.

"How much are we talking?" Mark asked.

The doctor tossed out a number twice what we had paid for the horse. "And be forewarned, after surgery you might end up with a horse that'll never be rideable again. You'll have to decide whether you want to put him down, or just maintain him for the rest of his life."

"You want us to pay for the operation and, after the fact, decide if we want to put him down?" I said.

"Or maintain him *forever?*" Mark added, imagining a future that prohibited our eating out for years to come because we'd be paying for this horse's care.

Floored by the potential expense of an operation or losing the horse all together, Mark told the doctor we needed time to think about what we wanted to do.

"Now are you ready to ask Tom to stop by for a second opinion?"

"I guess we should."

Mark called and explained the situation to Tom in his most businesslike voice. Tom responded by blowing a big raspberry into the phone receiver. "You called the vet! What did he do, get out of the car, give the animal a shot, wrap that leg, and charge you three hundred dollars? "

Mark was holding a vet bill for $312 in his hand. "Well, actually…
yes. That's exactly what he did. He wants to take x-rays. Says we
might have to operate."

"That'll cost a fortune and ruin the horse for sure. I'll come by this
afternoon and take a look. Whatever you do, don't be letting some
animal quack cut him up. I have some stuff that will fix that horse
up quick as a flash. You'll see."

As Mark hung up he said, "Tom thinks he can fix the horse with
some homemade potion he makes. He says we don't need X-rays."

"So, who shall we listen to? The vet who has a college education and years of professional experience, but happens to only work
with horses now and again, or the fellow whose entire life revolves
around taking care of horses, yet has a fifth grade education?"

"I say we listen to the country guy. His advice is free," Mark said.
"When in Rome…"

"For the cost of this horse we could have gone to Rome."

Tom stopped by later that day. "Don't act so nervous. This kind
of thing happens with horses." He ran his wrinkled brown hands
along the horse's flanks and the animal relaxed under his experienced
touch. "Your mare just wanted to establish her authority. Now that
she has, your horses will get along fine."

He handed us a spray bottle filled with a homemade concoction
consisting of iodine, peroxide and some secret ingredients he refused to divulge. For all we know, he might have added a dose of
moonshine because the stuff smelled mighty potent.

"Trust me. I use this all the time. It's an old family recipe. Spray the
wound twice a day, then throw some baking soda on top. Keep the
leg dry. In a few months that gelding will be fine and dandy."

"Baking soda?"

"Good stuff," Tom said. He leaned against his truck, his face filled
with relaxed humor. "Ya gotta trust nature to fix what goes wrong.
Call me if you need a refill." Then, whistling, he drove off leaving
the two of us swimming in buyer's remorse.

"How are we supposed to keep the leg dry when we don't have a
barn?"

"Maybe we could tie an umbrella to the horse's head."

"Maybe he'll just stand there under the trees until he gets better."

The horse hobbled out from under the trees into the mud and stared at us with distrustful eyes. A soft mist began, stirring up the mud at his feet.

"I guess we better put Tom's medicine on," Mark said.

"You do it," I whispered.

"He's your horse."

"Yeah, but you're the guy."

"You're the one with horse experience."

"You're the one who wants to fix the animal with Tom's magic medicine."

"You're the one who had to have *this* horse rather than the more robust one." Mark said.

Neither of us was going to tackle the chore alone, so we approached the horse, side by side, me with the spray bottle of foul amber liquid, and Mark with the box of baking soda.

The dance world never seemed so far away, but working together on a problem, even if temporarily, felt good.

"If a man does not keep pace with his companions, perhaps it is because he hears a different drummer. Let him step to the music which he hears, however measured or far away."

—Henry David Thoreau

DOGGONE

After two years in a BFA theater program at the University of Central Florida, our daughter, Denver, decided college—more specifically, a career in theater—wasn't for her. Her parents had left the dance world and couldn't stop spouting off about how much happier they were without the superficial trappings and insatiable egos prevalent in the business, so naturally, she didn't want to be left behind in the world of sequins and auditions.

She didn't know what she wanted to be or do, but she did know her siblings were wallowing in carefree family time while her years of childhood had been spent watching her parents run recitals. I had over 400 blog subscribers, mostly ex-students, reading the online diary I kept about our country adventures and my biggest fan, surprisingly enough, turned out to be my daughter.

So she quit college and moved to Georgia, diving into the world of hay, pickin' in the park, and gravel roads right alongside us. I had spent years struggling to pay into a prepaid college account with the idealistic dream that my child would hit the world running with a great education, so I won't say I was thrilled with her decision, but since "a closer family" was our primary goal, I recognized the positive element of her choice. Selfishly, I had to admit I missed her. I came to Georgia to be a mom, and she was one of the three people I longed to care for, so I was thrilled she would now become another character in our surreal life experience. Her moving to Blue Ridge would be temporary, of course, because I knew she'd discover a new path in time. For now, a detour through the mountains would give her a broader view of the world, just as living in the country was doing for us.

My husband's sister, and next, his parents, decided to follow us to Georgia, too.

"Family should stick together," they said, though they also said, "So what do you like about this backward place again?"

People are drawn to change for different reasons. We moved to the country to seek a totally different sort of life from what we had before. They moved to keep things as close to status quo as possible. Everyone's motivation differed, but the fact was, with family members arriving each month, there seemed to be less and less to go back to Florida for.

For example, for years we had a spunky little purebred Schnauzer named Sammy that joined me on daily runs, slept with my son, and sat in the front seat of the car as I ran errands. Just like us, Sammy was a conspicuous newcomer to the country with more enthusiasm than practical logic regarding about how to get along in the rugged, rural mountains. He adored the freedom and open spaces of Georgia, supplying us with hours of amusement as he darted through the underbrush of the woods, a highbred lap dog on safari.

Formerly, tufts of fuzz covered his legs and head, giving him the wise, bearded appearance of a traditional Schnauzer, but his fur was now constantly filled with burrs and thorns, so we had to shave him. The grooming bills added up to more than I spent on my own hair in a month, but what could I do? Sammy took to the wilderness with gusto, almost as if he had to combat his own embarrassment over being another prissy city slicker, as out of place in the rustic landscape as a plastic flamingo on a farmhouse lawn.

Our little dog loved the country, but try as he might, he couldn't subdue his terrier instincts and behave like a hound. He barked incessantly at the wildlife, terrorizing chickens and rabbits, and one day, overexcited by a wild run outside, he even killed our new pet bunny despite my screams for him to let go.

Canines and donkeys happen to be mortal enemies so our pint-sized schnauzer couldn't resist diving under the fence to torment our jack, nipping at his heels, biting his legs, and barking, barking, barking. As expected, the donkey made every effort to stomp the dog into the dust. A country dog would have known to dart out of range, but Sammy just rolled over in his pampered, babyish way, expecting mercy the moment he assumed the subservient position. Unfortunately, the donkey didn't understand the rules of this game, so he stomped the dog to within an inch of his life. This brush with death happened time and again, and more than once our hands shook as we wrote a check to the vet clinic, grumbling that a dog with half a mind would have learned his lesson the first time and stayed on his side of the fence rather than roll over and invite harm. Why was our dog having such a problem adjusting to the rigors of this new environment? The same could be asked of us, but we chose to ignore such questions.

One day, Sammy ran off to explore the woods and never returned. We looked for him for hours. Then days. Then weeks. We drove the streets calling his name. We talked to neighbors, put up posters, placed an ad in the paper, and left word at the local animal shelter. Months passed. He was never found.

For months afterwards, our eyes floated towards the woods as we speculated what became of him. He might have been shot by a farmer who lacked tolerance for some fancy city dog going after his chickens. He might have been killed by a coyote. Perhaps someone else's donkey did him in. He could have been stolen, or simply gotten lost and is now living with a new family. Whatever happened, the dog, a symbol of our suburban past, had disappeared leaving us with the Australian shepherd puppy Kent had randomly picked up while purchasing our horse.

Teddy, the new dog, grew to a rambunctious ninety pounds within a few short months. Just as Kent promised, he had trained the dog well. Teddy was an outside dog, the kind that slept on the porch with one eye open, ready to spring up and bark menacingly at anyone who dared intrude on his land. He was a herder, ready and willing to help me put the horses in the barn with a hearty bark and a few nips at their heels, but also keenly observant, darting out of the way whenever the donkey was cranky.

Teddy understood chasing possums and hawks was dandy, but he had to respect and protect the chickens and rabbits. One day, when our replacement pet bunny got loose, he chased it down and held the pet to the ground with his mouth. I panicked and rushed to rescue the poor thing, but unlike Sammy's killer Schnauzer instinct, Teddy hadn't broken the tender bunny's skin. He waited for me to get a firm grip on the rabbit, then let go, wagging his tail as if to say, *"There you go. I wasn't about to let him get away, silly rabbit."*

Teddy could run for hours alongside a horse, sit with unfaltering diligence on the porch, and he wouldn't dream of leaving the back of the pickup when we went to town. He was a low-maintenance, devoted country dog with a noble heart and I could no more imagine him in the stuffy environment of suburbia than we could imagine Sammy on a coon hunt. Fate had mercifully swapped out our dogs so we would never have to make such choices ourselves.

Several months after Sammy's disappearance, we picked up an abandoned puppy from a box in front of the local apple orchard. This floppy bundle of fur was designated as "Neva's dog" and Mark, who for some reason felt entitled to name every animal we adopted, called it Maxine. She quickly grew into a huge, inelegant plot hound with a thunderous, hillbilly bray. Without Kent's diligent training, she turned out to be a bit of a sneak, but we loved her regardless and she took to sitting on the opposite side of the porch from Teddy, the two of them like oversized, canine bookends, greeting visitors with the same noble attitude as the lions at the foot of the New York Public Library steps. With dogs like this, how could we live anywhere except on 50 sprawling acres?

Our dogs, like all the other random choices we were making each day, were creating tiny lifestyle adjustments that added up to a huge paradigm shift in our universe. We said we were just going to try this country living thing out to see if it made us happy, yet we continued to plant roots, as if, unconsciously, we wanted to narrow our options until there was no choice but to make this whole country experiment work.

"The language of friendship is not words but meanings."
—Henry David Thoreau

IMPORTANT LESSONS

After a few months of twice-weekly lessons, Kathy was finally starting to read, at least a little. Her finger traced short, simple words letter by letter as she sounded out *cat, dog,* or *run.* When the words were spelled exactly like they sounded, she could figure them out, but when a word was not spelled phonetically, there was little hope of her grasping definition. We were making progress, but reading comprehension was still a long way off.

I expected Kathy to associate these basic reading skills to writing as well, but alas, the first time I asked her to write a word she easily read, she couldn't think of the letters that matched the sounds she was voicing out loud. Apparently, teaching someone to read and teaching them to write are two separate things. I started putting more emphasis on Kathy's writing and gave her homework to write sentences using the few words she knew.

Her first attempt at writing cohesive sentences resulted in this:

There is a big fat man.
I see a big fat cat.
It is not fun to be big and fat.
The big fat boy ran.

I said, "Um, Kathy, not every sentence you make up has to be about big, fat stuff. Can you think of a sentence that isn't about a big, fat man?"

"How about I write, *that man is* not *big and fat?*"

"Never mind. Big and fat is good. You deserve a big, fat A+ for these sentences."

She took a sip of her Mountain Dew and continued practicing. "I like using the words I know. It's nice not to feel like a total dope."

"I can relate."

One of the reasons she had trouble sounding out words was because her accent was so countrified, and her missing teeth made proper pronunciation impossible. When she said the word "with" it sounded like "wit," so naturally she'd spell the word that way. The word "going" was pronounced "gun" for her. She'd say, "I'm gun ta the store ta git a sandwich," rather than, "I'm going to the store to get a sandwich," which made sounding out these words to spell them nearly impossible. When I corrected her pronunciation she'd look at me as if I were making things up, and say, "I believe you when you say that's the way them words are supposed to be said, but I always done said 'em differnt."

One day, I brought in a basket of cooking ingredients and supplies complete with utensils, a cookie sheet, and a recipe for chocolate chip cookies. That day's lesson involved teaching her how to use a measuring spoon and measuring cup, a fraction lesson as well as a cooking lesson. Two days later she brought me her "homework," three homemade cookies carefully wrapped in cellophane.

"These are from my second batch," she said. "My husband and son ate the first batch in one night. I tole them not to eat my homework, but they couldn't resist." Her smile was endearing. "I made more cookies the next day for my husband to take to work, and to show you I did it right. Now, I'm making cookies for everyone I know. "

I munched happily, the pride in her voice making me deeply grateful that I had found such a worthy volunteer project.

The next day, I bought her a subscription to a cooking magazine, and as I filled out the subscription form, I thought how good the practice would be if I asked her to fill out the form herself. I scoured the town seeking forms for Kathy to fill out, gathering job applications, credit card applications, memo pads, magazine subscription cards, and change of address forms. I never before noticed just how many forms surround us in an average day. Kathy filled out each form, carefully sounding out her name, address and phone number over and over.

"See, you might even win a trip to Tahiti," I said, as she filled in a post card for a travel contest. "Ever left Georgia?"

"Been to Kentucky to visit my cousin and been to Florida to see the beach once. That was far enough for me," she said.

"I'd like to see the entire world…if I can ever afford it," I said. "I've always wanted to witness firsthand how different people live."

"A person don't have to go half the way 'round the world to see new things."

Truer words had never been spoken. After all, I only needed to travel to Georgia to discover a world that was the polar opposite of everything that was familiar.

She handed me a contest card filled with neat, childish print. "If I win, I'll give you this trip to Italy," she said reaching out to pat my arm in a friendly way.

"Wouldn't you want to go yourself, considering it would be a free vacation?"

"I never thought about my going to such far off places before. I don't know if I'd like new places."

"Sometimes the only way to know what you do and don't like is to try something."

"That's how I got into meth," she said, laughing wryly.

"I guess some adventures do prove a mistake," I said, not liking the potential truths posed by such a statement.

Kathy addressed an envelope to herself and I told her to expect an assignment in the mail. Her task was to read the instructions and figure out what to do without me there to explain things. I also had her address an envelope to me, and told her to write and send me a letter about her big fat life. I spread a stack of junk mail on the table and together we went through the envelopes.

"I get this sort of stuff in my mailbox too, but I just toss it out."

"How do you know a piece of mail isn't a bill or something important?"

She waved a glossy flyer at me. "Nothing important is ever this colorful. Real stuff don't need bells and whistles."

Her comment was laced with the wisdom of a prophet.

I bought her an address book and showed her how the letters that stick out on the sides are like files, and inside, names are organized by the first letter of a person's last name.

Kathy flipped through the pages of that little address book as if it were made of gold. "I've seen one of these books before. My mother-in-law has one," she said. "But what do you expect me to do with it?"

"Fill the book with every friend, family member, and acquaintance you know, to practice writing addresses, and later we will send Christmas cards to everyone in the book. I'll supply the cards and stamps. You're in charge of writing the names."

"What about my friends who can't read?"

"Do you have a lot of friends who can't read?"

"Sure," she said. "I tole them they should come here like I'm doin', but they're not interested."

"We'll send them a card, too. Maybe receiving mail from you will inspire them to want to read," I said.

The next week I bought her a small, purse-size planner. Kathy had dozens of appointments to fit into her busy week. She typically had two AA meetings, a doctor's appointment, two reading lessons, a mandatory drug test, periodic court dates, and the usual school meetings and parenting responsibilities all parents juggle. When I asked her how she kept her schedule straight, she explained that learning to get by without knowing how to read had helped her develop a good memory.

"Nevertheless, fill out every obligation you have in this book. Flip forward to future months and list birthdays and anything else you can think of. Even if you know you will remember something, like our lessons every Tuesday and Thursday, write the appointments down just to get used to the process of taking notes. I want writing to be a part of your everyday life."

Kathy slowly wrote our reading lessons in for the next two months, then tucked the weekly planner into her purse. "This isn't really work for me, ya know. I enjoy getting organized. All I needed was to learn how these things are done."

Our lessons had indeed made me aware of just how word-intensive daily life is in America. Street signs, warning labels, and instructions on how to open a childproof lid help the average person get through the day with grace and proficiency. Illiteracy was not just inconvenient, but mandatory at the most significant level. Everywhere I looked, I saw words that, had they been nothing but random symbols, would turn the world into a confusing, frustrating, and dangerous place.

Practical application assignments were far more meaningful than reading *Moby Dick* together ever could have been. Nevertheless, watching Kathy's handbag fill up with the trappings of a busy life made me wonder about the old adage, "For everything gained, something is lost." Was I guilty of making her formerly simple life more complex? "Sorry if I'm giving you more to handle than you are accustomed to doing."

"The more I discover what I've been missing, the more sorry I am that it took me forty years to tackle reading so I could be like everybody else," Kathy said.

I nodded, feeling the same, but for exactly opposite reasons. My life was filled with gripping new challenges, too, as I struggled to understand a lifestyle more intimately earth-friendly and connected to things rather than being distracted by gadgets and modern conveniences. The only reason I didn't throw up my hands in disgust over the painful learning curve was because Kathy continually reminded me that ignorance has nothing to do with intelligence. Just as she was discovering how much she had missed in life as a non-reader, I was discovering all I had missed after living for so long with my heart and mind numb from too much work, effort, and focus on keeping up with the Joneses.

Kathy had her limitations, true, but she was also the first authentic example I'd ever met of a person free of consumer brainwashing. The endless bombardment of slogans and sales images that the average American mentally processes day in and day out bounced off her, because she didn't read magazines or newspapers and didn't recognize sales copy, billboards, glossy ads, influential packaging, or junk mail solicitations even when they faced her head-on. Kathy didn't use the Internet, or text message her friends, and she watched minimal TV. She lived in a world where family, church, home, and quiet pleasures were more important than *stuff*, and because of this, she was happy despite her lack of material wealth.

I was fascinated by her contentment; even envious. Teaching Kathy to read would change her life for the better in countless ways, but would her education lead to the very influences from which I myself was striving to break free? Her loss of innocence seemed slightly tragic, considering I was struggling so hard to break free of my own mindset and habits heavily influenced by a lifetime of consumption-driven behavior. I wanted to be content with less, but shedding a sense of entitlement and insatiable wants is more easily said than done.

We continued buying things like tools and tractors and furniture and rugs for a home we had yet to build. We had gotten rid of our two sensible cars and now had four gas guzzling vehicles, if you counted Mark's work truck and an old dump truck he bought from a friend. Mark insisted these things were necessary to set up the quaint vision of simplicity we dreamed of, a life where he would putter in a workshop and I would putter in the kitchen or at my writing desk. But as more and more tangible goods arrived, each one demanding space, care, and upkeep, the truly meaningful experiences—such as a vacation to forge togetherness or to expand our world aware-ness—slipped further away. I continued to introduce heart to heart talks with my husband, airing my concerns and voicing my desperate longing for more togetherness. Mark insisted the time for us would come later, after we had finally arrived at our romanticized country life where picnic dinners were served under blooming trees and the birds sang and our sweet donkey brayed to serenade our happiness as we strolled our 50 acres and slept in a log cabin mansion.

"Maybe we should cut our losses and sell this land, forget building such a grand dream house. We could buy a cabin that is already fin-ished like we originally planned," I said, knowing he found my end-less commentary on the issue tiresome but unable to keep my strong feelings to myself. "We decided to retire and move to the country so we'd stop striving, relax. We agreed we wanted to have time for family and each other."

"We will. When I'm done."

He was a man on a mission, having a ball as a builder working on an impressive project, thanks to a huge bank account available to feed his creative instincts. I was just a woman waiting for his obsession to end, dreaming the same tired dreams I had dreamt before our retirement. I didn't really care where we lived or how. I could have been happy in Florida, in Georgia or on the moon. The reason I wanted us to embrace simplicity was to forge a life with less distractions. If we had less to do, less to care for, and less to strive over, we'd start focusing on our relationship as a couple and on our family. God, how I missed my family . . . even when they were in the same room with me.

"You only need sit still long enough in some attractive spot in the woods that all its inhabitants may exhibit themselves to you by turns."
—*Henry David Thoreau*

WILD ENTERTAINMENT

Our world was filled with wildlife now, and rather than feel threatened or concerned by all the new creatures crossing our path, I was enchanted.

There was a hole in the tree by the front gate leading into our fifty acres. Sitting in the gnarly indentation at the crest of the trunk lived an owl with beautifully patterned wings and an expressive face. I started referring to him as our family owl, and got a tremendous kick out of the inquisitive pair of eyes glowing in the dark that greeted everyone who came to visit.

One day I spied an animal running across the road. I first thought I'd seen a mangy dog but the ears were long, the hair shaggy, and the contours of the animal's frame didn't seem proportionate. This dog was simply too thin, with oddly muscular thighs and a long snout, like Wile E. Coyote from the Roadrunner cartoons. *Ah, so this is what a coyote looks like*, I thought, watching him run with his tail tucked tight between his legs across the highway.

Once I spied four deer running along the fence inside our pasture. *How'd they get trapped inside?* I wondered. My mind reeled with excitement as I imagined feeding my new pet deer. But when I stepped out of the car, they raced across the field and with one mighty leap, cleared the fence and disappeared into the woods again. *Oh, yeah. Deer soar.*

We once saw a baby skunk in the pasture and though our actions may not have been wise, we all ran out to get a closer look. The scared creature hissed, we screamed, and then laughed ourselves silly because we were so sure we'd be victims of a stink bomb if we didn't skedaddle.

We watched blue jays build a nest in the corner of our porch. We hung hummingbird feeders outside the window to catch glimpses of the tiny creatures flitting about. I stood on the hood of my car to get a better look at the wild turkeys waddling across our gravel road. I even scattered corn about to keep them hanging around. People told me that bears were serious pests, but I didn't care. I prayed for one, like a little kid wishing for a temperature of 102 just so she could stay home sick from school.

One day, I heard a loud thunk against the glass door. A bird had flown into the porch, rammed into the windowpane, and fallen to the ground dead. This was the fourth bird to hit our cabin in a month.

I've always lived by the "I don't do dead things" rule. I firmly believe a man's job is to attend to gross or unpleasant dead creatures, so if the cat dragged a dead mole onto our porch, I'd put a bowl over the poor creature and Mark was left with the task of removing the carcass when he got home. No one wants to come home to a "honey-do list" that includes rotting carcasses, but I couldn't face the death of innocents as he could. Anyway, because of my rule, the day I found the little dead sparrow, I put a bowl over it.

The influx of suicidal birds was a puzzle. I stepped outside to study the cabin from a winged creature's perspective. The windows were very dark, and as such, should have been obvious to an animal flying about. *Why now?* I wondered. Is there suddenly an overpopulation of songbirds? Are so many birds taking to the sky that finding a safe flight path is difficult? Or are the birds eating something that makes them loco, like catnip causes felines to go crazy? Perhaps they're flying high (and I don't mean altitude) because some organic neighbor is growing weed (and I don't mean dandelions) which they can't resist eating (dude). Then again, perhaps there is a sudden onslaught of bird blindness, or an effect of wind and air pressure affecting the wildlife's equilibrium. Could global warming be the cause?

Later that week, a fifth bird hit the cabin door. I went to investigate with my trusty bowl in hand, but instead of a dead bird, I found a sparrow lying stunned in the corner of the porch. I bent down and picked him up.

"Boy, I wish you could tell me what's going on," I said.

They say a bird in the hand is worth two in the bush, and I can tell you now, that's absolutely true. I adore birds. I love to hear them sing and watch them zip through the sky and land on a bush right next to me. But years of bird watching couldn't compare to the thrill of holding this delicate, wild creature in my hand. The little sparrow felt weightless, yet as soft and warm as a toddler's hand. He looked up at me and blinked with resignation. Caught.

I stroked his feathers and held my palm open. After a moment, he abruptly shot into the sky. He was alive and free, one of the lucky ones, but then, so was I. Holding that bird was paramount to having a private audience with nature, a moment of intimate communion with an elusive, glorious element we usually must admire from afar. I was touched deeply, reminded of the true beauty and grace in the world.

In August, there was such a glut of butterflies in the area that dozens got trapped inside the porch. I saved them when I could, but sometimes, they'd beat themselves to death against the screen long before I could perform a needed rescue. They say if you touch a butterfly's wings, they can't always fly afterwards, so my dead-things bowl became a transport to lead them to freedom safely.

One day, as we were eating dinner, I noticed a wayward butterfly frantically flying against the screen. I excused myself from the table to help the creature out, but upon close inspection realized the butterfly was instead a hummingbird. I was delighted to have the opportunity to save the bird, especially since my dogs were eyeing the fairy-like creature as if it were a flying Reese's peanut butter cup. I shooed the dogs away and cupped my hand around the tiny bird, so frantic to escape that his bitty beak got caught in the web of the screen. I pulled him off like removing a dart from the bull's eye of a dartboard.

Holding such a miniscule bird was like catching a lightning bug. I opened my hand a small bit to peek at a brilliant little scarlet head. His ultra-delicate wings beat quickly against my palm feeling like an Eskimo kiss. After pointing out the miracle of this bird to my curious kids, and spewing romantic theory about the connection we were making with nature, I stepped outside, opened my hand, and let the little guy free. The entire episode was brief but glorious.

Life in the country was filled with these "trivial miracles." In the middle of taking a bite of lasagna, I found myself holding a hummingbird. How often did things like that happen in the hubbub of suburbia? Then again, miracles can and do happen everywhere in the world. The trick is noticing them. The beauty of the world had always been at my fingertips, but living at a slower pace was what inspired me to pause long enough to observe and reflect upon life's daily gifts.

Like the fact that the sky was ink black in areas where the city's glow didn't reach, causing the stars to strike the senses like pin pricks of pleasure, or that the absence of traffic noise never meant silence, but a mixed melody of wind, birds, and rustling leaves as soothing as a distant waterfall.

Life's volume had been turned up, and everything, from the feel of my daughter's hand to the hum of honeybees on the blackberry bushes, suddenly held my attention.

The gentle caress that simple experiences leave on the soul should have been enough. But true happiness demands a state of balance and I was realizing that for everything gained, something was also lost. I was enchanted by the quaint harmony of life in nature, but the absence of other things, such as intellectual stimulus and brushing up against people with intriguing life experiences, was sorely missed. I longed for the swell of inspiration that accompanies meaningful work.

I didn't forget that all the frantic spinning of wheels that we did while living in the city made for a miserable existence, but who would have guessed that too much leisure and a drastic withdrawal from contemporary society would feel equally out of balance?

Even with the world brimming with texture and awareness, hummingbirds and butterflies and stars touching my heart daily, I couldn't seem to shake my feelings of alienation and deprivation. I was savoring the world alone, when what I wanted most was to share the experience. My husband was busy building a cabin, then a house, then a workshop, with plans for a barn if money held out. His attention was consumed with shopping and delegating construction chores. He cared more about Ronnie's opinion and companionship than mine, choosing again and again to engage in projects for this man's benefit rather than our family's long term stability. My only friends were a girl who couldn't read and a donkey. I loved them both, but I loved and needed my best friend for life, Mark, much more.

To be a philosopher is not merely to have subtle thoughts, nor even to found a school, but so to love wisdom as to live according to its dictates, a life of simplicity, independence, magnanimity, and trust.
                                        —*Henry David Thoreau*

GOAT ECONOMICS

Herculean effort was required to clean up the endless weeds and downed trees on 50 untamed acres. We now had power machinery at our disposal, but still, we faced a daunting, endless task. What were we to do in those areas where we learned the tractor had no footing after the heavy machine sank into the muddy ground near the creek, forcing us to call Ronnie to bring his backhoe to drag us out?

"Now, I'm not claiming to know everything, 'cause I only have 'bout a sixth grade education, but seems to me you ought to employ a bit of nature to assist the job. Buy a goat," Ronnie said. "Goats eat everything donkeys and horses don't."

The idea that a goat would magically clean up our weeds like one of those automatic pool cleaners everyone had in Florida sounded mighty convenient. So we decided to buy a goat.

The problem was goats are not for sale at the local pet store. None on eBay either. I tried the classifieds. No goats. Clearly we would have to go the country route to get information, so we started asking around. Sure enough, in one day I learned that anyone looking for a goat simply had to go visit the goat lady. No name, just a title: the goat lady. When you spoke the name in these here parts, everyone knew just whom you were talking about, like Cher, or Prince.

With a vague idea of where the goat lady lived but no idea what the goat lady looked like, we set off to purchase a weed eater *au naturel*. The kids might have enjoyed the adventure, but if we brought them with us to a farm that looked like the equivalent of a goat pound, we might come home with a dozen goats, so we decided this first shopping trip would best be done while they were in school. After an hour of aimless driving, we seemed no closer to stumbling upon a goat farm than we were to stumbling upon a skyscraper. We pulled into a driveway to ask a local farmer for directions.

"We're looking for a farm that sells goats. Do you happen to know where that might be?" I asked.

The man nodded slowly, took off his hat and scratched his head. "Let's see," he said. He nodded again and slowly put his hat back on. He sighed, looked off into the distance, and winced at the sun. For all we knew, he might have been thinking about the goat lady, the weather, or how amusing sending some city slickers on a wild goose chase would be if he wanted to pretend he knew where the goat lady lived. The man spent a good eight minutes thinking and nodding and scratching. Clearly, he couldn't answer our question. Why wouldn't he just admit he had no clue?

Wanting to treat our new neighbors with the same respect and patience they were affording us, we didn't feel we could drive off until the man said something, but after those eight long minutes of watching him scratch his head we mumbled that we appreciated his time, but perhaps we'd drive a little farther.

He held up a hand as if to say, "*wait.*"

We waited.

Finally, he leaned into our window and gave us directions with specifics, like "You turn right at a big barn with a blue door, and then go down yonder some ways until you see a field with eight cows. Turn left on the gravel road, but not the one with the mailbox that looks like a John Deere tractor; wait for the next one with a dried cow skeleton on the fence. Stone's throw down that road you turn left again and the goat lady's place will be on your right after a small pond, which was a great fishing hole before the geese found it and ate every darn catfish. Least, that's where I recall the place is."

"Do you happen to know the address?"

He spat in the dirt. "There'll be goats."

We thanked him and drove on.

In the country, people take their time thinking, speaking, warming up to strangers. Patience is not just a virtue but a *necessity* if you want to build rapport with your mountain neighbors. When that man searched his mind for the directions, it was like Googling on a computer with a dial-up connection. It just took a while for the entire answer to come to him.

Still, the pace required to get an answer agitated me to no end. Efficiency was a firmly-ingrained attitude and a hard habit to break. On one level I understood that slowing down allowed a person to live more mindfully, but I also knew there was an opportunity cost for moving at a mellow pace. Dragging out the goat buying experience meant less time for other things, and I'm not talking about high achievement projects; I'm talking about what I longed for most: holding hands and watching the sun set, time for contemplation, intimacy, and more in-depth interaction with the man and children I loved.

We arrived at the woman's farm to the sight of a hundred goats lumbering up a sloped pasture to greet us. I scurried out of my car and leaned on the fence so the curious goats could nibble at my jacket and sniff my hands. The goat lady came out looking like a traditional farmwoman with a warm smile and gently graying hair. I don't know what I was expecting, someone with horns or a goatee perhaps, but this woman looked more reminiscent of Mrs. Claus than some mystical keeper of goats.

We explained we were shopping for a pet goat as I gestured to the crowd of animals at the fence. "I see you have plenty to choose from."

"Not exactly. These are all breeding stock for next season. Unavailable."

My face fell.

"What did you expect, showing up at the end of the goat season like this?" she said.

I nudged Mark's side with my elbow. "Gee, honey, we forgot to keep track of the goat season again, silly us."

"Do you have *any* goats for sale?" Mark asked.

"As a matter of fact, I do." We followed her to a corner of the pasture where the last of her salable stock, four young male goats, quietly grazed. "Two of these boys are already selected to be slaughtered Monday," she explained with neither remorse nor callousness. Hearing this was paramount to going to the pound and being told that the dog kissing your hand was due to be euthanized the next day. I crouched down to pat the horny head of a death-sentenced goat, thinking he had the very best personality of the lot.

"I really like this one. Can't you simply substitute an alternate goat and let me take him home?"

"People are very particular about what they eat. If they care enough to drive out here to hand-pick their meat, I'm honor bound to deliver."

Since we had only two animals to select from, we picked the next best goat. We felt quite charitable considering the animal would no doubt have become goat burger by the end of the week if we hadn't come along, so we considered adopting the last goat as well. The goat lady insisted he didn't have a "pet personality" and was better left for meat, so trusting her experience and goat expertise, we closed our eyes to his dismal fate and decided to wait for spring to get a companion goat. We christened our new goat "Freckles" because of the cute, brown speckles on his coat.

Now, you may be wondering what a goat costs. A boy goat is sold by the pound. That season goats were going for $1.25 per pound whether the animal was for petting or for the plate. To determine exactly what a goat weighs, a special measuring tape is placed around the ribcage. Freckles measured out at a healthy sixty-nine pounds.

Doing the math, I was surprised at the total cost. Eighty-six dollars! What would goat meat cost if it came prepackaged in the grocery store? Much of an animal, after slaughter, would be left to waste and $1.25 seemed a lot to pay per pound for a non-sliced-and-diced goat considering all the bones, horns, and inedible parts were tipping the scales. But things could be worse. Female goats, starting at $300, were more valuable because once bred, they would give the owner not only one baby but often twins or triplets two times a year. Females also provided milk for cheese and such.

For us, $1.25 per pound was plenty to pay for a pet whose primary purpose was to eat weeds. I wrote out the check thinking a mechanical weed eater would have cost us practically the same, but at least the goat didn't require electricity or gasoline.

Just like that, we were the proud owners of our first goat unless you count the goat from Heifer Corp., a foundation that provides livestock to families in third world countries. Over the years I'd sent donations to this worthy organization to purchase a cow for a needy family every spring. This year, I had bought a goat instead, harboring a romantic notion that looking out into the field to see my goat would remind me of another woman half a world away, looking with pride and gratitude at a sister goat of her own. Freckles was to be my tangible reminder that the world is filled with people who have less than we do and I need to be grateful every day for my life.

My Heifer Corp. goat cost $120, a fantastic bargain considering the third world recipients always received an impregnated female goat. You'd think the law of supply and demand would make girl goats in a third world country more expensive than one you buy in northern Georgia, but apparently, goat economics is complex.

I finished up with the goat lady while my husband put Freckles into the back of his new pickup truck. He gestured to me that we were ready to go and I hopped into the car. Just as we were pulling away, the goat lady leaned into the window and said, "Don't forget, that little guy will need a lean-to or shelter to protect him from the elements."

"Say what?"

"A shelter. You don't want him to catch a cold." She gestured to her lovely barn where dozens of goats loitered casually, not one of them sniffling. "If you don't have a barn, just throw up a simple tarp or something. Nothing fancy required, but he will need protection from the dew and frost. You don't want him to get wet."

Mark and I exchanged a worried glance. We certainly didn't want to be responsible for anything as sinister as melting a goat, so when we got home, we let Freckles loose in the pasture and talked of shelters. Staring at that small goat standing next to the massive weeds littering our creek bed, we felt rather silly. It would take 50 goats (or one hungry goat 50 years) to make a dent in that foliage.

"Get eating, buddy," Mark said.

"I think he's more interested in getting to know the donkey. Do you think the kids will like him?"

"Kids always love other kids," Mark said, grinning at his own pun. "I'm sure they'll be thrilled when we tell them they have a new pet, which will be in about fifteen minutes because school is almost out."

"Shouldn't we throw up a tarp for Freckles first?"

Mark looked at the clear sky and shrugged. "Tomorrow will be fine. We're running late, after all."

So off we went to attend to our daily chores of picking up the kids from school and my going home to fix dinner while Mark pored over building magazines for more construction ideas. After dinner and homework, playing with the dogs, and a quick game of cards since we still didn't have a TV, everyone went to bed, each of us headed for independent dreams, mine of travel and Mark's of methods to attach log beams to a 25 foot ceiling.

At five the next morning I got up and stood looking out the window.

"Is something wrong?" Mark asked groggily.

"It's raining. We should have thrown up a temporary tarp like the goat lady said."

"Freckles is just a goat, not the Wicked Witch of the West. A little water one time won't destroy him."

"You're a goat expert now?"

"Goats survived for a million years before barns were invented," he reasoned, scratching his hair and nestling back into the pillows.

"But the goats that survived were probably the ones living near caves for shelter, and the process of evolution and natural selection would make their offspring even less tolerant of rain."

"I'm going to cancel the Nature channel."

"We don't even have a TV," I said.

A thunderclap shook the windows. I lifted my eyebrows as if to point out that God was validating my theory. Mark had been married to me long enough to know that if he rolled over now, he'd hear a lengthy diatribe about goat health, rain risk, and mankind's responsibility to honor nature. He sat up, sighed, and pulled on his pants mumbling that if a million dollars wasn't enough to give a man a perfect house and a trip to Paris, that much money should certainly be enough to buy him a decent night's rest.

"But you're living the good life now. Land, a truck, and a modest living is all a man needs. You said so yourself."

He grabbed a baseball cap and stomped out into the downpour. "Now, I'm not claiming to know everything, 'cause I only have 'bout some college education, but it seems to me building goat shelters at 5 am isn't part of the good life."

Three hours later, the rain finally subsided and the sun came up. It was a Saturday so the kids were sleeping in. I was just putting on my robe, enjoying a cup of coffee on the porch, imagining my drenched husband putting the final screws into a makeshift shelter. I might have felt badly for him if I didn't know he had a donkey, three horses, and a perfectly healthy, wet goat leaning over his shoulder to give him his good morning kiss. Anyway, life wouldn't always be like this. As soon as Mark was finished building our perfect home, developing the land, setting up his new workshop, and ...well... one day, life would be relaxed and good and we would spend every morning in bed together rather than chasing after this very complex idea of a simple life. The only worry I should have in the end is finding someone to feed our goat when we finally got around to that trip to Paris.

"I have no doubt that it is part of the destiny of the human race in its gradual improvement, to leave off eating animals."
—Henry David Thoreau

INFORMATION, COUNTRY STYLE

It was going to be a cold winter. I knew this because Tommy, one of the construction workers, pointed out that the spiders were weaving their webs close to the rafters of the roof. I thanked him for this information, even though I was already privy to this year's winter forecast thanks to the kids at school telling my son that the wasps were building their nests higher in the trees, a sure sign a brisk winter is on the way.

"The weather is going to be cold tonight," I said, sliding into a seat across from Kathy.

"Yeah, I know. They were talking about what to expect at the feed store."

Forget CNN or Newsweek. Just buy hay and you could get the scoop on everything that might affect you in the country. Even so, I still felt compelled to read the local paper, needing a more reliable source than hearsay at the feed store for my basic information. The Blue Ridge Observer was published twice a week, Tuesdays and Fridays. I read the paper from front to back, even before browsing my fancy Atlanta paper for macro-news about the world at large.

The local paper was where we learned Billy Bob was celebrating his second birthday with a cowboy party at the local McDonald's. The paper featured articles about lifetime residents who had passed on, obituaries that included not only the deceased's occupation and surviving family members, but which Baptist church they were affiliated with and how they won the pound cake bake-off at the Moonshine Festival three years in a row. Sensationalized articles made the reader's heart beat faster, too. One week the mayor and two councilmen got arrested for gambling at a cockfight. Another week, a sting operation helped the sheriff close down a meth operation in a cabin not far from us. Sadly, a hound dog was killed in the process. A week later, the Piggly Wiggly busted a water main and all the veggies float-ed out to the parking lot. Great scandals like that made the paper entertaining and informative, in a surreal sort of way.

There were also announcements of things to do, such as watch-ing a local reverend playing fiddle at the Shriner's club on Fridays, festivals to visit, or church barbeques. Like all papers, there was a business section, too, and since building and tourism were the pri-mary commerce in the area, lots of talk about the ongoing war over building codes filled the pages.

North Georgia didn't have building codes until all the newer res-idents started arriving from Atlanta or Florida and began throwing their weight around, forcing laws to be put into place to protect the rights of homeowners. The editorials showcased the great bat-tle constantly being waged between the city folk intent on bringing "progress" into the area and the lifetime residents who didn't like change...or strangers...or Wal-Mart. Local residents wrote letters complaining about how all the halfbacks wouldn't leave well enough alone. (A halfback is a person from up north who moves to Florida, but when they miss the change of seasons, move only halfway back where the weather is milder, thus landing in Georgia.) The trans-plants retorted with facts about how the added income from their taxes helped inch the schools out of the dark ages, and of course they tossed in remarks about how, if the people around here were educated enough to understand economics, they'd appreciate what the new population was bringing to the table.

The city people (this included us) were drawn to the area because they had a sincere appreciation for the serenity of the surrounding nature. The slow, meandering lifestyle calmed a stressed-out soul and helped a person touch base with what counted in life. But after peo-ple like us got comfortable, they started missing convenience (and Starbucks) so they pushed for little changes. They campaigned to get the dry county ordinance lifted so they could enjoy a glass of wine with dinner at a restaurant. They voted to let the Ritz Carlton build on the lake so everyone's property values would go up. Of course, all these little changes added up to an unstoppable shift in the flavor of the little town, and the next thing you know, the very aspect that attracted everyone here was on the road to being lost. The property values would go up on paper, but living in a bustle-free environment, *sans* franchises, is what made the town priceless.

I understood the frustration of small town limitations, but Atlanta was a mere two hours away and I clung to the fact that I could always drive to the city to attend an author's lecture or visit a museum when I needed a metropolis fix. Every time I went into the city, I came home grateful for the lack of traffic, noise, and crowds in our small town. But at the same time, I felt smothered by the endless quiet and lack of intellectual stimulus. The tale of the country mouse and the city mouse was a poignant puzzle with no answer in regards to which was best.

Thankfully, living in the country was ripe with novel experiences for a city couple like us, so life continued to be educational and adventurous. On my daily mail run, I'd stare at a dozen or so chickens wandering about the post office yard, scratching in the dirt, cackling, and waddling about in the sun like stage props carefully set about to enhance the ambience of the post office. I'd watch them from my car, marveling at the birds' diverse shapes, colors, and quirky behavior. Then I'd go in to get the mail and spend a few minutes talking to the friendly postmistress, who not only knew me by name but had a pretty good clue about my personality, too, thanks to her checking out the mail I received. I'd return home thirty minutes later with arms full of mail that was now a mish-mosh of contradiction: *Fitness, Glamour,* and *Martha Stewart Living* magazines rubbing glossy elbows with *Country Living, Organic Gardening* and *Farmer's Almanac.* I'd stack them all by the door and start breakfast, then drop hints about how nice cooking would be if the eggs I was poaching were home grown.

Mark knew better than to take the bait when the subject was animals now, so he'd change the subject and ask if there was any important mail.

"There's an upcoming cow paddy bingo event. Tickets are $5.00.

How many do you think we should buy?"

"What's cow paddy bingo?"

"A field downtown is sectioned off with numbers and a well-fed cow is led around in a circular pattern. When he drops his *paddy*, the crowd goes wild because the person with the number the cowflop falls on has bingo and wins 500 bucks!"

"Can't beat Friday night entertainment in the mountains."

"I've also got a letter here asking for my support in a pig protection campaign, and I'll have you know the association is not a police activist group. No, these are real live pigs they're talking about and they need our help. I'm supposed to check the box that says, *'Yes! I want to make a commitment today to help FREE pigs from the crate'* and send in a donation of $20- $100. Quick, honey. Get out your checkbook. The pigs of the world need us."

Mark lifted one skeptical eyebrow. "You are already doing your part. You didn't make me bacon this morning."

I pointed to the letter and quoted, *"If we treated dogs and cats the way we treat pigs, there would be a public outcry and the abusers would be thrown in jail!"*

"I do like pigs." Mark said. "I like them best as bacon. Pork chops are good too."

"Dogs look up to you, cats look down on you – give me a pig! He looks you in the eye and treats you as an equal.' Winston Churchill said that!"

Mark sighed. "Didn't we send money to the Heifer Corp. recently?"

"For a goat, yes. I also sent money to the ASPCA, but we haven't done our part to protect pigs. Of that, I am sure."

"I'm going to the house site. If you really want to save a pig, go ahead and write a check, but remember we have limited resources. A donation might mean we have to skip something we need, like a decent stove."

I kissed the top of his head. "Don't worry. I want a good stove in the new house more than I want to save the world one pig at a time."

But after he left, I picked the letter up and read the text through, shocked to learn just how dire the plight of pigs really is. The poor animals are kept in gestation crates two feet wide, their movement so severely restricted they can't even turn around. They're forced to sleep, eat, and live in metal crates and continually produce litters of piglets. When the piglets are three weeks old, they're torn from the mother and the breeding cycle begins again. Apparently, pigs live in this misery for several years and then unmercifully they are slaughtered, ending up bacon on my husband's plate…when I remember to cook him bacon, that is.

I tossed the letter aside, thinking ignorance really had been bliss because I now had to add this picture to my growing awareness of mass farm production sins. A person may feel less guilt-ridden eating bacon from a pig they don't know by name, but I was starting to think that was like being an army general sitting in his cushy office, pushing a button to drop a bomb on an innocent village with no remorse. The fact that a person has distance from a moral dilemma doesn't relieve them of responsibility. I still had trouble understanding how my neighbors had the stomach to slaughter and eat their own dear pets, even though I knew (academically) that bringing up a happy, free-range animal in your backyard, and giving the animal a life of dignity and a reasonable length of time on this earth is better than supporting inhumane pig farming by playing dumb to the facts. I got it—farm animals are not pets—but live creatures who feel suffering.

A vegetarian lifestyle was sounding more attractive every day. I ended up sending $20 to the pig protection campaign because the pictures of *Sugar Bear,* a rescued pig at a Farm Sanctuary, tugged at my heartstrings. Then I went to the grocery store to buy bacon for Mark's breakfast the next day. My entire life felt like this, a huge complex struggle between my emerging new ideals and my old life patterns. The dichotomy filled my mind with clashing realities as much as it did my grocery cart.

"The common experience is that man fits himself as well as he can to the customary details of that work or trade he falls into, and tends it as a dog turns a spit. Then is he part of the machine he moves; the man is lost. Until he can manage to communicate himself to others in his full stature and proportion, he does not yet find his vocation."

— *Henry David Thoreau*

CHICKENS

One day, I stopped by the feed store to pick up grain and came face to face with a dozen incubators filled with day-old birds. The spring chicks peeped joyously, bouncing around like little yellow cotton balls with feet. Keeping a few chickens would not only be educational, but an economical thing to do, I reasoned. And offering a fifty acre home to chickens might create good karma to make up for my part in worldwide pig abuse.

I'd read that most chickens lay an egg a day. Each chick was three dollars. I did the math. With eggs selling for about $2 a dozen, each chicken, once grown, would pay for herself within a few weeks. I'd keep harvesting free eggs forever after that, a far more productive outcome than keeping a goat, and a drop in the bucket compared to horses.

Each cage contained a unique breed, all of which would grow up to have significantly different traits. I put on my glasses to get a better look at the pictures taped to the cages. Did I want the fat, traditional sort of hen with feathered feet, or the leaner chickens with afro head feathers and other fancy details? I knew I wanted chickens that were prolific egg layers and maybe a rooster with hearty vocal chords to wake me with a song, but beyond that, I didn't have much preference when it came to poultry.

The owner of the shop, Linda, was a remarkable source of livestock knowledge. She explained that all the females would lay eggs and all the males would crow, so my paltry poultry requirements wouldn't narrow the selection process at all. Some cages contained pre-sexed chicks, but others offered general run chicks, which meant their sex would be revealed as they matured. I could save fifty cents a bird by trusting the luck of the draw.

"You want brown eggs, white eggs, or green?" Linda asked, bending over to blow a little kiss to the pet chicken mascot that sat on the counter to greet and entertain customers. Her pet chicken wore a tiny red bow in her silky feathers. A class act, that chicken.

"Green? As in green eggs and ham?"

"Green, as in they aren't white or brown. You won't have to waste time coloring them for Easter, if that counts for anything. If you want big eggs, pick a Leghorn; if you don't mind smaller eggs, go with a Hatch Claret. They're survivors so you won't have to worry so much about predators."

"I don't see predators as being a problem. I just want good, natural eggs. Like the ones in the grocery store."

"The eggs you get from these girls will not be like those at the grocery store," she said, offended by my comparison. "Homegrown eggs provide better nutrition. They make your baked goods rise 30% more. You'll see. My advice is to pick the chickens you want, rather than thinking about egg color. You want sitters?"

"I don't know. Do I?"

"Sitters will get broody and hatch out eggs for you, but remember, they won't lay for a term when they sit, and they're slower, thus easier for a predator to pick off."

Again, with the predator comment. The woman must be paranoid.

"Chickens with feathered feet are generally good sitters. The bare-legged chickens will lay, but their natural instincts have been bred out of them so they won't sit on a nest. In other words, they'll never reproduce on their own."

"Where does the next generation come from then?"

"An incubator, of course. Science breeds the perfect chicken to meet our needs now. The hens that do their work diligently and produce well have no instinct to be mothers."

"That describes some of my friends."

Linda laughed. "You have kids?"

"Three."

"Well, kids love chickens no matter what kind you pick."

She wasn't wrong about that. When I picked Neva up from school and brought her back to pick out whatever chicks struck her fancy you'd think I had offered her the world. We lingered in the feed store a long time, marveling at the selection of ducks, chicks, bunnies and turkeys. An hour later we were driving home with a dozen peeping birds in a cardboard box and gleefully picking a fitting name for each bird. I suggested Cacciatore, Gumbo, and Fricassee, but she insisted on names like Rainbow, Princess, and Fluffy. Her impish smile and the gentle way she stroked the birds filled my heart with tenderness. I loved these simple moments with my children. Couldn't get enough of them.

I also bought a cage, a feed trough, a bag of chick starter feed, a water bottle, a clip-on light fixture and a package of light bulbs. My savings calculation in regards to home egg production was a bit off, I realized, as I stuffed the receipt into my handbag.

We set up the chickens in a heated cage when we got home, the little puffballs orienting themselves to their new environment with nary a glitch. For several weeks, the birds squeaked away in the corner of our cabin under the endless glow of the warming light. Neva spent hours gently holding the babies, talking to them and trying to teach them tricks. It was chicken nirvana, until one day we heard a squeak and our cat trotted by with a helpless, fluttering Silky chick in his mouth. The cat had stuck his paw between the bars of the cage and pulled the baby through like a kid sliding a cookie out of a bag. We ran after him shouting and throwing things, startling him enough to drop the chick, but it was too late.

I repositioned the cage on a high dresser and covered it with a towel so the cat couldn't strike again. Meanwhile, Neva spent the afternoon coloring a cardboard gravestone with the words: *Here lies Silky, little chick.*

We held a solemn funeral ceremony, complete with song, tears, and words of apology to the chicken gods. I wanted to treat the moment with the serious respect my little girl believed it deserved, but her sensitivity was so darn cute I just wanted to abscond her homemade gravestone to keep in a scrapbook for years to come. I avoided Mark's eyes to keep from laughing and settled with storing the memory in my mind for all time.

"When Linda said I had to watch for predators, it never occurred to me that *predators* included our household cat," I said to Mark that night.

"It's just that the chicks are so little. When they get bigger, taking care of them will be easier," he said, with as much confidence in his chicken expertise as Colonel Sanders.

The chicks did get bigger and soon started fluttering about the cage, burrowing into the shavings, and knocking over the food bowl. Nothing I did could contain the flying debris that littered the floor and left a film of dust on every piece of furniture in the room.

"These chickens have got to go!" Mark complained, distracted from his building magazines one night when the birds wouldn't stop their endless cackling.

The chicks had feathered out, which meant they looked more like chickens than furry Twinkies with feet now, so they were old enough to survive without a constant light bulb for warmth. I moved the cage out to the porch and bought a second cage, second feed trough, second water bottle, and more shavings so the bigger birds had more room to move around. Still, five or six adolescent chickens in each cage made a daunting mess. Our porch looked like a giant hamster cage. Smelled like one, too.

"These birds will be free ranging on our land soon enough," I said to Mark as I swept the porch for the third time that day while everyone else was getting ready for the family's big night out at the drive-in. "Once this stage is over, we'll have maintenance-free chickens forevermore."

"I'm counting on it," Mark said, slipping on a pile of slick chicken poop as he brought blankets and a bag of snacks to the car.

The movie playing at the drive-in that night was *Chicken Little*. All five of us huddled in the car sharing buckets of popcorn and Twizzlers. I had wonderful memories of going to the drive-in with my family when I was a kid, so every time we went I imagined we were forging memories that would last forevermore. The movie itself was but an afterthought. It was the togetherness I loved.

Two hours later we came home to find the dogs had knocked over one of the cages and apparently decided young chickens would make fun chew toys. The porch was a war zone of feathers and deceased chickens. Another funeral ensued. We were down to only five chickens from our original dozen now.

"It never occurred to me predators might include the cat *and* the family puppy," I mumbled, thinking Linda should have been more specific. Or perhaps I should have asked more questions.

Even five chickens were too many for a porch once the birds grew to be full size. For their own good and for my housekeeping sanity, these chickens had to go. But, where? I had planned on free-range chickens roaming our land, waking us every morning with a joyful crow and eggs to start the day, but our house wasn't yet finished. Then again, the donkey, horses and goat had taken up residence on our land already, so why not move the chickens out there as well? They could wander freely among the tall blades of grass, scratching and foraging just like the chickens at the post office and in yards all over town. I'd even set them up a nice box for shelter with food and water at the ready, and they'd be far happier living free and easy rather than trapped in a cage on our porch.

Mark agreed it was a good idea, so the next day, we brought the chickens to our land and set them free. The birds immediately scurried into the pasture to scratch amidst the horse dung. If it wasn't so darned corny, I'd have burst out in a rendition of "Born Free." I watched them revel in the sunshine for an hour or more until it was time to go.

"What if they're scared of the dark?" Neva asked as we left.

"Chickens have survived the dark for thousands of years. They won't mind," I said. "Besides which, they'll sleep in the little box I've set up. Tomorrow they'll probably be perched on the fence, waiting to be fed right along with the donkey."

Only the next day when we visited the land again, nary a feather was in sight.

"Do you think they ran away?" Neva asked.

"Perhaps they're hiding in the trees," I said, squinting as I looked into the branches overhead. No chickens.

We spent a good hour calling out to them, but in the end, concluded that those ungrateful chickens had indeed run away.

"I guess my chickens took off," I said to Ronnie when I stopped by to see the progress on the house later that day.

Mark looked away uneasily.

Ronnie dug his hands into his pockets and grinned. "You just let a bunch of chickens loose out here? At night? Without a chicken coop for shelter?"

"A chicken coop? Um… I did put a box up in a tree limb for them to sleep in."

His eyes crinkled at the corners. "I hate to tell you, but all you done last night was feed the coyotes and possums. I'm sure they appreciated it."

"No sir! You really think something ate my chickens?"

"Probably a weasel or a raccoon. Maybe it was a hawk or owl. Might be a stray dog or two. Could be a fox, of course. Just about everything eats chicken, 'cept maybe that donkey of yours."

"Cats and dogs like chickens, too," Mark said with a grin.

It occurred to me the list of potential killers was getting mighty long and I might as well add myself to it, considering my stupidity. "But what about all those free range chickens I see wandering around at the post office and in people's yards? Those birds somehow survive."

"Those chickens only free range during the day. They get tucked away at night in a chicken coop so they don't become sitting ducks."

"Oh."

Not much in the mood for more funerals, I decided to stick with the *they ran away* story for Neva and I suggested she pick out a few more chicks at the feed store. This time, we'd build a chicken coop before setting them free. Since young girls are far more enamored with chicks than with adult chickens, Neva didn't mind starting over. Another dozen chicks took up residency in our family room. They too moved to the porch a month later. They too made a debilitating mess that made everyone feel as if we were living in a barn and they too drove Mark to eventually put his foot down and order a chicken removal.

"If you want me to install them on the land, I'll need a chicken coop," I said. "Can you pause a few hours from building the house and make me one?"

"No way. I'm busy. You should have thought about that before you began the experiment."

I had come prepared for his answer. I pointed to an ad in the local paper that read, *Local carpenter and handyman. No job too big or small.* "Why don't we hire this guy to build us a little chicken house?" I opened a book on small animal housing to a page featuring a basic chicken coop and held it up so Mark could stare at the plans.

Mark flipped a few pages, nodding at the nifty animal housing options in the book. "Okay. But I want to talk to the guy and make the arrangements myself."

Delighted, I set up a meeting. The handyman, Erick, met us the next day and we gave him the plans. The picture of my coveted chicken coop was simple, just a little shed with a door and a cartoon drawing of a little chicken going into a small, square hole, like a doggy door. I told Erick not to bother with the inside of the coop, because I had ordered ready-made chicken nesting boxes.

Mark arranged for Erick to go shopping for the materials that afternoon so the project could get underway the very next day. A few hours later Erick called Mark, asking if he could drop by the receipt for reimbursement. The materials bill came to $1,600.00.

Mark called me. "What did you ask him to build? We could fly to Europe and order an omelet for what our eggs are going to end up costing us!"

"I showed you the plans in advance. It was just a little shed with a little chicken dancing by the door. How was I to know wood cost so much?"

"I buy wood all the time and it doesn't cost that much!" Mark yelled.

I winced, thinking the grand total would be even more when labor was included. According to the book, we would need to erect a fence around the coop as well. How was I going to spring that one on Mark?

"I'm sorry, but something just doesn't seem right. I really thought a coop thrown together by a handyman would be more in the range of $400. Just how big was that chicken coop, anyway? Did you notice?" I said.

Mark paused. "I'll call you back."

Turns out the plans in the book were for a chicken house that could easily house 200 chickens. I had under a dozen birds. Oops.

"I didn't pay attention to dimensions when you showed me the plans," Mark said sheepishly. "So, I told him to make it smaller, but this chicken house is still going to cost us about four grand by the time he adds his labor. You better really like harvesting your own eggs, 'cause it'll take about thirty years to make this project cost-effective."

"Not everything in life has to add up on a balance sheet. Raising chickens will be a learning experience, and perhaps I'll use the coop for other things as well. Like raising a turkey."

"To eat?"

"I couldn't possibly."

"Then no turkeys. I hereby declare that you can only raise what you are willing to eat. I hear turkeys are smelly and dumb, anyway."

"OK, no turkeys. I wouldn't want dumb poultry hanging around."

I vaguely wondered what birds I *could* keep that my husband wouldn't expect me to eat because my animal husbandry experiments were the only thing filling my days while the kids were at school and he was devoting our wildly amazing newfound freedom and resources to his own personal interest of building. The animals weren't simply a hobby. They were my lifeline.

"Will you be a reader, a student merely, or a seer? Read your fate, see what is before you, and walk on into futurity."
—*Henry David Thoreau*

THE GIFT

I once thought New York was the Santa capitol of the world. Every December in the city Santas rang bells in front of Salvation Army collection pots on every street corner. I'd throw in a few quarters as I passed, smiling and wondering, *Are you the real one?* Sometimes these Santas had dark skin, bushy eyebrows, or the wrong colored eyes. They might be abnormally short or tall. They might even be women, young yuppie types, elderly, or just a guy lacking "jolly-ness." I wasn't fooled a bit.

As Christmas came to Blue Ridge, I noticed men who looked like Santas everywhere, and not one of them wore a red suit or rang a bell. Here, a Santa went about his day like everyone else, with a twinkle in his eye and his bushy, white beard ungroomed. Often, he wore overalls over a Henley shirt and well-worn work boots. I even saw Santa at the hardware store one day. He was loading his truck with two-by-fours. As I passed, he nodded and winked.

One morning, I spotted two Santas having breakfast at the Waffle House. Their round stomachs filled the booth, leaving little room for expansion after they finished off their plates of biscuits and gravy. White hair and beards covered the collars of their flannel plaid shirts. One wore a John Deere baseball cap. They were talking about how the endless rain was making a mess around their barn. *Must be tough on the reindeer*, I thought.

Blue Ridge also had a few Good Samaritan Santas decked out in red velvet. Santas passed out gifts at the bank or made an appearance at fundraisers. A traditional Santa rode the train to the Light Up Blue Ridge ceremony every season. He would sit in a decorated gazebo in the park to take pictures with the kids. Mrs. Claus handed out peppermint sticks by his side. I enjoyed the festivities, but my eyes couldn't resist slipping to the crowd where, it seemed to me, more authentic Santas lingered, the kind with a bit of chew in their cheeks and mud on the hems of their work-worn jeans.

In the country, commerce didn't drive Christmas so much and people were not too frazzled to pause for a cup of homemade eggnog. The holidays were as wholesome and natural as the holly growing in the woods outside our cabin door. For the first time in as long as I could remember, Christmas was not a flurry of malls and boutiques. I didn't spend evenings reading about Christmas traditions in *Martha Stewart Magazine*. Instead, I had the time and inspiration to actually dabble in wholesome holiday projects. I sent Christmas cards to friends who hadn't heard from me in years and made baskets of goodies for my neighbors. I spent an evening with the kids stringing popcorn and cranberries to go with ornaments made of bagels and birdseed, and decorated a tree outside for the wildlife. I cooked homemade dog biscuits with my daughter and mixed up a batch of horse cookies and placed them in festive containers. We watched *It's a Wonderful Life* in front of a roaring fire while I crocheted my husband a homemade scarf.

But although our country Christmas was not focused on presents, I was excited to buy one special gift because the holiday provided me with the perfect excuse to buy Kathy something useful without the gift seeming like charity. The problem was, what? Kathy could use a new coat, but perhaps that was too personal? A gift certificate to the grocery store would be nice, but maybe that would seem like a handout.

One day, as we were talking about our children's wish lists, Kathy told me she'd met a man employed at a fancy dentist office in Atlanta who makes false teeth "under the table." Her husband had given her one hundred dollars for Christmas to put down as a deposit, and she was going to set up a payment plan for the rest so that, in a year, she would eventually get dentures. She was thrilled.

We'd never really discussed her dental problems beyond acknowledging how her lack of teeth made pronunciation difficult, but with the subject now open, I gently asked questions about her experience of living without teeth at age forty. In her honest, unassuming way, she shared stories of her self-consciousness and the ongoing physical and emotional pain that came with having no teeth. Kathy's wants were few, but getting a healthy set of teeth was high on her wish list.

"I just want to be pretty and like other people," she said shyly.

"I've been trying to think of just the right gift to give you for Christmas and I'd really love to pay off your teeth if you'd let me," I said.

She didn't respond immediately, so I added, "After all, teeth will make my job easier since it will help you pronounce words correctly. This will be a gift for us both."

I had put aside money for a gift for Kathy and several hundred dollars was tucked in a compartment of my purse. I pressed the money into her hand, insistent and encouraging. Her resistance melted away and she took it graciously as we ended our lesson.

We were scheduled to take a break for two weeks while the kids were home on Christmas vacation, and Kathy called to tell me she was getting fitted for her new teeth the next week. When we returned to our lessons in the New Year, she'd be a new woman, or at least a woman with a new mouth.

On the day she actually got her false teeth, she called to share her joy, her voice lisping slightly as she struggled to adjust to a mouth full of dentures.

Finally, the day for resuming our lessons came. I arrived early with donuts to celebrate. Promptly at nine o'clock, Kathy walked in, purposely holding back a smile.

"Oh, no, you don't. Let me see," I said.

She flashed me a euphoric grin and I caught my breath. Her teeth were straight and white. The dentures filled out her face, making her chiseled features look softer. She looked more intelligent with teeth, too. With only three rotting teeth, she had looked like the stereotypical illiterate country gal, someone from a skit on the *Hee Haw* show. Now, she looked like an upper middle class housewife, and a very pretty one at that.

"You look gorgeous. Do they hurt?"

"They feel weird. I don't think I'll be eating any donuts for a while."

"What does your husband think?"

"He said I was a knockout and insisted other men will want to take me home now." She giggled. "It's funny, but I swear people treat me differently, like the checkout girl in the grocery store. Used to be she wouldn't give me the time of day, but suddenly she's talking to me, asking me how my day is going."

Of course people are going to treat you differently, I thought. *You no longer look like an indigent, ignorant bumpkin. You look like an intelligent, beautiful woman and no one would ever guess you are handicapped by the inability to read.* I felt no small amount of pride over my part in her transformation; a self-serving feeling I suppose. Mostly I felt deeply happy for Kathy, a woman who seemed to appreciate every small advantage afforded her with a reverence I couldn't help but admire.

"A lady from church offered to get me a makeover and a haircut, and I think I'm gonna do it," she said, fondling the ends of her long, shapeless hair shyly. "It's been so long since I've felt good about myself."

"Well, this will come in handy for you then," I said, handing her a Christmas card with a small gift card to a neighborhood clothing store. "I wanted to get you a more traditional gift for Christmas too, something you can open."

She looked over the card, thanked me, and slid the envelope aside.

"Read it," I said.

She looked embarrassed. "I can't."

"Of course you can; I picked this card specifically because you know the words."

Kathy looked at the card again and shrugged her shoulders. "What kind of writing is this?"

I grabbed the card to point out how simple the sentiment was, and only then realize that I'd chosen a card with cursive writing. Oops.

So I explained what cursive writing was, and promised we would practice that too, in time. Then, because she hadn't made any comment about the gift card I decided to ask her what she thought of that, too .

Her jaw twisted.

"Do you know what that card is?"

"Not really."

"The card represents a certain amount of money. You swipe the card in machines by the register in a store and you get credit to use, like cash."

Kathy flashed her new, brilliant smile. "Hey, I've seen people do that before. I've always wanted to try it."

I was deeply aware of Kathy's limited exposure to society's systems, and yet I missed this one. Kathy had never had a bank account and so, of course, had never used a credit card, much less a gift card. She also never applied for or used food stamps, coupons, or anything else that required reading to maneuver through rules or regulations.

I walked her through the motions of using a gift card, realizing my gift wasn't at all going to be the new sweater or pair of jeans she would pick out with the little fifty dollar certificate. My gift would instead be something more meaningful - a new experience and expanded awareness.

On a grander scale, the same theory applied to all the acquisitions Mark and I were accumulating. None of the trappings of a country lifestyle that we seemed to be stockpiling were really needed or warranted for the life of simplicity we originally planned. The stuff we kept buying was more about what the lessons and new skills attached. Were these the lessons we needed to learn? Tractors and chickens and living in a home-made cabin of rustic logs with animals outside our door felt nobly organic, but our consumer attitudes and drives were not unlike those we had before, when we were living in bustling suburbia. The reserved, quiet life we set out to achieve, a life that was available to us at anytime and anyplace if we just chose to embrace simplicity, was in fact, still being put off until later. There was simply too much to do to prepare for the simple life to allow us time to pause and actually live simply.

Had we stayed put in Florida where we had an established business, house and community and chosen to reprioritize our life and make small changes, we would likely have created our coveted life transformation easier, quicker, and with far less upheaval to those we loved. So, what were we really striving to do by moving to the country?

"Perhaps the facts most astounding and most real are never communicated by man to man. The true harvest of my daily life is somewhat as intangible and indescribable as the tints of morning or evening. It is a little star-dust caught, a segment of the rainbow which I have clutched."

—*Henry David Thoreau*

SOMEBODY'S GARDEN

As an avid cook and someone ultimately curious about the world, raising chickens was more about seeing nature's process firsthand than raising birds for practical reasons. I'd read dozens of magazines about hobby farming, and now I had a hankering for a garden too. I wanted to plant, prune, weed, and harvest. I wanted to feed my family homegrown organic vegetables and fruit picked right off the vine. Local eating was considered the socially conscientious thing to do, and with a garden of my own, I could bring food to our table without consuming the gas an avid environmentalist would use to drive to the local farmer's market.

I dreamed of homegrown tomatoes, beans, peppers, garlic, melons, asparagus, and squash. I had a basket in my kitchen filling up with seed packages to prove my intent, and *Organic Gardening, Herb Enthusiast, Vegetarian Times*, and *Georgia Gardening* magazines began fighting for space in my overstuffed mailbox. I read books with titles like *The 64 Dollar Tomato* and *Animal, Vegetable, Miracle* as if they were academic textbooks rather than inspirational memoirs.

All I needed was a place to do the planting and help getting started. I'd never grown anything beyond a house plant. Mark, on the other hand, had been an avid gardener for years. In Florida, due to the weather and the size of our yard, his interest hovered primarily around orchids and flowerbeds, but he was enthusiastic about planting a vegetable patch to feed the family. He shared inspirational stories of a neighbor he much admired as a child, telling me how much he loved helping put vegetables up for winter. He spoke with such reverence and passion that canning sounded like a great aphrodisiac to him, and if the ability to make my own pickles would make me sexy in Mark's eyes, I was game. I missed his touch and his earnest attention terribly.

Mark deemed the garden should go in a corner of the field adjacent to our pasture. We didn't have a source for watering plants there yet, but we might be able to rig something from the rambling stream nearby.

Despite the array of tractor appendages we'd purchased, we hadn't included a tiller, so Ronnie dropped by with his tractor to turn up a huge swatch of dirt for the garden. Mark also purchased a freestanding push tiller for additional preparation. For two days, I tossed rocks aside as Mark made defined rows, mounding the dirt into neat humps for future lettuce, beans, carrots, beets, corn, cantaloupe, and squash plants.

A month later we undertook stage two. Mark made impressions with the handle of a rake in the earth, and I crouched over to push tiny seeds into the holes, gently piling dirt on top. We planted some tomato starter plants and, as a last minute thought, scattered pumpkin, gourd, and watermelon seeds on a nearby hill. The ground in this area had not been prepared for a garden, but we figured a planting crap shoot for gourds couldn't hurt.

*Inspired, we continued to purchase additional plants a*nd seeds like someone at a buffet table piling their plates to overflowing because their eyes are bigger than their stomachs. As the days grew warmer the extra plants shriveled in the garage. Other seed packets never made the journey out of my to-do basket. We ended up planting only one half of our proposed garden, but the truth was, starting a garden from scratch was far more labor-intensive than I had anticipated, so starting with only half a garden turned out a blessing.

Mark came home with a huge bag of daffodil bulbs to plant around the new house. The flowers may or may not bloom in the first season, but we'd have an explosion of color to curl anyone's toes from then on, he explained. Never averse to working towards a promising future, I devoted a weekend to planting bulbs. My husband, always a master at delegating manual labor, stood upright making holes with a hoe and I was the one expected to bend down, nose and fingertips in the dirt.

"Stomp on the dirt to pack it down. Any air that gets into the root will make it rot," he said, leaning casually against the hoe handle.

I stood with a groan, holding my aching back as I stomped on the dirt.

"You don't have to do a daffodil dance on every one. Just stomp on it."

"I *am* stomping. Who said gardening can't be done with finesse?" I continuing to do my little cha-cha-cha on top of each potential flower as if dancing might bring good luck to the bulb.

Mark had purchased 450 bulbs at the neighboring garden center. The fifty sale bulbs I bought on-line seemed paltry at best but demonstrated my enthusiasm and desire to be a part of the landscape planning if nothing else.

"Whatcha got?" Mark said, looking at my purchases and wrinkling his nose. "Mixed bulbs? We hate mixed bulbs."

"We do? Since when? Mixed bulbs offer diverse color. See, that's written right on the package. Besides, they're pretty."

"They aren't *naturalized*," he said.

"Of course they're natural. They're plants."

"I said natural*ized*. Flowers grow and multiply on their own, so for the landscape to look natural, using one color is best."

"Anything we plant will multiply on its own and over time and become naturalized, right? Problem solved. Besides, why does a flower bed have to look natural? Not like bulbs would spring up in nice rows along a house if someone didn't plant them in the first place. "

"Mixed flowers are corny."

"And yet, companies sell mixed bulbs and people do buy them."

"They also sell Day-Glo pictures of naked ladies painted on black velvet but we don't buy them and hang them over the mantel."

"Why plant a garden with only a few primary colors when you can offer a rainbow?"

He looked at me as if I had just suggested we cover the sofa in the living room with plastic.

"I also bought hyacinths," I said, thinking my knowing the name of such a fancy flower might impress him.

"They're too small for a huge plot of land, and... um... looks like you bought them in mixed colors too."

"Because I like mixed colors."

Again, his reaction was as if I bought a mermaid lamp with a clock in its stomach for the living room. To his credit, he did try to feign appreciation for my bulbs and made a few polite suggestions for where they might look best, such as planting them off to the side of the driveway half way into the forest, or maybe on the far side of the house near the air conditioner, perhaps behind the big rock.

I decided to give him an out. "If you feel that strongly about my bulbs, I guess we could plant them near the chicken house."

"Good idea! Why don't you plant them there some other day?"

"You're not going to help me plant them today while we are on a bulb planting mission? I'm helping you plant the 450 expensive bulbs you purchased."

"Landscaping this house is a big project and I'm busy creating just the right look. I don't have time to waste playing around in the animal area."

"But it's OK for *me* to waste time in the animal area?"

"The animals are your thing. Building this house is mine."

"OK," I said with a sniff, not relishing the idea of hours spent alone planting unwanted bulbs in a place where the only creature who would notice was my donkey. The barnyard was becoming a symbol of my loneliness now and I spent many a quiet hour there, wondering what I could do to entice my husband to join me for a nice roll in the hay, or at the very least, a little hand holding.

As it turns out, planting bulbs is a little like buying a new couch. You add a dash of something new to your home and suddenly everything else looks lacking, so you're compelled to paint the living room. No sooner had we finished planting the bulbs than Mark had us back at the garden supply store for more plants. Now we needed trees.

"How about we get a bunch of those?" I said, pointing out apple trees on sale.

His eyes widened. "You only need a couple of apple trees for a grove. Just buy one of each type. You can't handle more. Trust me."

"I want lots of apples," I insisted. "Enough for cooking and for horse treats too."

"Four trees will provide enough apples to drown in."

I chose one Gala, two Granny Smith, and one Golden Delicious. For good measure, we picked up peach, plum, and pear trees, too.

"Hey, there's a fig tree," I said, spotting a small tree off to the corner of the garden center. "What can I make out of figs?"

Mark's brow crinkled. "Um… figgy pudding?"

"Of course. Figgy pudding! But that's only for Christmas. What else can I make out of figs?"

He thought some more. "Fig Newtons?"

"OK. So not a lot of fig recipes come to mind, but if we ever want to run around naked playing Adam and Eve, the leaves will come in handy. Come on. Let's get one."

I put the small tree in our cart, but when the checkout girl explained that Georgia fig trees don't really bear fruit, I put the bucket back on the shelf.

When we got back home, we used the tractor to plant the trees. Mark sat in the seat of the Kubota drinking lemonade while I plunged my hands into the dirt to smooth out the topsoil, ever the laborer bending to his orders. I chose to focus on the fact that our Garden of Eden was taking root, a metaphor for the future I imagined us living where we existed in harmony with nature and each other.

Each morning thereafter, I gazed out at the vegetable garden looking for signs of life. Within days, small sprouts emerged from the warm earth.

"Lookie! Our plants are growing!" I squealed, delighted to watch nature on autopilot.

"Um, honey…those are weeds. Somebody's going to have to pull those."

I waited a few days for 'somebody' to pull the offending weeds.

They grew taller. Thicker. Eventually, I figured out that 'somebody' was going to have to be me because Mark was too busy doing his own thing to ever again join me in the garden after the initial planting day.

I pulled the weeds, but the next day, more weeds had taken their place. I was reminded of the roaches that used to return to my apartment in New York City even after I had fumigated the place. That was a lifetime ago. Feeling warrior-like now, I marched out and pulled the new offenders. The next day, more weeds appeared. I pulled them again. And again. And again.

Our vegetable plants made a meek première and I started worrying that I couldn't distinguish between weeds and legitimate plants, so I dragged Mark to the garden to help me figure out what was what. He gave me a quick lesson on how to tell plants from weeds so I could continue my daily vigil.

One morning, while giving Donkey a morning carrot, I spotted something fat resting under a tangle of leaves. Sure enough, there hidden among the thick leaves was our first homegrown vegetable, a 14-inch zucchini brimming with sun-generated goodness. I also spied a yellow squash, a more normal sized-zucchini and some banana peppers. Gleefully, I returned to the house to show Mark my bounty. He commented that lots of zucchini grew as big as the one I was holding. My veggie was no big deal.

It doesn't take a brain surgeon to keep a zucchini plant alive; zucchini is a prolific grower and all, but I thought my first homegrown vegetable deserved more recognition from the master of the house than received. I myself couldn't help but prance around doing the 'I grew a veggie' dance, which is far funkier than the daffodil dance, I assure you.

That night, I sat down at my computer and searched epicurious. com to peruse the 271 zucchini recipes available. My first round of produce already sat simmering in a veggie chili, but I had to plan for the windfall ahead.

The next day, I revisited the garden again, hoping to see new produce, but all I found were hundreds of little yellow hairy bugs on my bean plants. I quickly beckoned the man of the house again, hoping a seasoned gardener might know what to do.

"You can always use a pesticide, but if we want an organic garden, somebody will have to have to pick those bugs off by hand."

"Somebody?"

I was now privy to the fact that 'somebody' meant me, so, grumbling, I spent three hours picking little yellow hairy bugs off of bean plants. Organic gardening seems a romantic ideal, but in reality, going au natural can be yucky. I couldn't even get my little nature-loving daughter to help. She took one look and said, "This is gross. Besides which, I hate beans. Who cares if the bugs eat them? You're on your own with this one, Mom."

For all that I tried to explain how noble and important organic gardening is to our health and the planet, Neva couldn't be swayed, so I devoted the afternoon to bug annihilation all by myself.

The next day, just as in the case of the weeds, my garden had been infiltrated with more yellow bugs. There was no way I could spend every afternoon picking them all by hand, so I decided to employ home remedies. I sprayed the plants with soapy water. That night, we had rain and the bugs had a grand time playing in the bubbles, but they didn't desert. I went back to hand picking.

A few weeks later, Mark drove by the garden, came home and said, "The plants look great. Why haven't you been picking the beans?"

"No beans yet," I said.

"By now, there must be beans. Are you sure?"

"Of course I'm sure. *Somebody* has to be involved in this gardening party we started. *Somebody* is pretty busy picking weeds and bugs. Trust me; *somebody* would know if we had any beans."

After dinner he dragged me down to the garden and slipped his arm around my waist. "Um, honey... the plants are so loaded with beans they look ready to cave. What are you waiting for?"

"No, sir...." I crouched down, and dang if there weren't hundreds of string beans hanging off the branches, hidden in the leaves like praying mantises. Not knowing what to look for, I hadn't seen them. "They look like a part of the plant."

"They *are* a part of the plant," he said. "And ready for harvesting. *Somebody* has to pick them."

Since picking beans was far more interesting than picking bugs, I didn't mind being *somebody* this time. In fact, my enthusiasm for the task was so contagious, that Mark and the kids started picking too and in half an hour we had two huge baskets filled.

The squash plants proved to be overachievers too. I gathered a basketful, and from that day on, added squash to every meal, until Kent no longer asked, "What are we having for dinner, Mom?" and instead commented, "What will we be having with our zucchini tonight, Mom?"

I put zucchini in bread, cookies, and brownies. I sautéed, stuffed, and fried zucchini, put it into soups, and blanched and froze a dozen bags.

We ate beans till we burst. I froze some, canned some, and even tried my hand at pickling beans, though I knew at the time there was scant chance anyone in our family would eat a pickled bean. Preserving wasn't so much about good eating now but more about taking advantage of our 'free' food in a way that would allow me to brag all winter about my new self-sufficiency. I made salsa, tomato sauce, and dozens of jars of pickles: traditional dill pickles, bread and butter pickles, sweet garlic dill pickles, lemon dill pickles, and more.

Still harboring hope that canning would improve my sex life, since a woman with canning skills seemed high on my husband's list of remarkable women, I did my best to present every batch of canned produce to Mark with a sultry bat of the eyelashes.

"That's a lot of pickles," he said, seeing the counter overrun with jars of green spears, and a huge bowl of cucumbers brining.

"I figure, any food that gets you to pucker up is worth making," I quipped, trying to look sexy as I hoisted another gallon jug of vinegar to the counter.

"They look great," he said, turning away.

Sigh.

Every day, I walked down to the garden with a big bowl and scissors to cut lettuce for our evening salad. I'd mix the fresh dark greens with walnuts and feta cheese and throw in anything else I found ripe that day. Every meal began with my pointing out how healthy the menu was, my not-so-subtle demand for praise from the troops. I was spending an awful lot of time in the nourishment area of our life, but since gardening was only going to last the summer, I considered it a short term grand experiment rather than drudgery. I marveled at each vegetable's natural form, fascinated that these tasty items were imperfect cousins of the Stepford vegetables found in shrink packaging at the grocery store. I got a kick out of the fact I could walk right outside my door with an empty bowl and return moments later with that same container overflowing with the makings of a healthy meal.

Of course, some of our efforts fell flat for no explainable reason. We planted cantaloupes and the plants flourished and flowered, but nary a melon grew. We planted corn, but only skinny wormy stalks came out. I was willing to pick bugs, but drew the line at worms. The corn become treats for the chickens. I should mention here that my chickens were real slackers in the egg department so far, and all I did was feed them, rather than them feeding us. We still had not seen a single egg.

Then, one day, I came upon 'the globe.'

A vine had popped out of the dry dirt where we had tossed the random seeds. Huge flowers bloomed along the stem and the bees buzzed so loud that echoes inside of those big flowers could be heard from ten feet away. Nevertheless, only one single globular thing developed. I stood at the edge of the hillside and stared. Might that round thing be a pumpkin? Perhaps a watermelon? But why wasn't the surface turning dark green? The ball didn't look like a gourd. If anything, this ball looked like a honeydew melon, except we hadn't planted any of those.

After two months of speculation, the globe turned orange, revealing that we'd grown our very own foot-wide Halloween pumpkin. I was mighty proud to have grown something so substantial, so much so I couldn't bear to carve it. The pumpkin sat in a place of honor on the mantel, as a seasonal decoration. I was so proud of that pumpkin that when Halloween passed, I added some cornhusk pilgrims as a fall tribute. Soon snow fell, and that pumpkin, still as fresh as the day picked, was crowned with a Santa hat, which made for an odd Christmas decoration, I agree, but still nice evidence of our farming finesse.

Spring came and I tried nestling the pumpkin in a wad of Easter grass, but even I couldn't justify the pumpkin's presence when spring offered a bounty of fresh flowers for decoration instead. So, the pumpkin found a new home on a bench outside of the kitchen door. I patted the gourd whenever I passed, marveling that months had gone by and there wasn't a speck of rot on the thing.

By May, I started wondering if pumpkins lasted forever, or if this specific one was enchanted. I started wishing the thing would wither or rot because I couldn't bring myself to just throw my prized pumpkin out now. I was deep in the throes of planting a new spring garden, and ready to retire any vestiges of the former year to make room for the new produce. Finally, I took the pumpkin to a hillside and, with a whispered "*sorry*," smashed the gourd for the chickens to pick through. A month later a new pumpkin plant made a shy entrance into the world and young eel-like vines spread across the hillside like Medusa's hair. Yellow globes began to bud on the tips. I'd unintentionally begun a heritage pumpkin patch, and our Santa Pumpkin had become the grandfather of many pumpkins to come.

And so my garden adventures continued. By each September I was tired from months of bending over to weed, harvest and water. I hated to see the garden fade, but after a full summer I was ready to take a break from harvesting to start opening the jars of preserves and sauces I'd made instead. Some days the effort and expense of organic gardening made me question the true value of growing food at home. I could buy a can of tomatoes for half the price of growing them, and finding locally grown produce was easy since every corner had a neighbor farmer selling wares from the back of his pickup. The industrial revolution was considered good for humanity because inventions rescued people from endless manual labor, right? But despite all the reasons why home gardening might be impractical in regards to a utilitarian equation, nothing compared to the sense of accomplishment and the fascination I gained from growing food myself.

Before moving to the country, my understanding of food sources was limited to an academic awareness that food grows on plants or in the ground, bacon comes from pigs, and hamburger from cows. Living closer to the earth made me see everything in life has a season and a purpose. Witnessing the life cycle of a bean, from planting of the seed to watching the mature plant wither and die, brought a certain reverence to my meals.

I still wasn't ready to raise livestock for eating, even knowing the meat for sale in the grocery store came from animals subject to a horrible, pitiful existence. The methods corporate food companies developed to feed the masses cheaply and to please our palate are truly inhumane. But however passionately I felt about the need for humane farming practices, I couldn't bring myself to kill my own dinner. I just had too much empathy for any creature I looked right in the eye to be the instrument of its death. My weakness was my shame.

As a compromise, we purchased one half a cow and a whole pig from Ronnie. Mark agreed to share the cost of the animals with him, with the understanding that I was never allowed to see them. I guess he feared I'd crack and lead the beast home on a rope as a new pet if I ever saw my cow up close.

One day that fear was put to the test. I wandered down to Ronnie's pasture to admire his property and accidentally came face to face with my cow.

"That black and white one is yours, you know—well, at least half of him," Ronnie said.

For an instant my stomach dropped, but watching that cow meander lazily across a field ripe under the sunshine made me reconsider my gut reaction. This cow would live two years on a clean pasture, while others I consumed spent six months in darkness and dung because the poor creatures were unlucky enough to be born and raised by a corporate meat company. True, in both cases, the animals were destined for slaughter, but death would come quickly and gracefully to my cow. I'll feel better when my freezer fills with hormone-free packaged meat from a cow who had known the pleasure of sun and kindness during his time on earth.

Like so many others of my generation, I know I rationalize my behavior when stress or frustration has me headed to the McDonald's drive-through. I don't always eat with mindful awareness. But tending a garden and watching animals graze naturally has taught me to consider the difference between food raised with respect and dignity, and the alternative. I guess you can say that instead of saying grace with my meals, I began to *feel* grace as my relationship with food changed.

"There is no beginning too small."

—*Henry David Thoreau*

BEE YOURSELF

Two bees ran into each other. One asked the other how things were going.
"Pretty bad," said the second bee. "The weather has been really wet and damp.
There aren't any flowers or pollen, so I can't make any honey."

"No problem," said the first bee. "Just fly down five blocks, turn left, and
keep going until you see all the cars. There's a Bar Mitzvah going on with all
kinds of fresh flowers and fruit."

"Thanks for the tip," said the second bee as he flew away.

A few hours later the two bees ran into each other again. The first bee asked,
"How'd it go?"

"Fine," said the second bee, "It was everything you said it would be."

"Uh, what's that thing on your head?" asked the first bee.

"That's my yarmulke," said the second bee. "I didn't want them to think I
was a wasp."

(That's a beekeeper joke, don't ya know?)

As I pored over gardening and environmental magazines, I kept
stumbling over articles that focused on "an impending epidemic of
monstrous proportions." Bee colonies were collapsing without clear
cause and science was in a tizzy over the loss of our beloved pollinators. The world's food supply would collapse without bees, the
articles proclaimed. Meanwhile, honey was at a premium due to the
decline in production as more and more independent apiaries were
giving up the struggle to stay in business.

My new role as guardian of the land made me feel responsible for
doing my part to save humanity.

Theories about why the bees were disappearing ranged from
global warming and the overuse of chemicals to the possibility that
cell phone towers were interfering with the insect's communication

skills. New, heartier Russian bees, more aggressive in nature, yet less inclined to go belly up, were being bred. Even so, the bee population was still dwindling.

Despite the scientific facts, I didn't see a lack of bees as much of a threat where I lived. My blueberry bush was always humming with honeybees, bumble bees and all manner of wasps and butterflies. The ground vibrated from so many flying insects hovering over the clover and whisking through the fescue, I had no doubt my plants would be visited by enough pollinators to get the job done. The whole bee scarcity thing seemed an exaggeration, but the focus on bee colony collapse disorder did bring my attention to just how vitally important bees were to my garden. If I wanted to do this organic and environmentally friendly gardening thing right, I should get some bees.

I began studying beekeeping. As creatures of distinct habit and remarkable social structure, bees can be second-guessed and even controlled. Hive placement, estimated flight path, and a bit of basic math can leverage bees so they'll impact a garden in the best of ways. Furthermore, local raw honey is one of the healthiest foods a person can consume; the honey from the pollen of the very plants that plague residents with allergies helps a person develop natural immunity.

I didn't have allergies and my garden was producing well, but the lure of jars and jars of free honey to cook with was as much a motivation to me as performing the ecologically conscientious act of raising bees.

The problem was going to be Mark. If a miniscule little sweat bee buzzed anywhere near, he would flap his arms and dance about like a terrified little girl, so I knew he wouldn't be very enthusiastic about my adding fifty thousand bees to our back yard.

"Honey, I was thinking about how to get the most from our garden, and beekeeping might serve us well," I said one night.

"No."

"Can't we talk about it?"

"We just did. You asked about keeping bees. I said no. Case closed."

"That's not a very good attitude. When the world's supply of food dries up because there weren't enough bees to pollinate plants, won't you feel guilty?"

"Maybe so, but bees sting. Isn't it enough that you have chickens and zucchini plants?"

"I need bees to pollinate the zucchini. Just think of all the sweeties I can make you with a vat of honey at my disposal. Honey's expensive, you know, but with bees, honey will be free." (I prayed he wouldn't compare this to my egg production equation, which as yet, hadn't saved us a cent since my birds hadn't laid a single egg.) "I'll put a hive in a far corner of our land. I promise."

"I hate bees," he said.

"I know you do, dear." I felt a twinge of guilt when his heavy sigh of resignation filled the air.

He said no more, so I thought the case was closed. Bees had been vetoed. But a month later, he joined my sister in giving me a starter beehive kit for my birthday. He no doubt felt railroaded by my sister's enthusiasm and figured I'd be getting bees one way or another so he might as well get credit by giving me his generous permission rather than having his preference ignored. Nevertheless, I was touched. It's easy for a man to give his wife a sexy nightgown or a lovely dinner out for her birthday. But a beehive when you absolutely despise bees? That's love, or so I chose how to view the act.

I went online and bought some beekeeping books, bee food, a bee smoker, and tools. I subscribed to *The Beekeeper Journal*, joined the Georgia Beekeepers Association, and signed up for a weekend beekeeping course.

When the hive kit arrived, I put the pieces together, painted the parts, and went back online to purchase bees, only to discover orders for bees are taken in January and since this was spring, all the bee companies were sold out.

Mark suggested I talk to the Indian at the flea market who sold honey on weekends. Perhaps he would know where I could get some bees. So, we visited the honey booth, and I interrogated the Indian while Mark leaned down to peer into the jars of gleaming gold sweetness.

The Indian was a gruff, quiet man with dark eyes and tobacco skin. He offered to sell me a nuc (a small colony) of bees, and for a reasonable fee offered to help me set them up. The next day he came to our place in a rattling truck filled with a dozen gallon jugs of honey and a box holding five frames of bees. Mark immediately announced he had important errands to run and skedaddled. Alone as usual in my country adventures, I showed the Indian beekeeper where to set up the hive.

I took him to a shady corner of the forest where Mark agreed I could keep the bees. The man grunted, looking about with a shake of his head. "If you want the hive to succeed, the box needs to be out in the open where the sun shines. Somewhere near your garden. Why would you want to hide bees in the forest anyway?"

"My husband thought it might be safer to keep them out of sight."

"Not for the bees," he said, stepping to the open field and pointing to areas that were good for a beehive. "I take it your husband is not much of a farmer."

"He likes the idea of farming, but a practical application of his ideals is not exactly his forte."

A change of bee plans would not make Mark happy, but I was about as savvy about bees as I had been about mules, and I admitted I was agriculturally ignorant and tired of wasting money when we did things 'our way' instead of the right way, I told the man to set up my bees wherever he thought was best. The Indian drove to the very front of our land, selected a prominent, grassy spot right at the entrance, and wordlessly set up the hive. When this was done, he made his way back to the car to write out a bill, his face a mask of stoic intelligence. For some ridiculous reason, I felt my bees were of better quality than any I might have purchased from a bee farm because an authentic Cherokee delivered them.

"Don't forget to feed them." he said as he started up his truck.

"How?"

He nodded towards the box on the top of the hive. "That thing you have on the top of the hive is a feeder. Just fill the box up with sugar water and the bees will stick to their new digs."

"Sure. Okay," I said, trying to feign confidence. As soon as the dust settled from the Indian's truck rolling down the lane, I rushed to the house to crank up the Internet. An hour later I returned to the hive with two pounds of sugar diluted with water for that thing on top of my hive, which I now knew was a feeder.

There didn't seem to be any sort of bee mutiny going on yet, but I filled the feeder anyway. Bees came and went from the small opening in the front, seemingly happy with their new home.

Mark was perturbed when he returned to find the bees out in the open, but he wouldn't dare move the hive, so they remained right where they had been positioned. A new hive of bees pretty much takes care of itself, and since flowers were blooming like gang-busters, there was nothing to do but watch from afar. Having bees was rather anticlimactic until a month later, when the time came to officially check the hive.

The books said I could handle the bees in jeans and a long sleeve shirt. Gloves and a headpiece are all you truly need to work with bees, and even then, the thick leather fingers of the gloves make it hard to get hold of the closely spaced honey files in the hive. Nevertheless, I decided to slip on my bee suit, partly because I was a nervous newbie and partly because I wanted to pretend I was a big-time beekeeper. A bee suit is really nothing more than a stiff jumpsuit made of canvas. A plastic safari hat with a bride-like veil protected my face. A beekeeper suit looks a little like a spacesuit, truth be told.

"Take me to your leader," I said, the first time I put on the suit and gave the family a fashion show. I walked around the living room in slow motion like someone walking on the moon.

"We could get a suit in your size so you could get up close without risk," I suggested to Mark. "It's pretty cool to witness how nature works, and I'm told a honey-filled hive is heavy. You could help me lift and harvest the honey. Beekeeping can be an adventure we share."

"No interest."

I sighed, then loaded up the car alone. I had a second hive box at the ready in case the bees were ready to expand their living quarters. I also had my trusty bee brush to sweep bees out of the way, a hive tool, and a lighter for the smoker. I figured with the hive only a month old, all the beekeeping paraphernalia was unlikely to be necessary, but I wanted to play with my new toys and the bee suit made me feel serious and infallible.

I lit up the smoker using pine needles for fuel. Within seconds the pot oozed a heady stream of thick, gray smoke. The hive top was sealed with propolis: a sticky residue bees create to seal their homes. Good! This gave me an excuse to use my hive tool. I pried the lid open and peeked inside feeling ever so professional. A million bees stopped what they were doing, turned around, and stared at me with disdain. Their eyes spoke of raw hatred, I tell ya.

I reached for the smoker and shot little whiffs of smoke under the lid. Hopping back, I tried not to hyperventilate. Slowly I crept forward and lifted the top again, only to discover the bees had all crawled down into the recesses of the hive. Sigh. That was better.

I leaned in closer to inspect the frames, staring with wonder at the brood embedded in the new comb. Using the pry end of my trusty hive tool, I lifted the center frame. A hundred bees scurried about eating honey, a natural reaction to the smoke. The frame was shockingly heavy, dripping with sweet amber. I wanted to dip a finger in and get a taste, but the glove and my awkward hold on the frame made that impossible. Gingerly, I set the frame aside.

I shifted things about to look at the other frames, but rather than do a full inspection, I just peeked at the active frames from above fearing I'd crush the single queen like many dopey inexperienced beginners do.

I had put together a new hive stand that very morning, so I moved the hive to the ground so I could install the new part and crushed a handful of bees in the process. Oops. When I tried to set up the stand, the box didn't fit on the concrete blocks, so I ended up putting everything back in place, crushed bees and all. I poured more sugar water into the hive top feeder. This wasn't necessary, but feeding the bees was the only thing I knew how to do with confidence and I was the kind of girl who always felt feeding her loved ones was a way of nurturing and caring for them.

I wanted to put an entrance block in front of the hive to keep out honey robbers; however, the entrance was swarming with active, annoyed bees. Apparently, they don't take kindly to strangers killing their kin. Determined, I tried to put the device in place, but two bees landed on me and tried to sting my arm. Protected by the suit, I brushed them away, grabbed the smoker and puffed in their direction, only to discover my smoker had burned out! The bees were now buzzing louder, no doubt spreading the word that I no longer had a weapon. Quickly, I bent down and stuffed a handful of pine straw into the smoker and squeezed the air vent until more smoke puffed up.

"Take that," I said, sending a few extra shots their way. They say bees can sense your attitude, and the most important thing you can do is remain calm and loving when working with bees. Obviously, this particular lesson would take practice for me.

Satisfied at surviving my first hive check, I put everything back in place, backed away, took off my veil and gloves, and leaned against the car to watch the bees swarming in the air. My hair was sweaty from the bee hat, but a warm breeze blew through my bangs. The bees outnumbered me by the thousands, but having come through a successful first encounter, I felt oddly in tune with them.

Wildflowers dotted the field around my feet and the blackberry bush was in bloom, as were dandelions and clover. I formerly picked daisies, cosmos, and coneflowers for my table this time of year, but now decided to leave the flowers to their greater purpose. I knew the bees would fly in a two-mile range, and return to this very box to do the famed bee-dance to communicate where each flower was located. Imagining this, I considered my grief over dance disappearing from my life. Perhaps my greatest love had simply been reincarnated, lurking in the background of my existence quietly, in the dance of the bees. Perhaps everything I had been in the past and everything I was learning to be now was fusing, the shadows of one life gently morphing into another.

I sat there in the field for over an hour wondering how I could possibly describe the poignancy of this moment to my husband. The astounding resonance of this quiet adventure would unfortunately end with me, because some things cannot be shared secondhand despite our desire to try. I felt sad for all Mark was missing, sadder still for what I myself was missing as I witnessed the beauty all around me, alone.

"Do not be too moral. You may cheat yourself out of much life so. Aim above morality. Be not simply good, be good for something."
—*Henry David Thoreau*

HOME CHURCH

Friends from our former life often asked, "How are the kids coping with the move?"

"Our kids have never been happier," I'd say, only to receive a condescending smile, as if I were lying.

We no longer had access to expensive gymnastic or karate schools promising to develop a young person's grace or self-discipline. There were no afterschool computer labs or SAT crash courses to enhance a child's learning capacity, either. We didn't even have competitive cheerleading squads promising a perfect cartwheel, the key to popularity and a lifetime of success in some circles. As such, friends were convinced our previously popular pop culture kids could never be happy. How could hip people like us live in a backward town without malls, movie theaters, or designer clothing outlets?

They didn't get it. Our life had become a great experiment, and collectively, we saw promise and beauty in the simple things that forged togetherness. We dived into family adventure like a starving person would dive into a buffet table.

We laughed at ourselves as we stumbled through daily country experiences, partially because we didn't fit in, and partially because we did. There really was very little to do in the country, and because of this, we just hung out. We sat around a fire ring at night and shared dreams, embarrassing moments, and jokes. We went apple picking and tubing down the river. We picked beans from the garden, had snowball fights with the dogs, and dared each other to eat homegrown guinea eggs. When we had no place to go, we brought entertainment home, not a rented video, but things to do, such as making baskets, cartoon drawings, or homemade Christmas ornaments of clay. We ate meals together for the first time in years, and sometimes hopped into the car for a late night treat at the Dairy Queen, a venture made all the more appealing because nothing else was open past six o'clock.

Our theater of choice was the local drive-in, the trunk of our car packed with thermoses and treats. Our favorite dinner out was a picnic in the park on Thursdays when local bluegrass musicians gave free concerts. We went to festivals, craft fairs, and meandered through the local flea market to pick up antique bottles, socks, and books. We swam in the lake, hiked to see waterfalls, and picked blackberries. Our time together was leisurely and casual, with meaningful conversation cementing our feelings of togetherness. No single event was cause for great enthusiasm, yet the general attitude was that life was good. The lack of constant suburban stimuli forced us to look within ourselves for fulfillment, and the mass-produced products and experiences so carefully designed to make people feel fulfilled seemed anything but fulfilling from this distance.

"Life here feels like a vacation," my son once said. Indeed. But as the novelty of family time spent together wore off, my kids chose to spend their free time with new friends. My husband, wanting desperately to be embraced by the local crowd, preferred laughing about country antics with Ronnie rather than talking about the day with me.

My new confidant became Kathy. As each member of the family struggled to fit in and become 'naturalized' in our new environment, the desire for companionship became a personal challenge each of us chose to solve independently.

Mark and I worried that our suburb-raised kids wouldn't be able to relate to their new peers. Here, youngsters were learning to drive a tractor at the same age their former friends were learning to maneuver a skateboard. But the Internet makes the world a smaller place, and even the most countrified kids had a respectable handle on pop culture trends and styles. Some kids were indeed cowboys or farmers in the making, but they knew what bands were popular, what clothing was cool, and they spent enough time on YouTube to keep current with the fast paced culture of the world at large. The kids in Blue Ridge were as comfortable in a barn as at a GameStop, a combination of MTV and Huck Finn influences balancing their lives. They didn't hang out at the mall. Instead, they went camping, whitewater rafting, and swimming in the lake, all healthy activities that I thrilled to witness my kids trying.

I suppose the fact that we moved just before my son entered high school made the peer issue less threatening. Kent had had his fill of pop cultural influences and his personality was set. He was definitely going to college and had a broad view of the world. Moving to the country simply gave him a reprieve from the endlessly competitive environment of the rat race, time to redefine his moral and emotional center. He would charge back into the "real world" within four short years, and when he did, he'd be fortified with good memories of family togetherness.

Denver was an adult, taking a year reprieve from her life path to rebalance and get her bearings. Her time with us wasn't unlike a college kid taking a year off to backpack Europe before getting that first job, and thereafter taking on a lifetime of mortgages and responsibilities. I trusted she would be fine.

Our daughter Neva, however, was more of a cause for concern. She was younger; still in her formative years and more apt to be influenced by local attitudes and influences. I loved that she constantly had a chicken under her arm rather than being a slave to fashion and the latest iPod accessories. Neva was a budding environmentalist and animal rights advocate, an avid reader and deep thinker. She was smart, self-reliant, and happy. The problem was the wholesome environment of the country came hand in hand with constant exposure to a narrow mindset, a darker side of the country where ignorance ruled behavior.

Kids didn't talk much about religion on Florida's suburban coastline, but in Blue Ridge, a family was defined by what church they attended. On the first day of school, my kids came home baffled because every student they met opened the conversation with the same question. *"What church do you belong to?"*

Kids just didn't ask that kind of thing in Florida, at least not before asking someone their name or where they got their cool shoes.

When Kent and Neva innocently commented that our family didn't belong to a church, they were barraged with hard-sell tactics to attend this church or that one, as if the locals got a commission for each soul they saved.

"Why didn't you just tell the kids at school that we don't go to church?" Mark said.

"I did. They started calling me a Jew," Kent said.

"Did you tell them you aren't Jewish?"

"Of course, but they still said things like, 'Hey Jew, give me a pencil. They aren't doing it in a mean way. They're joking…I think."

"Is everyone who doesn't go to church a Jew?" Neva asked innocently.

Mark and I exchanged a look of chagrin. We may not be big church people, but we obviously were remiss if we hadn't instilled a basic understanding of religion in child number three. Shame on us.

"No matter what I say or do, they keep bothering me about what church we're going to join," Kent said. "It makes me feel weird."

"Me, too. I told everyone we haven't decided which church to join because we liked our old church in Florida so much. Lying is easier. I don't want everybody here to hate me because I'm a wicked sinner," Neva said.

"You are not a wicked sinner, and you shouldn't lie to avoid confrontation. A family doesn't have to be involved in organized religion to be decent and spiritual."

"Why don't we just join a church so they don't keep bothering us? We don't have to actually go," my son suggested.

"We're not the sort of people who do things we don't believe in just to fit in," I said with enough emphasis to remind everyone that comment applied to much more than just our choice of worship.

"Easy for you to say," Kent mumbled. "Once they tag you as godless here, you're doomed."

For a month, we tried to come up with a comfortable way for our children to thwart the awkward religious grilling they received at school. How could we explain to our offspring that being called a Jew wasn't an insult, even though in this case the name-calling was clearly meant to be one? How could we explain that a good Christian doesn't hate gays and blacks and Catholics and anyone else who isn't a Baptist? How could we convince them that people who drank or cussed or didn't choose to sit in a steepled building on Sundays were not doomed to hell?

Finally, Mark came up with a solution. "Next time the kids ask you what church you attend, tell them you're home-churched."

Kent lifted one eyebrow. "What does that mean?"

"You know how kids are home-schooled around here because the parents don't trust school to educate them with strong-enough Christian values? Well, tell everyone you are home-churched because your parents believe that is the only way you'll be taught our family's deep faith and wisdom. That'll shut them up."

And it did. Our kids became known as the home-churched Hendrys.

One day Kent mentioned he was going home to Florida to visit relatives. A kid at lunch asked, "Are you taking a gun?"

Kent laughed. "Why would I take a gun?"

"To shoot the niggers. You can't walk the streets down there without niggers jumping you."

Kent relayed the conversation, thinking I'd find it funny since the kid had said the stupid comment with absolute seriousness.

"What did you say to that?" I asked, trying not to grind my teeth to dust.

"Nothing. That kid's a stupid redneck. I wasn't about to tell him some of our friends are black. I'm not stupid!"

"Do all the kids at school talk like bigots?" I asked, giving Mark one of those *we simply can't raise our kids here if prejudice and ignorance is gonna be the norm* kind of looks.

"Not all. But lots do. Face it, Mom, there are rednecks here. *Lots* of them. Don't worry; I hang with the right crowd."

The right crowd. That comment alone made me uncomfortable.

Obviously raising kids in a place where you have to step around a minefield of ignorance was going to take work. A country upbringing was all well and good when living here provided us the time and inclination to sit around the campfire to enjoy nature's stillness and the inspiration of changing seasons, but exposing my children to an endless stream of drugs, teen weddings, and ignorant attitudes was more than a little threatening.

The country was genteel and charming, but the more I came face to face with life under the surface, the more I questioned the integrity of our life choice. Ninety percent of the girls in the area wanted nothing more than to get married and have kids on or before their eighteenth birthday. Thirty percent of the girls in our area were married by the time they were 16! Would one of these empty-headed Daisy Dukes date my son and get pregnant, expecting him to step up to the plate and spend the rest of his life in this nowhere town? (How quickly "quaint" turns into "unacceptable" when it involves your child's future.)

Worse yet, would my youngest daughter decide to get married and pregnant on or before her eighteenth birthday, influenced by peers who enthusiastically claimed it was *the* thing to do if you were really in love? How would Neva know marriage at the age of 15 was not a normal part of the adolescent dating experience in America today? She may grow up one of the sexually responsible few, but still, I wanted my daughter to become a female of substance and purpose, not one of the country belles whose primary concern was her looks, her popularity, and forging a family based on the traditional dynamic of the fifties.

Complex and important life issues would continue to rear their ugly heads as long as we stayed in the country, forcing us to throw sticky subjects out on the table to reaffirm our family mindset. If we were going to stay in Blue Ridge we really would have to home church our children.

In the end, I came to the conclusion that the great task of raising conscientious, responsible kids wasn't easier or harder due to geographical location. Just different. I loved that our kids were growing up less consumer reliant and with less stress, but diligent and mindful effort would be needed to hardwire their minds to be less prejudiced, less close-minded, and less likely to pass judgment on others here, too.

The problem is, no matter how mindful parents may be, it takes a village to raise a child.

"As a single footstep will not make a path on the earth, so a single thought will not make a pathway in the mind. To make a deep physical path, we walk again and again. To make a deep mental path, we must think over and over the kind of thoughts we wish to dominate our lives."

— *Henry David Thoreau*

THE MILLION DOLLAR QUESTION

Old friends continued to ask me, "What are you doing with your life now?"

I explained we were taking a few years off to live in the mountains so we could focus on family.

They inevitably said, "Wow, you two are living a dream."

It took all my self-control not to blow a big raspberry right into their faces.

I don't want to kill anyone's idealism. We all want to imagine contentment is waiting for us if we just turn our back on worldly pursuits and remember what counts. Everyone agrees money can't buy happiness, but deep down we all believe money can, at least a little. But be careful, lest your dream become a nightmare, too.

On any given day, I'd drive all over the county, shuttling the kids to school, feeding the animals, tutoring Kathy, taking a pump class at the closest gym, 40 minutes away. On this particular day, as I was driving to pick up my kids from school, the family's new puppy began whining and circling as if he had to go to the bathroom. My new car had already been ravaged by rustic living fallout. Hay was between the back seats and two fifty-pound bags of grain had leaked into the trunk. That week, Mark put a tree stump in the trunk, and though he eventually reclaimed his prize, he didn't bother to remove the bark and moss residue left behind. All things considered, a puppy accident, while unpleasant, would hardly be noticed in this car. I tossed a towel on the floor, hoping that the puppy would find this more inviting than my coat, which happened to be resting on the seat next to him. Of course, my coat proved a more appealing toilet, probably because the coat smelled like a donkey.

I was trying to simultaneously steer and take care of the puppy when my husband called to share the day's slew of frustration and conflict regarding his log home project. He ended with yet another explanation about why we wouldn't be moving into the dream house on schedule.

He also told me that even though he had spent the entire day at the house site, he ran out for some more materials before bothering to feed the livestock, as he had offered to do that morning. I now had to drive over myself to do the task or let the horses go hungry. I picked my kids up from school and took them to the land, grumbling about wasted gas and time. They argued the entire way about who should hold the new puppy. I tuned them out and turned up the music on my CD player. The CD skipped.

Rain fell nonstop all day. Our pasture, formerly a rolling valley of green grass, had turned into a mud pit with no hope of repair anytime soon. Having never encountered this kind of problem in suburban Florida, I was exhausted from lying awake nights listening to the rain, watching the temperature drop, and feeling increasingly bad about the conditions my animals had to endure. My still-injured horse, Peppy, deserved a safe, dry place to heal, and since there wasn't an ounce of grass left in our pasture, he needed dry hay too. I didn't know where a person could buy a full load of hay, nor did I have a place to store a bunch of bales if I did. So I kept buying one bale a day at the feed store for three times what hay cost in bulk and toted it home in my car's back seat because my husband's truck bed was reserved for the things he felt were important, like new tools or grapevine for wreaths he might someday make. I felt guilty about the cost, frustrated by the inconvenience, and dismayed by my quickly deteriorating car.

I parked my mud-encrusted, puppy pee-and-hay-filled car in the grass, and went trudging into the pasture, ankle deep in mud and horse dung. This wouldn't have been a problem except for the fact that I was wearing my best pair of high-tech sporty workout shoes, which I had donned because I was assured I wouldn't have to make this trip today.

I checked the injury on Peppy's leg, dreading the fact that I'd have to spray the putrid homemade medicine on the wound and fling baking powder over the area myself. The leg was covered in a hard, wrinkly brown shell and I couldn't tell if this was a scab or hardened mud collected in the wound. If the shell was mud, I'd have to remove the mess to get the medicine into the wound. If I started pulling scabs off a horse's hurt leg, he might kick my brains out. There was no plumbing on our land yet, so the only water source was the creek.

I batted my eyelashes at my son. "Help your old mom out, will you?"

Kent grudgingly slopped through the muddy pasture to bring me the first of several buckets of creek water, his new Reeboks instantly ruined.

I poured the freezing water down the horse's leg and pulled at the gross, compacted wound. A leaf came loose. Fairly confident the hard shell was just dirt now, I spent 20 minutes picking and rubbing the wound with a towel while dodging four annoyed, stamping feet. The rain came down with more force. My fingers were frozen.

The mud that had been up to my ankles now reached my thigh. It splashed up onto my t-shirt, which didn't exactly make me look like a contender for a wet t-shirt contest, but more like some out-of-shape, middle-aged hillbilly wearing a soaked camouflage potato sack with a hundred dollar pair of brown Nikes oozing goo. Not cute.

With the wound cleaned up at last, I asked Neva to get out of the car to help her brother. Kent's designated role was to catch the goat and drag him by the horns to a tree so we could tie him up. Otherwise Freckles would make himself a nuisance and get between the horses and their feed.

The goat ran this way and that in an excited frenzy, my son hanging on and slipping and sliding behind him like a surfer dude riding waves of mud. Watching the drama of the badly behaved goat, I couldn't help but wonder if goatburgers were a delicacy we might one day consider trying after all. I turned my attention back to the injured horse.

Meanwhile, Kent was so intent on keeping a handle on the goat's horns, he'd forgotten to shut the gate. The other two horses and the donkey came charging out. Loose now, the big animals started running every which way, their eyeballs rolling back in their heads as they snorted and whinnied.

So, there we were: three crazy huge animals running loose, two city-bred kids running for their lives, and me, anchored in place with the wounded Peppy, shouting for the kids to calm down and help me corral the animals. My brave offspring were sure they'd get trampled, so they ignored me, screaming in such a panicked way the animals grew more agitated. Neva high-tailed her butt back into the car. Kent released the goat and dived behind a tree, shouting in bloodcurdling fear that we were doomed. Of course this meant the goat could now join in the rampage as well. Thanks, son.

Goliath, the largest and most spirited of our horses, was behaving like a loco stallion from an old John Wayne movie. I tried to cut him off, but he headed the other direction, snorting and bucking. I wasn't so much nervous as I was pissed, imagining I could develop a taste for horseburgers, too, at this point.

After about ten minutes of this fruitless equestrian chase, it occurred to me that hungry horses would come for food. Oh.

I poured some feed into the bucket and Goliath trotted up. I stared him in the eye and plunked the bucket down. He stared back at me, leery. I held his halter over the bowl, an obvious sign that the fun was soon to end. He lowered his head to nibble, his nose neatly fitting into place. I tied the lead, whereupon he instantly became the docile and sweet horse I needed. Just like a man to put up a fight and then turn into a big baby the moment he realizes the girl has control.

The horses were finally situated and eating. My fingers were frozen. My ears were frozen. I was mourning my shoes. My daughter was waving, humming happily because she got to stay in the warm car with the puppy during most of the ordeal. Meanwhile, my son was flailing his arms dramatically.

"Did you see that? Goliath was charging at me but I dodged just in time! I'm lucky to be alive."

I lifted one eyebrow. "Yeah, thanks for the help, cowboy."

Peppy hobbled forward. He hadn't eaten much and his leg looked even more swollen than yesterday. I petted his nose and apologized for the fact that I didn't have a dry, clean barn for his convalescence. He ignored me, except to look for apples in my pocket. The rain made his hair sleek against his skin, revealing his now-protruding ribs, so I gave him all three apples.

Donkey looked on with gentle eyes, as if to say, *"This wouldn't happen if it were just the two of us."* He leaned into my side, the only creature in my world that seemed to understand I could use a tender nuzzle once in a while. I gave him some extra feed and a cookie.

Before driving home, I stopped by the chicken house. No eggs still. Damn birds.

I would describe my car after that episode, but I do not possess the required eloquence to paint a picture of the filth and unbelievable mess our mud-laden shoes made. Ah, well. I loved my car. I loved my land. I just had to be resolved to loving one inside the other.

I came home to the find the construction crew had disconnected my washer again which now sat on the porch, rusting. That morning they'd promised my laundry facilities would be up and running by that afternoon, but clearly, cleaning clothes at home would not be an option for days, if not weeks. I wanted to kick the machine, but thought better since mud was oozing through my socks.

We all undressed in the cold at the front door and left our muddy clothes in a pile. The kids showered while I cooked dinner. As the stove heated up, I tried to clean my shoes, now looking like they'd been worn on a trek through Mongolia. I would have thrown them out except for the fact that, gross as they were, they looked better than my other six pairs.

We'd been living without a TV for eight months, so after cleaning up the dishes, there was not much to do but go to bed with a magazine. I read an article about how easy teaching horses perfect manners could be. Obviously, this author hadn't met my horses.

I fell asleep and dreamed. My dream was not of Paris and Porsches, nor of the peaceful life I thought would be ours without question once we unloaded our business, but was instead filled with visions of mud and loneliness and fitful worry about money.

I awoke to another day. And more rain.

WHINING, DINING, AND WINING

On one of our first visits to Blue Ridge, Mark and I checked out the one and only decent restaurant in the little town. We were enchanted by the quaintness and earthy quality of antlers and Appalachian wildlife taxidermy teeming on the walls.

A waitress wearing the nametag "Trudy" asked us what we'd like to drink. I hadn't even looked over the menu, so I just ordered a glass of wine.

Trudy blinked dully. "No can do. This is a dry county."

"What does dry mean exactly?"

Trudy smacked her gum. "Most people in these parts consider drinkin' a sin. We don't serve liquor in Fannin County. If you want to get drunk, you need to go to Ellijay." (Ellijay is a town 35 minutes away.)

"I don't intend to get drunk. I just want a glass of wine," I muttered. I ordered a diet Coke and couldn't resist adding, "If residents are forced to drive to the next town to drink, aren't we likely to have more intoxicated people driving on the roads around here?"

A couple from another table leaned over to explain that beer and wine could be purchased at the grocery store, but no hard liquor could be purchased anywhere in Blue Ridge. There was a BYOB system in effect, however, that allowed customers to bring their own bottle of wine to some of the restaurants.

I glanced around at all the other couples enjoying a nice meal in the rustic restaurant. No one had a bottle nestled in a paper bag on their tabletop—no doubt because of how awkward it would be to request glasses from someone who thought of wine as the nectar of sinners.

I have never been much of a drinker, but my not being able to order a glass of wine made me want one now for reasons I couldn't explain.

"How do you suppose a restaurant like this survives without liquor to build revenue?" I said, knowing how important a bar bill is to a restaurant's bottom line.

"I guess they don't need liquor sales to get by," Mark said.

But over the next few months, the establishment changed hands three times. Eventually, the place closed altogether. Word was the owner moved his business to Ellijay so he could meet an upscale restaurant's overhead by offering a full service menu—meaning liquor.

Visiting a dry county on vacation had been quaint, but now that we lived in the area, "quaint" felt annoying, if not a bit controlling. Popular franchises steered clear of the town because the strict liquor law made implementing their successful formats impossible, and independent restaurateurs couldn't survive without the high return from premium beverages. That left the town with a Dairy Queen and a smattering of burger joints to meet the area's culinary needs. Meanwhile, what could have been much-needed local tax dollars landed in the next county's coffers as residents took their dining business one town over.

The local economy struggled as a result, so the residents grew divided on the issue of liquor sales. The people who wanted to lift the drinking ban argued that the ordinance was threatening the town's economic stability. They also argued the Bible doesn't really state drinking is a sin, so religion is no excuse for disallowing beer and wine in area establishments. The die-hard Southern Baptists responded that scripture does point to drunkenness as an undeniable evil. They claimed the ordinance was in place to protect citizens.

The arguments ping-ponged back and forth over the net of economics, religion, and free choice, but in the end, the issue was mostly about change: those who wanted change and those who didn't.

As happened every few years, the ordinance was challenged by a local vote. For months the landscape was littered with "vote no" or "vote yes" signs. People wore buttons proclaiming their stance, and conversations around the post office or feed store hummed with passionate opinions about alcohol sales.

On voting day, churches brought buses of senior citizens from nursing homes to the polls. The elderly were closer to meeting their Maker and thus more inclined to embrace His teachings, (especially after hearing a few passionate lectures on the evils of alcohol en route.) Ministers demonstrated at the voting booths in hopes of "saving" the less pure of heart or at least intimidating guilty folk into avoiding the polls. Meanwhile, the people who believed the dry county ordinance was unconstitutional stomped by the demonstrators to boldly place a vote that might jumpstart the flagging economy.

I found it remarkable that we lived in the one place left in America where the lure of commercial success could still be thwarted by a 1950's mentality. 'Change' had become the buzzword all over America. Our new black president had proven the concept of *change* was powerfully seductive, but in the mountains, no one wanted anything to do with progress of any kind.

Personally, I understood the need for the economic boost that would come with lifting the dry county ordinance, and I resented others thinking they had the right to decide whether or not I could order wine with dinner. At the same time, I had an aversion to franchises, and secretly I was grateful that the self-righteous attitude of the Bible thumpers kept the quaint town at a growth stalemate.

Nevertheless, I voted to have the ban lifted because, for me, living in a place where liquor was treated like liquid leprosy was simply too darn inconvenient.

I no longer enjoyed eating out. Driving 40 minutes to find a place that would allow me to order comfortably was cumbersome, and I had no interest in bringing a bottle hidden in a brown paper bag to the local eateries like some kind of wino who can't go a few hours without. I continued to drink a glass of wine with the meals I made at home, but suddenly this felt weird, too, like I'd become a closet drinker. The strangest part was I never cared much for drinking before, but the fact that alcohol was prohibited in our town had me more focused than ever on the joy to be gained in a heady sip of wine at the end of the day.

I guess if you tell people they can't have something, they want it all the more. History shows that speakeasies and illegal clubs tripled in number in our country during Prohibition. This led to a huge surge of mob-related violence. With the income potential from crime sky-rocketing, bootleggers and mob bosses grew more powerful than our elected officials. People who were not much interested in spirits before Prohibition now kept a hidden bottle behind the books in their libraries and secretive drinking became all the rage. Did the religious anti-alcohol population have any clue what a boon their efforts were doing for drinking in the bigger scheme?

Having friends to dinner became a minefield of correct behavior because you just never knew on which side of the debate acquaintances stood. Wine complements a refined meal, but when I offered up a fine bottle to accompany a fancy dish, the alcohol often languished, untried.

Wine was on my mind, historically, experientially, and philosophically now.

"I want to learn to make wine at home," I announced to Mark one morning. "There's a class offered on how to make country wines at the Folk school and I want to sign up. The way I see things, wine-making is just one more form of cooking, like making jam or canning pickles."

He looked at the description of the class in the brochure. "Sounds fun, actually."

"Want to take the class with me?" I asked, even though I knew my husband was about as likely to pause from his building project to spend time making wine as he was to fly to Paris for croissants that weekend.

"I'll stick with driving the get-away car when we start transporting rotgut across state lines," he said. "But I might be interested in taking a blacksmithing class on the same weekend. I'd like to learn how to pound iron for house garnishes. We can have lunch together on the breaks."

It was a date. A date in two separate rooms, but a date neverthe-less. Within a few weeks, my bedside table was brimming with wine-making books and my first issue of *Winemaker* magazine. I diligently studied chapters on how to use a hydrometer and how to rack wine from a primary fermenter to a carboy. I read about the importance of potassium metabisulfite, pectic enzymes, bitartrate, and potassi-um sorbate. I learned about yeasts and supplements, refining agents, acids, carbonates, and bacteria. A person needed a degree in chemis-try to understand how to make wine at home.

Winemaking turned out to be a popular subject at the folk school. The class was full of wine enthusiasts and nearly everyone had tried making wine before, mostly from kits. In a kit, all the ingredients are rationed out in little pre-measured packets and all you have to do is follow the day-by-day, step-by-step instructions to create a fool-proof wine. I was much more interested in rolling up my sleeves to do things the old-fashioned way, even if the project meant wrestling with the learning curve once again. Most traditional wine is made from grapes, but country wines are blends made with fruits, vegeta-bles, and herbs. Since I had an abundance of garden delights right on my fifty acres, I determined country wines could be my forte.

At the first class, the teacher said, "The greatest thing about home-made wine is that people can't deny the beauty of taking natural ingredients and laboring over them for over a year to create a refined beverage that is a celebration of harvest, friendship, and life. Rarely do people turn down a glass of homemade wine."

If learning to make homemade wine did indeed make a non-drink-er soften to the idea of a harmless drink, I had found the perfect solution to the dry county dilemma. I was inspired!

The class started with instructions on how to make a batch of strawberry wine. The last strawberry wine I drank was Boone's Farm, right out of the bottle in the back of my boyfriend's Chevy at the drive-in in 1977. Good stuff, as I recall, and to my recollection, strawberry wine was quite the aphrodisiac. I pictured opening my first bottle of homemade wine in the backseat with Mark. The pos-sibility of rekindling the passion my high school sweetheart showed me way back when made me even more inclined to take winemaking seriously. I wrote the recipe down in my notebook, because we just so happened to have a drive-in in Blue Ridge.

"First, we need to clean and prepare some bottles," the teacher said.

The class scraped labels off the surface of used wine bottles. Since this fell in line with my earth-friendly goals, I scraped happily. We sterilized containers, heated five pounds of sugar in a pot of purified water, and cut fruit to fill a mesh bag. We measured chemicals while receiving a quick lesson on how to use a thermometer and a hydrometer to determine alcohol content after fermentation began. The process wasn't nearly as complicated in the classroom as books made the process seem. The only difficulty would be remembering the details because we began sampling wines in different stages of fermentation at nine in the morning and kept sampling until five. Eight hours of wine sampling does not bode well for accurate note taking.

Homemade dandelion-chamomile, kiwi, and strawberry wine sweetened with fresh lemonade all flowed, most of which tasted similar to a good Chardonnay with a dash of summer flavors tossed in. We were served blackberry and elderberry reds, and potent golden mead, too.

Most helpful was being able to sample batches of wine in different stages of fermentation. We tasted strawberry wine just after the batch was mixed, then tasted a batch six days old, and again after six months. The experiment concluded with a one-year-old bottle that went down smooth and delicate.

By 3:00 we had finished our winemaking lesson and the country winemaker happy hour ensued. The teacher was a member of a bluegrass band, and the crew showed up to give us a rip-roaring standup comedy show filled with backcountry wine jokes. The bass player was also a beekeeper and between sets he gave a short lecture on how to make mead with honey. I jotted down notes, giddy with inspiration.

There I was, drinking blackberry wine while enjoying the song

Take Me Away from Concrete and Greed played on a homemade percussion instrument complete with a tin can, plunger, washboard, and bicycle horn attached to a walking stick. This was a far cry from the sophisticated world where I once sat in fine restaurants sipping imported wine and listening to a jazz trio.

I stomped my foot to the silly songs and watched the crowd of carefree, suburban deserters who, like me, had taken a break in their middle years to come to the folk school to learn something new. I liked these people. Liked this wine. The moment was sweet. I was no longer questioning my life choice or struggling to validate my existence by stacking up pros and cons of what life was like now compared to what life was before. I wasn't questioning my identity or wondering how making homemade wine might save enough money to justify the expense of the class, as if all of life was a balance sheet requiring a practical return on every investment. True, drinking all that wine might have helped me reach this personal nirvana, but nevertheless, I was happy doing nothing of great servitude or purpose, just savoring the flavors of homemade wine and good company.

Later I met up with Mark and I listened to his news of the blacksmithing experience and all the new things he was learning, too. He talked of house building and how he wanted to make copper trims for railings. He talked of all the new tools he'd seen in class that he wanted to buy. Mark almost never drank, but I offered him a glass of my homemade wine anyway.

"Well, if you made this yourself... why not?" he said, filling his glass to the brim and holding the wine up for a toast.

"To us," I said.

"To the things I can now make for our house," he corrected.

"I had this advantage, at least, in my mode of life, over those who were obliged to look abroad for amusement, to society and the theatre, that my life itself was become my amusement and never ceased to be novel. It was a drama of many scenes and without an end. "
—*Henry David Thoreau*

ANIMAL HUSBANDRY, SANS THE HUSBAND

Raising animals may be called *animal husbandry*, but in my case, tending to the farm creatures was entirely a wifely pursuit. Sometimes, I felt foolish taking on so much unnecessary work in the name of experimentation. The mud, effort, commitment, and endless routine of animal care curtailed my freedom more than I ever imagined. More than once, I tallied the time and cost of keeping animals, imagining just what kind of vacation in Europe we could have taken instead, if only Mark been up for the trip. But he had made absolutely clear that he wasn't planning to take me anywhere anytime soon, so I focused instead on the meaningful lessons I might discover in each barnyard endeavor. I was contemplating not just man's relationship with animals, but all human food sources and man's impact on the natural world. These were lessons my soul longed for, an in-depth awareness of nature's basic mechanics beyond the surface education I was given from schoolrooms or a book.

I was fascinated with small discoveries, such as the fact that chicken eggs are not fertile until several days after the hen has mated because a rooster's sperm doesn't affect the egg already half-formed inside her, and instead impacts the egg yet to be developed. The chicken maintains 'reserve sperm' and her eggs might become fertile for weeks after one mating. See, I never knew that.

A drone (male bee) has no stinger. Neither does a bumblebee. You can hold them up to your arm and nothing will happen. All those years of my running away from anything with stripes and wings were for naught. A worker bee will indeed sting you, but stings are good

medicine for arthritis. Many people use sting therapy to heal themselves. See, I never knew that either.

A horse is pregnant for 11 months.

It takes 39 days for a duck egg to hatch, 31 for a chicken.

A rabbit is pregnant for 39 days. A queen bee can live 7 years, but
her workers only survive a few weeks.

Slowly and surely, despite many mistakes, I was learning about
the natural world. I could doctor wounds and groom, medicate, and
train all manner of creatures now.

My attitude regarding animals could all be summed up by my relationship with the donkey. After months of tugging fruitlessly on
Donkey's lead rope to get the stubborn beast to budge, I discovered
that if I stood calmly beside him, he would walk side by side with
me anywhere I wished to go. When I tried to force him to move, a
frustrating battle would ensue. Only when I treated him as a friend
and partner would he eagerly follow my lead. Now, if that isn't a
metaphor for living in harmony with nature…

I had but to call out to my horses and they would come running
as good-naturedly as a dog to his master. My chickens came running
when they saw me, too, comfortable to peck in the dirt around my
feet or to take a powdered donut from my fingertips. My rabbits
would sit docilely in my lap. My goat…well, he never did learn to
behave, but that's another story.

I felt like a cross between Dr. Doolittle and Mr. Hyde. I had a
wonderful affinity for animals now, but the joy came with steep associated costs. I'd created a monster of inconvenience and hard work
for myself, and the closer I came to nature, the more alienated I felt
from my marriage.

My horses would accidently push me into the barn door and I'd
have a bruised shoulder for days. My rabbits would panic when the
dogs came sniffing and I'd end up with arms covered in bloody
scratches. Occasionally our rooster would start feeling his oats and
attack, creating a small gash or two on my calf before I could boot
him away like a feathered football. I couldn't go anywhere without
undertaking a complex schedule of feeding and care arrangements,

calling in favors from friends and family. But as battered or tired as I sometimes got, I never considered throwing in the towel because this was the life Mark and I had chosen together under the pretense that a simple life would bring us closer, and I wanted so much to make our new life work.

One day, my husband's horse got his foot stuck in the fence. I had just tied the horses up for a feeding; Goliath pawed the ground and caught the bottom wire of the fence between the back of his hoof and the horseshoe. The more he pulled, the deeper embedded the wire became, not a good thing for the horse or the fence.

I climbed under Goliath and wedged my shoulder under his leg to free both hands to pull, but for the life of me, I couldn't get the wire out from under his shoe. The horse was busy eating, but soon the grain would be gone, and then he was bound to start fighting the fence. I needed to free him or there would be hell to pay.

I tried using a horse pick (a device used to clean rocks and dirt out of horseshoes) to dislodge the wire. No good.

I cursed, but that didn't do a thing either.

My fingers were frozen, my temper hot. I called Mark to explain the situation; Goliath was his dumb horse, after all.

"What do you want me to do about it? I'm at Wal-Mart, 45 minutes away," he said.

"Where are the wire cutters? I'll simply cut the fence away."

"I don't have any."

I was certain he had wire cutters. Hadn't I watched him cut away the fence once when the goat got stuck, only days ago? I reminded him of that.

He was silent for a minute and then said, "I don't know what you're talking about. We don't own wire cutters."

He was always deeply possessive about his personal things, so I assumed this answer was really just his way of saying he didn't want me touching his tools.

"I'm having an emergency here," I said through gritted teeth. "Just let me use your wire cutters."

"I don't have any. Honestly."

"If that's the case, will you please buy a good pair to keep with my tack for the next time this happens?"

"Wal-Mart doesn't have any."

I was pretty sure our Wal-Mart had every basic tool imaginable, considering the store carried rifles and chicken feed to serve the area's consumer needs. Perhaps this conversation wasn't about Mark protecting his wire cutters at all, but about the fact that he didn't want me to cut the fence.

"If I leave the horse stuck to the fence, he's gonna bring it down. That or he'll get hurt, which means a big, fat vet bill. I've tried everything. I can't free him."

"I'll call the fence guy. Maybe he can run over and help you," Mark said.

The horse was getting more and more agitated, pulling at the fence with greater force. I turned to Goliath with renewed determination, wedged my foot on the bottom of the fence wire, and yanked with all my might. Nope.

I tried slamming a piece of wood against the wire. Nope.

All that was left was for me to do what any resourceful, independent girl would do in a situation like this. I cried. After indulging my self-pity for several minutes, I wiped my tears on the back of my sleeve and gave Goliath more grain. How much could I feed this horse without harming his constitution? I offered a prayer to the horse heavens as I sobbed. I put my head between my legs, too tired even to cry anymore. Eventually I turned around to discover Goliath's horseshoe was no longer caught in the fence wire. His foot was conveniently resting through the wire mesh now. I pushed him away with all my might before he did something stupid like jam his foot into the fence again. Drama over.

"How was your day?" My kids asked that night at dinner.

"Uneventful," I responded.

Crying over an animal and getting into an almost-fight with Mark because I felt vulnerable and inadequate and he showed no sensitivity or concern for my wellbeing was an everyday occurrence now. No biggie. Nothing to do but accept that frustration is a part of raising animals—and a part of being married.

That is, except in the case of the goat.

There was no denying the goat was cute, running to greet us with enthusiasm and delight, but he didn't seem to understand he was a goat. Freckles thought he was a hood ornament, clambering up onto the roof of my car and stomping back and forth while I yelled and tried to swat him down. He played king of the mountain and I was left with a hundred little dents marring the roof of my new SUV.

Sometimes Freckles thought he was a puppy, thrusting his muddy body up onto our laps whenever we sat by the fire ring. He'd eat our marshmallows and knock over our coffee mugs, leaving us dirty, sore, and inclined to throw a goat on the fire rather than another log.

The goat was forever getting stuck in the fence, or sneaking out of the pasture. He ate our flowers, broke into the feed bins, and trampled the chickens. We'd expend great effort to catch him and put him back in the pasture, where he'd force his way in front of the horses' food buckets to cause an equestrian uproar. He bit holes in our jackets, butted anyone who was foolish enough to bend over in his vicinity, and ate everything and anything EXCEPT the weeds swallowing our pasture. Even the passive donkey had enough of his shenanigans one day and finally kicked him good, breaking one horn tip completely off.

Still, we were tolerant until the day Freckles discovered our neighbor's garden and wreaked havoc on the elderly man's carefully tended vegetables. It was all well and good for us to endure the goat's destructive antics, but we were not willing to invite open warfare with our country neighbors.

"The goat has got to go," Mark said. "He's too destructive, too annoying, too… goatish."

"I agree, but where do you send a goat that he won't become chunks of meat packaged up in butcher paper? Neva loves that goat and she'll never forgive us if her beloved pet is slaughtered."

"I know someone with several female goats looking for a stud goat. I told them they could have our male for free if they promised to give him a good home."

Somehow, this seemed too good to be true. But rather than ask too many questions, I said, "Sounds good."

So the next day, the goat moved to a new home. I reminded Neva that we were soon to have a baby horse, infinitely more exciting than a goat.

She wasn't entirely convinced raising animals had to be an either/or prospect.

"I'll miss him," she said with a sniffle. "But I understand he was trouble. Maybe someday, when we have a fenced area that a goat can't escape from, we can get another."

"Maybe."

Fat chance.

And just like that, the dynamics of the barnyard changed.

Country people don't have a problem understanding that a goat is just a goat. Obviously, we were going country, because for the first time ever, Freckles wasn't a romantic symbol of my caring for a family in a third world country. He wasn't a pet deserving the same consideration as our dog just because he had the luck to be adopted by a family charmed by the country ideal. He was just an annoying goat. And sending him off to an unknown fate was easier than I ever expected.

"And I am sure that I never read any memorable news in a newspaper.
If we read of one man robbed, or murdered, or killed by accident, or
one house burned, or one vessel wrecked, or one steamboat blown up,
or one cow run over on the Western Railroad, or one mad dog killed, or
one lot of grasshoppers in the winter, - we need never read of another.
One is enough. If you are acquainted with the principle, what do you
care for a myriad instances and applications?"
—*Henry David Thoreau*

IN THE NEWS

Kathy took a test every few months to check her reading level, and after two years of lessons, she was reading at the third grade level. I was told the newspaper is written for a fifth grade mentality, so I started thinking reading the news wouldn't be too far a stretch for her.

"Do you know what's in a newspaper?" I asked one day.

"News?"

"Well, yes. The Atlanta paper has national coverage, but our smaller, local paper has mostly information about our community. I thought you might want to start reading the paper so I bought you a subscription."

She sat up in her seat.

"All newspapers are set up the pretty much the same. The front page is the big news."

I read her the headlines and paraphrased the news.

- The mayor had been arrested three times for cockfights and people were clamoring that he should be given more than a small fine.
- There were yellow ribbons all around town because one of our local boys died in Iraq and his body was being shipped home for the funeral on Sunday.

- Town councilors were lifting the alcohol ban and giving pouring licenses to select businesses outside the city limits in hopes of jump-starting the flagging economy.

I turned to the second page, and pointed out the arrests reports, explaining what they were.

Kathy's face grew ashen. "Does that mean my name was in the paper the year I was arrested?"

"I suppose so."

She bit her lip. "I had no idea information like that was printed for the world to see. Doesn't seem very respectful."

"I think you lose your right to privacy when you break the law," I mumbled, turning to the editorials. "This is where people write letters to share their opinion on community and world events." I read a few of the heated letters, two of which were taking opposing sides on a local signage law.

Kathy pursed her lips. "Those two letters say the exact opposite things."

"A newspaper doesn't take sides, at least in theory. The editor prints everyone's opinion so readers will be exposed to different views. By hearing all sides of an issue, people can come to their own conclusions. Which side of this issue strikes you as fair?"

She waved a hand in front of her face. "I don't know. Let the politicians take care of running things, I always say."

"But we pick the politicians, so how things are run is a result of our choices. Ever vote?"

"Naw. Nobody in my family has ever voted."

"Maybe if you start reading the paper, you will vote someday."

"I don't even think I'm allowed, having been arrested and all."

"We should find out." I flipped another page, turning to the obituaries.

"Is everybody listed in the paper when they die?" she asked.

"Someone has to submit the information to the paper first."

"I guess my mom's name wasn't listed then," she said, her fingers tracing the picture of a deceased woman. "I wish I had known to do that."

"Next time someone close to you passes away, you will be able to send in an obituary."

"Yeah…" She sighed. "But nobody will know how to do that for me. Ain't nobody in my family understands such things. "

"You never know. Things change. Look at how much you're learning."

She nodded, but did not look convinced.

On the community events page, we learned of a free bluegrass concert, a bird watching lecture, and the two-dollar pancake breakfast for the Shriners. Social services were also listed, such as the Empty Stocking program helping disadvantaged families get Christmas presents, and the health clinic giving free flu shots.

We reviewed the TV and movie listings, compared prices in grocery ads, and read about the animals up for adoption at the local animal rescue. Kathy seemed only mildly interested until I got to the classifieds. She leaned in closer.

"They list jobs? I thought the newspaper only had news."

"Think of the paper as an information source, rather than just news. The paper is entertainment as well," I said, pulling out a page I'd saved from the Atlanta paper's Sunday comics. "I thought for fun we could read the funnies today." I pointed to a comic called "Kathy," hoping the name would amuse her.

She leaned over and started sounding out the text, but the sentences unfolded so slowly the humor was lost.

"Do you know why the words are written in those little white bubbles?" I said.

She sat back in her seat looking overwhelmed. "I have no clue."

"See the way the bubble points to a character's mouth? That's because the bubble represents a voice. When little dots go from the bubble to a character's head, the writing is a thought. You can follow the conversation without 'he said' or 'she said' tags this way."

"Well, that's certainly clever. Whoever thought of using bubbles for a voice must have been really smart. "

"I suppose."

The rest of the day I couldn't stop thinking about the innovative artist who came up with idea of bubble captions rather than putting text under the picture. Was the innovative artist renowned for his contribution in the world of funnies, or did other artists just copy his gimmick until everyone had forgotten where the original idea came from? Perhaps cartoon bubbles just evolved over time. Why had I never thought about or noticed these things before? I took cartoons, like so many other things in life, for granted. Since meeting Kathy, I was seeing the world with fresh eyes. I left feeling grateful that day—for newspapers, for comics, and for a reading student who taught as much as she learned.

"Any fool can make a rule, and any fool will mind it."
—*Henry David Thoreau*

EGG ON MY FACE

After a year of trial and error and the loss of at least a hundred young birds, I finally had eight full-grown chickens mature enough to start laying. I was determined to keep them alive.

I installed a bigger pen for my birds, burying the fencing into the ground so nothing could burrow underneath and since I now understood these eight birds may not ever make it to maturity, I ordered additional chicks online from a poultry company, the most cost-effective way to buy chicks, according to Ronnie.

If you've never done this yourself, I should warn you that Internet poultry shopping is dangerous, especially when your ten-year-old daughter is sitting next to you expressing little gasps of delight every time you add a different baby chick to your spring hatchery order.

Neva had been pining for the chickens with wispy fur-like feathers (Silkies) ever since her all-time favorite chick had become a cat snack, so I ordered half a dozen, along with the twelve Leghorn super egg layers I wanted for myself. We were both enchanted by Frizzles, so I thought I might as well get a few of that breed, too. Might as well get some fancy Cochins for diversity, and I don't have any green egg layers so I should probably throw in a few Ameraucanas. What are those cool things? Sultans? Gotta get a few of those crazy looking birds...well, you can see how things escalate. Before you know it, you've ordered 68 baby chicks.

A few weeks later, the post office called to tell me a box from a poultry house had been delivered. Clearing his throat, the postmaster said I may have a problem because the box was oddly quiet.

I rushed to the post office, drove home quickly to open the package, only to find 58 dead chicks lying in the synthetic grass like lifeless Easter peeps. The few birds that had survived were huddled under the dead bodies as if they'd pulled their friends over them for a blanket. Devastated, I called the company and was told the chicks must have gotten a chill.

"These things happen," they said, promising to replace the order.

I didn't necessarily want another order. I wanted to sue for mental anguish. Do you know how horrible opening a package is when you anticipate cute chicks and instead find tiny carcasses? The guilt was crushing.

"We're going to send you a few extra chicks next time, just in case," the woman said.

Quickly, I put the remaining live chicks in a box with a warming light. It was a chilly day, so I covered the plastic tub with a towel thinking they would appreciate a toasty environment. If nothing else, I might head off potential chick pneumonia. What I didn't know was that a cover would make the temperature inside the box spike. An hour later the remaining chicks were now dead, too. Not from the cold. Nope. I had cooked them.

Naturally, I went to bed and cried myself to sleep.

When Mark came home he said, "What gives?"

"Because of me, 68 innocent chickens are dead."

He tried not to laugh. "I know how badly you want to raise chickens so we can eat organically like the family in that book you are reading, *Animal, Vegetable, Mineral.* Maybe everything you are learning lately will help you write your own bestseller." A mischievous smile curled about his lips. "We'll call yours *Animal, Vegetable, Funeral.*"

A few days later, my replacement chicks arrived. Another sixty-eight adorable live peeps in a single box with a few extra birds for good measure. I carefully removed the perky, chirping chicks, only to discover a few random baby chick pancakes on the floor of the box. Five chicks had been crushed during the mailing cycle, and three more by the time we reached home. I felt badly for them, but at least I didn't feel as guilty as if I had dropped a dictionary on their heads.

I cared for the helpless birds with diligence. Newborn chicks are only about the size of a soft golf ball. But they grow. And they grow fast. When placing my order, I wasn't thinking about where I would house 68 chickens for the months *before* they were ready to be released into the main pen. I was simply thinking that, predators be damned, I'd get enough chickens to assure survivors so I'd have egg layers six months hence.

I now had over 60 healthy baby chicks peeping away in two cages by my desk. In a week, they were hearty enough to move into the garage where the temperature was less controlled, but because they were growing so quickly, I had to divide them into four groups. This required my buying more lights, water bottles, feed troughs, and cages. So much for my cost effective plan for buying chickens *en masse*.

Two months later, I had to move the growing birds into a bigger pen again, so I fenced a corner of my permanent pen as a holding area for adolescent birds. They needed to be kept apart so my adult chickens wouldn't bully them. Two months after that, I finally introduced the young chickens to the new and improved chicken run. Unfortunately, I now had so many chickens I needed a second chicken house, so the little shed I was using for horse tack had to be sacrificed. Gee, this living the simple life was endlessly complicated.

For six months I fed and tended my flock, checking the nesting boxes everyday as I eagerly awaited nature to kick in. Every day I looked hopefully for eggs. Every day I was disappointed. Finally, when I almost gave up hope of ever seeing an egg, I spied a small round, brown globe in the chicken house.

"I got an egg!" I squealed.

Mark was outside the henhouse waiting for me. We'd only stopped by the henhouse for a moment on our way to pick up the kids from school. He called out, "That's nice. Come on, we have to go. "

"Come see! Come see!"

"I get it. You have an egg."

"You *have* to come see it."

He poked his head into the shed. "Yep, that's an egg all right."

"I don't think you understand the significance of this egg."

"You have chickens. Eventually, you're going to get eggs. It's not rocket science."

"This is not just an egg. This is an organic egg, only minutes old. This egg came from a chick I raised to a hen all by myself after a

year of chick death and disappointment. For your information, this
egg is edible. That means *free groceries*. Certainly you see the miracle
in this egg now!"

"If I knew you'd get this turned on by an egg, I would have snuck
out here with a dozen from the Piggly Wiggly and shoved them under your chickens a month ago."

Were the egg not so precious, I'd hurl the damn thing right at him.
"I'm going to leave this egg and let Neva collect it herself."

A half hour later, we picked the kids up from school. I shared the
exciting news. Since we had a few errands to run while we were in
town, I told everyone I encountered about our egg. The girl behind
the counter at the coffee shop, the feed store owner, and the woman
at the bank all smiled in a patronizing way, as if I were a seven-year-
old kid telling strangers I lost my first tooth. Granted, I had about
the same degree of childish enthusiasm, but still, I wanted the world
to know I finally had raised an egg from scratch. I thought the entire
experience was cool.

I called my eldest, Denver, and told her I found an egg in the
chicken house, and invited her to breakfast.

"We're all going to share that one egg? How big is it?"

"It's a rather small egg, but that's not the point. I'll be making a
ceremonial breakfast."

"Gee, sounds great, but I'm working," she said.

She'd rather work than share my special egg? Her loss. I'd wow the
other two kids with my egg. When we got home, I drove everyone
straight to the henhouse. The kids went inside to see the historical
egg while I looked for my cell phone, planning to take a snapshot of
the egg for eternal prosperity.

Kent called out, "There's no egg in here."

"Of course there is. Right on the ground."

"Nope. There is, however, part of an egg shell."

I rushed in. Sure enough, some stupid chicken had broken my
precious egg. There went my ceremonial breakfast. There went my
picture. There went my pride and joy.

"Don't fret. You'll probably get another egg tomorrow. Once

chickens start laying, they keep at it," Mark said.

"Yeah, but I wanted THAT egg. That was my first. That egg was special."

"It's just an egg," he said.

The kids nodded in agreement. Clearly I was the only one who understood the magnitude of the loss.

Determined to combat the obstacles standing in the way of egg success, I bought oyster shell to scatter about the cage for my chickens to peck at, having read shell makes chicken eggs harder and more resistant to cracking. Linda told me the first few eggs a chicken lays are like practice eggs; they might have a weak shell, or even a missing yolk. No cause for worry. I'd be getting perfect eggs in time.

"The eggs will taste like whatever you feed the chickens. If you feed your chickens veggies, your eggs will taste like veggies," she said.

If this were true, my eggs were going to taste like powdered donuts because Neva had long since discovered sharing donuts was the way to the hearts of feathered friends.

"Doesn't that mean you'd have to feed your chickens eggs to get eggs that taste like eggs? That would be cannibalism, right?"

"Trust me, if you like broccoli, feed 'em broccoli and you'll get eggs that taste like broccoli," she said.

Interesting theory. Maybe my chickens would enjoy a glass of wine. I'd rather enjoy eggs that taste like Chardonnay.

For the next few days, I searched the henhouse expectantly, until, at long last, I got another egg. It was small, brown and cold to the touch. I wondered how long the egg had been sitting in the house. An hour? Half a day? I took the egg home to show everyone, announcing that this would be our breakfast. But for all that I'd been waiting for months to cook a homegrown egg, I was now unnerved by the idea of eating something that had been sitting in a bunch of dirty nesting shavings for who knows how long. Eggs were supposed to be kept refrigerated, right? A person could get a serious case of salmonella from an egg that wasn't stored at the right temperature. Was I really supposed to eat an egg that had been sitting outside in a dirty nest for hours? For all my belief that home grown eggs were supposed to be good for you, picking up an egg off the ground suddenly didn't seem sanitary. Perhaps there was a step in the process I didn't know about, like I was supposed to refrigerate the henhouse or pasteurize the egg.

Tentatively, I cracked the egg open in a frying pan. The yolk was a deep, vibrant orange rather than the pale yellow I was accustomed to. The insides seemed thicker somehow. Certainly this meant the egg was old. Perhaps toxic, in decay, or just filled with bacteria absorbed from sitting in hen poop for an hour. All I knew was this egg just didn't look like any egg I'd ever cooked.

With no small trepidation, I cooked the egg for my husband. If he dropped dead, well, I'd know that home grown eggs were not for us.

He took a bite and smiled. "Good."

I reached out to cover his food with my hand, compelled to confess before he took another bite. "I don't know if you should eat this egg. The yoke was kinda orange, like it was fathered by a pumpkin rather than a rooster."

"I believe that's normal." Mark said taking another mouthful. "I was told free range chicken eggs have more nutrients and that makes the yolks more colorful." He polished off his breakfast, proclaimed he felt healthier already, and went off to cut down and sand a dozen trees for our new porch.

I headed for the Internet to read more about eggs.

The more I read, the more foolish I felt. Eggshells have a protective coating that keeps an egg from spoiling after being laid, but not all organic eggs are equal. The organic, free-range eggs I paid an extra dollar for at the health food store came, perhaps, from chickens that most likely had one hour a day in the sunshine on a four by four concrete pad. Hardly "free range" compared to my birds. No wonder I didn't recognize a healthy egg when I saw one.

Homegrown eggs have 30% more protein, higher nutrients, and less cholesterol than commercially raised eggs. An orange yolk signifies a more healthful egg; the watery pale yellow yolk of store-bought eggs is due to synthetic filler in cheap food. The poor nutrition and lack of natural food sources like bugs or greens, denied the commercially raised layers, are what makes their yolks lackluster. The greatest chefs in the country use only free-range, organic eggs because of the benefit to their masterpiece dishes.

I was committed to growing my own fresh eggs more than ever now, so every day I checked the hen house. I had lots of chickens, but still, I wasn't getting lots of eggs.

I started complaining about my slacker chickens to anyone who would listen.

"Tell my wife that if she's patient, she'll eventually get eggs," Mark said to Ronnie as they hoisted a huge log into position at the house site. "She's obsessed with the idea of home grown eggs now."

"They'll come," Ronnie said, his hands running along the bark to be sure the log was set correctly.

"I think I have the only chickens in the history of the world that refuse to lay."

"Give 'em time."

For three weeks, I visited the chicken house, then stomped up to the worksite to complain some more. The house was changing in shape and design, getting bigger and looking more upscale than we originally discussed, but Mark assured me going bigger saved us money somehow.

"Now, I'm not claiming to know everything, 'cause I only have 'bout a sixth grade education, but seems to me what you need is some guineas," Ronnie said, nailing narrow tree trunks to our Adirondack kitchen bar. He took some nails out of his mouth to explain. "I don't know why, but when you have guineas hanging out with chickens, the birds lay more, as if chickens are competitive or something."

Like all the odd little details I was discovering about animals, this concept struck me as fascinating. "Do guineas get along with chickens?"

"Sure. They're just a different kind of chicken, after all. I saw some guineas for sale this week at the flea market. If you want, we can go down tomorrow and have a look-see."

Since I didn't know what guineas looked like, I perused the Internet for a look-see, only to discover rather ugly birds with a vulture-like face, a huge shapeless round body, and a horn on the top of their head. Dark red gills make their white faces stand out with the same stark villainous appearance of the joker in *Batman*.

"What do you think?" Mark asked, looking over my shoulder at the game bird website.

"Did you know guineas make a weird sound, like a raspy flute, the female calling out in a two-syllable screech while the male makes a single toot?"

"I didn't know that."

"Guineas make a racket when danger comes around, so they're considered 'watch birds.' Their eggs are smaller and pointier than chicken eggs. One drawback is they lay in the bushes, so I'll have to hunt their eggs down if I want to cook them, but since I just want the birds to inspire my other chickens to lay, I don't care if or where they lay eggs."

"You're a virtual encyclopedia of guinea knowledge."

I nodded smugly. "You may now add 'guinea expert' to my ever-growing list of talents. I'll have you know people who raise guineas don't get Lyme disease, and dogs come home clean because these birds clear away all ticks for a mile. Fly control alone is reason enough to keep poultry."

"Then go for it, dear."

I found no reference to guineas being a natural encouragement to get chickens to lay. I also didn't mention that guineas have been known to park themselves at the entrance of a hive and eat bees as they fly home from foraging pollen. The birds can gobble up a beekeeper's entire bee population in a few days if given the chance. Uh-oh.

The next day we all went to the flea market and I bought three silver and three black speckled guineas. I also bought six game chickens. Game chickens are recognizable because their legs are green, and sure enough, these chickens looked as if they were wearing Grinch tights. The game chickens were lean and wiry, and in my opinion lacked personality.

I took the birds home and introduced them to the flock. The next day I found two eggs. I rushed to the worksite to tell Ronnie and Mark the guineas were doing their job. The boys were standing in front of a hole in the wall that would soon be the fireplace.

"Just wait. Once they get the chickens going, you'll be overrun with eggs," Ronnie promised.

Mark waved his hand in a distracted way, clearly wanting me to go away so he could get back to work. "They'll come."

And he was right. The next day, seven eggs were softly resting in the shavings. I showed them off proudly promising I'd make the boys egg salad for lunch.

The third day, I found 19 eggs and one chicken was in the hen-house laying right as I visited. She had an ornery look in her eye, so I left her alone, but I collected a basketful of perfect brown eggs, all the same size and shape, with one little white egg in the mix. I took them to the worksite to show off.

"How do you suppose you have 19 eggs when you only have 17 grown chickens?" Mark asked, taking a bite of his egg salad sandwich. "And why so many brown eggs? Aren't some of your chickens green and white egg layers?"

"Well, sure, but I have one white egg," I said, holding up the meager, oddball egg. "Obviously, my brown egg-layers are just over-achievers. Must be the influence of the guineas."

"It's always the brown egg layers that respond to guineas first," Ronnie said.

That night, I ordered a quiche recipe book on Amazon and made Eggs Benedict for dinner. I whipped up a meringue pie, because that was the only dessert I could think of that used lots of egg whites. If I was going to get another 19 eggs the next day and every day after that, I'd have to become a master at egg dishes. Perhaps I'd make lemon curd. I might even begin a lemon curd business and sell my product at the flea market on weekends!

"Eggs for dinner again?" my kids asked.

"Why not? I plan to take advantage of each and every egg I find. From here on, our dogs will have the dreamiest fur coats, everyone's cholesterol will go through the roof, and I'm going to learn to use natural egg as face masks for vibrant skin."

But the next morning when I went to do my morning rounds, there were only two little white eggs in the chicken house. I went to the house site to ask Ronnie what he thought had happened. He and Mark were talking about light fixtures, but they took a break to give me their full attention.

"Do you think the effect of the guineas wore off?"

"Might be," Ronnie said with a chuckle. Then he laughed. He started laughing so hard he had to sit down. He laughed so hard that he had tears in his eyes. He pointed to Mark and laughed harder. "You didn't tell her."

Mark was fighting a smile. "I forgot my saw at the workshop. Be right back."

"He didn't tell me what?" I said, growing increasingly suspicious of Ronnie's mirth and my husband's guilty exit.

"I bought a flat of eggs at the flea market when we bought them guineas and I've been putting them under your chickens all week. I couldn't resist. You didn't really believe a game bird would make your domestic chickens lay, didja? That don't make no sense a'tall."

I stood there, blushing hot and red. "You say Mark knew about this?"

"It was his idea."

"Hmmm......"

"When he told me you went on and on about your eggs last night, bought an egg cookbook, and even talked about starting a lemon curd business, I told him he had to tell ya. That's why today I stopped with the eggs. Honestly, I never dreamed you'd think all them eggs really came from such young chickens. Especially since the eggs are all uniform in shape and size. That can't be when you have a mishmash of chicken breeds. Certainly a smart college girl like you knows that."

"This is what I get for having an honest preacher as a friend."

He hung his head. "You really mad?"

"Me mad? Over eggs? Couldn't happen. But do be afraid, Ronnie."

I looked at him out of the sides of my eyes. "Payback is a bitch."

He took a bite of the quiche I'd made and smiled at my threat. "Miss Ginny, you've got more country in you than anyone would guess."

A month later my eggs finally started coming for real, and as he predicted, the eggs came in a variety of sizes and colors, everything from little pale green and brown eggs to jumbo shades of off-white and tan. In time I figured out which birds were laying which eggs. When I found guinea eggs, I cooked them too, and as soon as I had more eggs than I could use or give away, I left them under a brooding chicken and hatched my own chicks.

I was amazed at how easy keeping chickens was now, considering how complex the project seemed in the beginning. The chicken experiment was like our entire life makeover; a process filled with hard life lessons. At least laughter took the sting out of the hardest lessons. I had to remember that as long as we didn't take ourselves too seriously, we had a chance at happiness.

"Most of the luxuries, and many of the so-called comforts of life, are not only not indispensable, but positive hindrances to the elevation of mankind. With respect to luxuries and comforts, the wisest have ever lived a more simple and meager life than the poor."

—Henry David Thoreau

SUBURBAN WITHDRAWAL

I often paused to watch my children interacting with our new world, constantly needing assurance that everyone and everything was well. Kent had started camping and learned to drive the four wheelers. He played soccer and drums. With a subtle tan, and a body changing from boy to man, he looked rugged and happier than I ever saw him before. Neva constantly had dirt on her hands as she wandered our land as my sidekick, helping me plant or care for animals. She was fearless, a tomboy, and quick to show empathy and care for anything living. My children's broadening lives made every frustration bearable, because I loved them more than I cared for my own satisfaction. I still worried about Denver acclimating to the area, but a part of me saw her discontent as a gift too. I had huge hopes for my daughter, and Blue Ridge seemed too small a canvas upon which a woman like her could paint a life masterpiece. But I savored her time with us now nevertheless.

Mark had adapted to rural living with chameleon-like ease. Within a month of our moving, his car radio blasted country tunes. His wardrobe began filling up with plaid flannel shirts and he talked with a twang. His well-groomed beard grew bushy and he allowed his truck to grow an inch-thick layer of dust. He gained seventy pounds and became Dairy Queen's best customer.

I continued to keep my acrylic nails, and colored my hair every six weeks. My wardrobe was up to date with fashionable clothes, at least if you include jeans and countryish sweaters. I may have moved to the country, but a style-less bumpkin I'd never be, or so I vowed. My car stereo still chimed jazz or classical music. I listened to NPR, determined to keep up with liberal world news and the latest literature. I may have moved to a different location, but I was still *me*. Just me enjoying and embracing the country lifestyle.

The problem was inside I felt more like a dancer on an extended vacation than a country girl. When no one was around, I'd thrust my leg up on a fence post to enjoy a deep stretch. I cranked up music in the cabin and dance steps oozed out from me as I cleaned. I couldn't see a child pass by but I didn't imagine her in a leotard and tights, her hair in a neat bun.

When the weather was fine, the lush trees swaying, and the birds making lazy circles in the sky, I was inspired to move. *Dances With Wolves* had nothing on me—I had dancing with Donkey down pat. After a lifetime of movement, I just wasn't ready to stand still. So I danced in private. I danced because it felt good. I danced because I was happy. Sometimes, I danced because I was sad. I danced because moving made me feel alive at a time when my body and mind felt lulled to sleep by too many gentle country breezes.

Dance wasn't all I missed. I longed for intellectual stimuli and a dash of pop culture. I missed feeling driven to achieve, to consume, to compete. Was I really such a slave to my cultural upbringing that I couldn't slow down and be happy with less? There were so many good things about our life now. I had time to be a focused parent, an environmentalist, a reading mentor, a student in a challenging Master's program. How could I possibly feel something was missing?

But something *was* missing—my husband. Lost in his obsession to build his dream log home and to fill up his ideal workshop with tools to indulge his creativity as a rustic interior designer, he was treating me as nothing more than an annoying obligation. He encouraged me to play with bees and plant a garden with a pat on the head, like when a parent plops a child in front of a TV set because they don't want to deal with raising kids.

Sometimes, I was fine with the long hours of solitude. I'd be filled with such a deep sense of contentment I could feel my heart beating in a sure, healthy rhythm, my blood flowing with vitality and ease, as if the peace of this natural environment was removing the garbage that a lifetime of superficial struggling had packed inside. I'd stand in the driveway at night, awed by stars above shining bright enough to pierce the heart. The sound of the wind in the trees felt like God's whisper.

I loved that my children were experiencing this connection to nature, too. One day Denver urged Mark and me into the car so she could drive us to a field to look at thousands of lightning bugs illuminating a huge pasture.

"Isn't this the most beautiful thing you've ever seen?" she said, her face soft and tender as she gazed at the sight before her.

"Yes," I said, but I was looking at my daughter's face, recognizing the depth of spirit I had prayed would someday be in my children. There it was, undeniable in her sensitivity, eye for beauty, and connection to the environment.

I tried to concentrate on that same depth of spirit in myself. Perhaps if I tapped into my talents to better the world in this corner of the universe I'd be happier. I volunteered to teach dance for free at a local dance studio, but they turned me down. I contacted every studio I could find within an hour's drive. No takers. Proud of my new MFA, I volunteered to teach writing for free at the local art center.

"People around here really aren't looking for the kind of teaching you do," I was told, meaning a trained professional from the city was more an invader than a resource in their eyes. After a lifetime of being admired for my skills and experience, I couldn't give my skills away. For the first time ever, I was treated as obsolete and valueless, so the best I could hope for was keeping busy with everyday things like laundry and cooking, things that seemed overly common and not much of a contribution to the world at large. Focusing solely on my personal growth felt a tad too self-serving to me. I always believed a good life began with selfless service, and compassion not just for yourself, but for others. To feel better, I wrote while Mark shopped.

Wal-Mart was the only store within casual driving distance (40 minutes) so we found ourselves making excuses to go almost every day. Need a rug for the new bathroom, a meat thermometer, or some plastic containers to hold horse feed? Wal-Mart, Mark's on the way. And I'd usually join him because I wanted to be with my husband whenever I could be. The life I invented for us 'on paper' just wasn't enough.

While we were there, we'd throw unnecessary things into our cart, like clothes, new car mats, or DVDs, not because we needed them, but because they were on sale. Consuming was such an ingrained habit that we continued to shop even while lecturing to each other that consumerism was ruining the world. I bought books like *Affluenza*, *Simple Prosperity*, and *Your Money or Your Life*. Mark said they sounded good, and that he'd read them when I was done, but he never bothered.

Mark had built not one but two large workshops for himself on our land, and he purchased loads of tools and supplies. Unopened crates of woodworker paraphernalia littered the dysfunctional shop like an overturned hardware warehouse. He justified the glut by insisting he shopped the sales. Mark always proclaimed he was saving money as he spent. His newest windfall of tools was an investment, he claimed. He was going into the rustic furniture-making business.

The problem was, after all that shopping, he didn't have the energy to tackle getting the workshop organized, much less make furniture. Instead, he made trips to more stores to buy another set of clamps, non-slip cushioning for the floor, or wood, wood, and more wood for future projects. He soon had enough supplies for years of woodworking, but he had yet to build a workbench on which to make a simple birdhouse. He justified the indulgence by insisting he was 'preparing' for the good life when we would once again spend some time together as promised. We both took classes at the John C. Campbell Folk School. I'd write about whatever craft I had explored and even won a literary contest for one essay. Mark believed every craft he made belonged in a gallery so he would make a deal to buy tons of supplies from each teacher he worked with, preparing for that fateful day when he would actually start producing crafts for a living. But the stock remained heaped in piles in his crowded workshop, untouched.

There's always tomorrow to write the book or set up the workshop, we said, hanging on to the thread that the better life that awaited us made our current circumstances somehow more acceptable. But the next day, we'd be busy again. After all, one of our daughters had a soccer game. I had to feed the animals in the morning. Mark was going to pick up some more wood slabs from a fellow with a saw mill who was offering wood at a good bargain.

We had always been achievement-oriented people, the kind of people who believe luck is really just the result of hard work and commitment. Our adopted town offered a prime opportunity for establishing ourselves in a new field, and yet we just couldn't stay focused to make the vision of our new life manifest. We chalked our dysfunction up to our being burned out and exhausted from eighteen years of running a dance studio, telling ourselves we needed time to heal, but the truth was that living in the country alters a person's inner time clock. The country was slow. Living here, we became slow too.

Perhaps ego, or social conditioning, made accomplishment paramount to feeling alive. Perhaps the money at our disposal drained us of motivation, because in the past, the need to pay bills and the desire for a more comfortable life kept us at the grindstone. Now the only motivation we had for anything other than marking time was a nagging sense that we were not living up to our potential. We had walked away from the one thing we were truly good at, and for what? A bunch of wood slabs collecting dust in a workshop that wasn't even broken in? For a donkey? Our money wouldn't last forever, and our inability to start our inner engines to begin something new gave us a sick sense that our life was like a train chugging along a track that would soon run out of rails.

They say six weeks of changed actions will break a habit, but for us, change took a year. Perhaps the reading material, when I finally got around to digesting the messages, helped. Perhaps the lack of shopping venues took the thrill off the shopping experience. Perhaps the failing economy was making frugal living trendy, or the country mentality was slowly seeping into our hearts and minds and we were shedding old behavior patterns as result regardless of our weak personalities. But one day, we were pushing the cart through Wal-Mart, and both of us suddenly realized there was really nothing we needed. We were tired of 'stuff' and deeply tired of our days being eaten up by driving to get that stuff. The idea of purchasing anything we didn't really need seemed not only wasteful, but slightly gross.

We checked out with the one item we had come for, a bottle of Liquid Plumber. Then we drove through Starbucks to grab a cup of coffee, but instead of sighing into the steam, we both winced because the coffee tasted bitter and burnt. The high dose of caffeine no longer appealed to our taste buds because we had finally re-conditioned ourselves to enjoy a cup of smooth, homebrewed coffee. The drinks languished in our cup holders, growing colder, just as our connection to shopping had.

Were we really embracing simplicity, or had we spent so much that only when the sands of resource were running out could we in reality embrace the simpler lifestyle we claimed was so important to us?

No lifestyle is perfect. Knowing what will bring you contentment is like the little ball that hides under a cup, getting juggled and quick-changed by a swindler with sleight of hand. The fellow moves the cups so quickly you can't figure out where the prize is, so you gamble and take a guess. Eventually, you just point to a cup and whatever is underneath is what you have to live with. But oh, how I wanted to make mindful choices rather than be a slave to circumstance as defined our history.

Denver was now twenty-one and she had spent the year enjoying family time, communing with nature, and taking pleasure in the simplicity of life in the country. She had developed a greater understanding of the environmental, educational, and emotional issues attached to a country lifestyle, so she was not sorry for having dropped out of college to join us. But enough was enough. She was done with the entire slow country thing. She was ready to venture to a place where life would be more stimulating.

"I gotta get out of this town," she said, with no small amount of desperation in her voice.

"I understand completely. You still have a lot of living to do. You need to go places, meet people, and do things to stretch your awareness of the world. Someday, you may want to live in a place like this again, but for now, you need the energy and opportunity that comes with living in a city," I said, inwardly applauding her revelation.

"Don't think I don't appreciate nature and the quaintness of this town. I'm just ready to have some fun," she said. "Everyone my age around here is already married and divorced with two kids. I can't stand this place anymore. I want to date someone with a decent vocabulary. A guy who doesn't chew tobacco and have a gun under the front seat of his truck."

"You should go," I agreed.

The problem was, she had cashed in and spent her college fund as well as the seed money we gave her for establishing an alternate career. For a year, she had enjoyed independent living while only working a part time job. Now, she had aspirations to go to school for jewelry design in California, but the Bank of Mom and Dad had closed its doors for lack of capital. She'd have to work and save her own money if she wanted to escape.

"It's impossible to make a decent living here. Every job is minimum wage," she complained. "Even if I do want to get away and move somewhere with better work options, it's hard."

"Putting money away to build up your college plan during our leanest years was hard, too," I said. "But we found a way. You left school, and now you have to live with your choice and figure out what you're going to do next. Changing your life takes work, sacrifice, and planning."

"I'm missing the best years of my life. A girl could rot here," she said with a melodramatic sigh.

"Not if you decide now you won't let that happen," I said. She was so young and had so much to learn about life. Like it or not, her existence would reinvent itself over and over as time wore on, for life tends to unfold that way. That said, a girl wouldn't rot in Blue Ridge unless she did so by choice. Sadly, I knew the same sentiment applied to me.

"We must walk consciously only part way toward our goal and then leap in the dark to our success."
—Henry David Thoreau

CONNECTED IN THE COUNTRY

I bought Kathy a copy of Webster's Youth Dictionary, thinking the text might help with spelling. She gave the book a blank stare.

Holy cow, she doesn't know what a dictionary is!

So I gave her an overview, teaching her how words are alphabetized. We devoted a full lesson to looking up the meanings of words, which also challenged her basic spelling skills and reading comprehension. I'd give her a word she didn't know, like "tundra" or "allocate" and ask her to find the spelling in the dictionary. After several minutes of fumbling through the pages, she would find the word.

Kathy's homework came back differently after that. When I asked her to write sentences, she'd bring me descriptions copied directly out of the dictionary, evidence that she was indeed using the book. I started wondering what other resources might expand her base of knowledge and promote more at home practice.

Mark and I had all kinds of computers in our storage unit, castoffs from our business that were older models and slower processers, but any one of them would be perfect for a person who'd never sat at a computer before. Learning to work a computer was certainly important if Kathy were to become self-sufficient.

The card catalog in our little town's library was on a computer system. Driver's tests were given on a computer here, and government offices used computers to make appointments. Our small schools put basic information and schedules online, and e-mail was the medium of choice for teachers wanting to communicate with parents. The country may be backward in some areas, but citizens here were hooked up like everyone else in America.

At our next session, I said, "I have an extra computer I could give you to set up at home if you're interested."

Kathy's eyes grew round. "I'd love a computer. Then my son could do his schoolwork at home like the other kids. Maybe I can learn to work on a computer, too. I'd love to find out how to use the Internet."

So the next week I brought her one of our used computers and a small computer desk. I was more than a little confused about where to start. Kathy had forty years of practice steering clear of anything that required reading. She had never had a bank account. Never used an ATM. Never swiped a credit card in a grocery store. Never bought gas outside at the pump. She had never ordered anything online, never looked up merchandise on a store computer, or even plugged in numbers on a jukebox to play her favorite song. Kathy had no clue how a computer worked, didn't understand what applications were, didn't know how to move a cursor, couldn't type, and probably wouldn't have a clue of how to turn the machine on. Operating a computer was going to be a huge challenge for someone still learning to master a BIC pen.

So, I bought her the *Jump Start* and *Reader Rabbit* programs for levels K-3. I wasn't allowed to use non-credentialed materials on the college computers which were plunked right in the room we had our lessons, so I brought in my laptop to teach her some preschool game basics. For weeks afterwards, Kathy came to every lesson gushing about how much fun she was having practicing at home, and she confessed she had to fight for computer time with her family, which meant everyone was engaged in learning at home now. She even got the Internet hooked up, which I thought amazing for someone with such limited resources, until I read an article about people in third world countries spending money to build a community Internet station for the village children to gain access to the world before even drilling a well for water. Perhaps the Internet wasn't a luxury item anymore.

I was proud to bring Kathy into the technology age, yet sorry too when I imagined her someday wasting hours on YouTube and tweeting with friends, rather than spending her time cooking or reading poetry.

I couldn't fight the direction that innovation and progress was taking our world; only act responsibly regarding my own choices. So I swallowed my resistance, and introduced my simple friend to the very same fast-paced technological world that I was trying to escape. Meanwhile, I struggled to understand and embrace the slower, natural world Kathy maneuvered with such grace and acceptance.

If we met somewhere in the middle, we would probably both be better off.

The greater part of what my neighbors call good I believe in my soul to be bad, and if I repent of anything, it is very likely to be my good behavior. What demon possessed me that I behaved so well?
                                                        —*Henry David Thoreau*

THINGS STAY THE SAME

More than half of the women in our small town were blonde, with fashionable doo's that heightened their femininity. They wore impeccable makeup and clothes that were flattering to female curves, kept their nails manicured, had regular pedicures and facials, and used the tanning booth all winter long. Country gals almost seemed compelled to enhance their womanliness as a way of balancing out the raging masculinity of the local men.

The country boy's basic attire consists of jeans and a dirty t-shirt, perhaps a cowboy hat or baseball cap to keep the sun off of their tanned skin. Often their hands are stained and their faces sport a day-old growth of beard. The country boys' fitness levels are impressive, not because these he-men are hanging out in gyms pumping iron, but because their modes of work and recreation tax muscle. The typical day for a country boy includes hunting, training horses, putting up a shed, or working on the truck's carburetor. This lifestyle makes for a manly man. Stacked up against the girly girls, the population is balanced as a whole.

Since balance is something Mark and I both craved after years of frustrating imbalance, we found the old-fashioned male and female roles on display endearing, if not downright fascinating. The men ruled the roost at home and the women let them.

The Southern belle country women, however, were not spoiled housewives such as some we knew in Florida, the type whose husbands made a lot of money and all they had to do was take yoga, get their hair done, and tote the kids around to dance lessons or soccer games. No, the women in the country all worked in female-oriented jobs, as teachers, hairdressers, nurses, or real estate agents. With pay

scales low in a small town, the entire family had to pitch in to make
ends meet, but since most country females had a disinterest in forging an ambitious career, their focus was taking care of the husband
and children.

Amazingly, the fact that these hard working women made significant financial contributions to the family did not earn them a say
in family decisions. The women worked to earn money and secure
insurance from stable jobs while the men did piecemeal work in construction, spending the money and making the decisions. When a
woman dared voice an objection, her opinion was viewed as anarchy.
("And that's the way it's supposed to be in a good, Christian family,"
Ronnie explained. "The Bible says so.")

Mark admitted he was envious. How nice to be married to a woman who knows her place and allows the man to be the man! There's
comfort in age-old attitudes designed to build up the man's self-esteem. Happier husbands lead to happier wives. Theoretically, at least.

Mark's desire for a traditional marriage dynamic wasn't because
he was unenlightened or chauvinistic, but born from a nagging scar
that we'd been nursing as a couple for some 17 years. We operated as
virtual equals, not so much because Mark respected me and relished
my ambitious nature, but because he had no choice in the matter.
Our dynamic had been established at the very beginning.

When I met Mark, I had just left a viable career as a leading cho-
reographer and dancer in New York. I was the 29-year-old owner of
a growing, hugely popular dance school business and I had a home
of my own. I was a single parent who earned enough to care for her
child responsibly. Mark was my dance student, and barely an adult at
23. He had no job, but quite a bit of debt. He lived with his mother,
and had never been employed unless you count waiting tables a few
nights a week and teaching an aerobics class. He fantasized about
becoming a star, and had no career aspirations aside from acting or
being a dancer. I wasn't really interested in a man who brought so
little to the table, but he pursued me diligently and as time went on,
my reservations eroded away.

I was drawn to the unique creative synergy between us. I adored his company. I loved his laugh, his looks, and the way he gave lip service to liberal or new age attitudes, even though he rarely lived the ideals in practice. I loved his arrogance and sense of self-importance, and I excused his spoiled attitude as an unfortunate side effect of his high strung, artistic temperament. I fell, slowly but inevitably, in love with him despite his being so high maintenance.

I supported him financially for the first year or so that we were a couple, because he had no money. He just wanted to study dance and pursue his passions. Daily, I bought him lunch and let him hang at my place for free. The general attitude for us both was that I was the grown up with the business, and he was the young kid "artist" who couldn't be tied to such worldly anchors as a job. Once we were married with a family to care for, I insisted he start contributing financially. I had no interest at all in being the only breadwinner saddled with an adult dependent, and since he couldn't come up with anything he wanted to do on his own, he started working at the studio for me. We had a baby, and after some five years, another. As time wore on, Mark had no choice but to grow up and become a key player in my world of endless struggle and responsibility. I shared my business, my home, and my firstborn with him without reservation, but rather than feeling honored or lucky, from the very beginning he resented the weight of responsibility that came with being my partner.

I considered us equals in every way, but this didn't change the fact that I was his boss and my name was on everything we owned— mortgage, business, car, etc. This created feelings of inferiority and further resentment on his part. He was my business partner, not just a husband, and he understandably wanted recognition for the sacrifices he was making as a fellow teacher. Unfortunately, I couldn't relinquish power any more than I could conveniently wipe out my history as the founder of the school since people knew my background as well as his. Mark was exceptionally talented and he made significant contributions to the business, but the fact was, I was the one with a reputation in the dance field, and the one who drove the business and managed our affairs to keep revenue coming in. My stepping aside as the figurehead was never an option, even if I wanted to, which I did not.

We worked side by side for years, the synergy created by the combination of my experience and pragmatic approach and his natural creativity the success factor that made our little company eventually worth a million dollars. But deep down, Mark never felt amply recognized. The elements that he found so very attractive about me in the beginning, such as my talent and drive and the way people looked up to me, became the qualities he hated most about me later, as is often the case in the complex story of love.

Mark now had 17 years of hard feelings built up, and his animosity leaked out in a myriad of ways, beginning with his inability to sincerely celebrate any achievement I made, and eventually by punishing me with constant long periods of physical alienation. Sex was the only thing he had total control of in our relationship, and he wielded his power by ignoring me with a vengeance. Our relationship had long since turned into something more like siblings or best friends than lovers.

Fourteen years into the marriage, driven by the oppressive circumstances of our ongoing lack of physical connection, I had a fall from grace. I forged a connection to an old friend on the Internet, and so moved was I to be on the receiving end of a man's interest and appreciation that I stupidly had a one night stand on a trip out of town. Remorseful, I confessed to Mark. This flung open the door to the traditional drama that befalls a marriage when trust is broken. The episode lead to our living apart for a month, and we seriously contemplated divorce. But like many couples in crisis, we worked through the horrible breach of faith with accusations, tears, and apologies, and in the end, we determined that we loved each other and would stay together.

I was ashamed and regretful of my mistake, and would have done anything to undo my folly. Mark took responsibility for his part in the sad ordeal, promising he would never leave me untouched for months (or years) again. Our love was authentic—certainly authentic enough to recognize what our mistakes were and how they came to be—and we both stated our love would be stronger once we over-came the problem.

All of this drama and the close call of divorce was a contributing factor in our decision to sell the business and escape our stalemate existence in Florida. Moving to the country represented a clean slate and the opportunity for a new dynamic and a fresh beginning. Mark insisted he wasn't that young financial mess living with his mother anymore. He was a man with a deep desire to prove himself, and he desperately wanted to assume the leadership role to show the world, and *me*, what he could do if only he was totally in charge. If he had the power to make the decisions about our money and our future, then our intimacy issues would smooth out too, or so he assured me.

All I had to do was let him be *the guy*.

Now, you might think I would be uncomfortable giving up my independence so completely, but in truth, I wanted to reverse roles as much as he did. Loving someone who resents you, who can't resist making little digs about your behavior, or who can't bring themselves to show pride or interest in any of your achievements because every accomplishment is viewed as a sign of your swelled ego is no fun. Being deeply in love with someone who won't touch you with ten-derness is no fun either.

Mark had made infinitely clear that since he'd been wronged, he had the right to take additional liberties in the give and take of household equality. I was serving my penance, which meant I had no right to stop him from spending, and if he wanted to leave me bitter-ly alone while he shopped himself sick, that was his prerogative too.

I was deathly tired of the energy required to be the driving force of the business and, at the same time, a fulltime wife and mother. I was tired of balancing finances and being the boss and having to 'force' my husband to accept projects (and the work involved) to keep revenue coming into the family. I was sick being the one to take out the trash and get new car tires and all the other traditionally male tasks that fell on my plate because I married a guy who considered me capable. Deep down, I was just as jealous of other marriages as he was. I envied women who were married to men who made decisions, paid the bills, made love enthusiastically, and took care of all the mechanical and masculine details of life with confidence. I wanted to be *the girl,* and giving Mark the reins to our life seemed to be the key.

Just as we had flipped the switch from being city dwellers to country residents, dancers to farmers, obsessive workers to retired people, we flipped roles in our marriage, too. Mark took over all the decisions and assumed complete control over our finances. Overnight, he became the ultimate authority regarding what we bought, where we lived, what we could afford, and how our life would unfold. He occasionally asked for my opinion about the color of a new couch he wanted to buy or what kind of tile I thought would look best in the kitchen, but if I voiced a preference that was in any way opposed to what he wanted, he forged ahead and did whatever he wished anyway. That was okay by me. I couldn't care less what color the couch was, really. I just wanted us to be happy and to interact in a healthy way *on* that couch.

Old habits are hard to break, so when some of Mark's decisions set off warning bells, I couldn't help but ask questions about our finances, such as when he canceled our youngest child's college plan to free up more money for his building project. Mark's opinion was we couldn't afford her college plan now, but we would have plenty of money to attend to her educational needs later. Unable to satisfy my desire to keep up her little savings plan, I went ahead and paid off the last of my son's prepaid tuition, facing Mark's displeasure stoically.

"Certainly you can build a house without canceling college plans too. We have so much to work with, " I argued, a sick foreboding of doom settling around my heart as more and more I saw evidence that we had very different priorities.

The reinvention of our life was now in full force. We had changed locations, careers, and life attitudes. Our wardrobe was different, landscape was different, furniture was different, dogs were different, friends were different, recreational choices different, diet different, cars different, reading material different, and our family dynamic too was different.

The problem was, no matter how different everything was externally, inside we were still basically the same. Mark still felt undermined and controlled when I voiced even the simplest concern about his spending and priorities. He maintained control in the only way he knew, by avoiding physical intimacy and alienating me when he was displeased. We were back in our dysfunctional rut, only this rut admittedly had a prettier landscape.

Everything I had wanted in life before we retired, I wanted still. Peace. Romance with my husband. Family time. Expansive opportunity for my children. A life that was more about experiences and togetherness than "stuff." The business, long blamed as the cause of our problems, was gone, so why was I so lonely, and still shattered because my husband found endless excuses to put off physical togetherness? How come, no matter how much money we had, we were constantly in debt and financial stress continued to chase us as if it was tied to our tails by a string?

I couldn't put a voice to my disappointment or frustration, because admitting a few million dollars and total freedom wasn't enough to fix what ailed us meant we had to look deeper. We had seized an amazing opportunity to create whatever kind of life we wanted. We began this journey with a beautiful family, a long history as a couple, and a solid marriage. We had several million dollars in property, pledges, and the bank, and the time and freedom to do anything we wanted from this day forward. To be anything less than grateful for a life filled with such blessings would be a sin, right?

So, instead of questioning why our life reinvention was not working in the areas that counted most, Mark and I dove into change with more conviction than ever, almost frantically, trusting that once the metamorphosis was complete, happiness would be ours.

We kept changing, changing, changing… and not changing at all.

"Follow your genius closely enough, and it will not fail to show you a fresh prospect every hour."

—Henry David Thoreau

COUNTRY ELEGANCE

Baby chicks and bunnies are the Easter gifts of choice for an animal-crazed kid. My daughter had hands-on experience with both by now, which took away any hope that a little ball of fuzz would assure her ultimate joy on Easter morning. But an incubator... now that would be breaking new ground. Not only would hatching chicks at home be fun, but educational as well. Mark muttered that a chocolate bunny and a stuffed toy would suffice, but gave his consent, so on Easter morning Neva received candy nestled inside an eighteen-inch-square still-air incubator.

The incubator was nothing more than a small box made of Styrofoam with a light for warmth and a grid bottom. Water was poured into grooves in a lower panel to create humidity. A four inch plastic window on the lid allowed eager owners an opportunity to view the contents without disrupting the temperature, but four times a day the lid would have to be removed to hand turn the eggs inside. Incubating eggs was an interactive activity. Cool!

The family members all had an opinion about what eggs we should try to hatch. Mark suggested starting with a few of our own (free) random chicken eggs, but we had more than enough chickens now, so I was pushing for something novel like quail or duck eggs. Kent thought we should hatch an ostrich and claimed that if we did, he would ride the bird someday (his idea of a joke, I think). Neva didn't care what we hatched, as long as she could watch a real live baby bird come into the world.

The day after Easter, Neva found one little bantam chicken egg in a pile of hay, which she happily put in the incubator. We drew a cute smiley face on the shell with Magic Marker so we could keep track in the turning process. In my opinion, one little chicken egg didn't justify a 30-day commitment to egg rotation, so I was on the lookout for more eggs.

The feed store didn't sell eggs for incubation, and the only other store around was Wal-Mart, which had a lot of farm needs but no fertilized eggs, so I typed "bird eggs" into a search on eBay and sure enough, dozens of sources for fertilized eggs popped up. Neva and I were leaning towards ducks, so I bid on several breeds and ended up winning a dozen Appellate duck eggs. To celebrate, I made a quick visit to Amazon for poultry hatching books. Then, I went back to eBay to browse a bit more, mostly just to gawk at the offerings. That's when I stumbled upon peacock eggs for auction.

Peacocks! A glamorous, sophisticated bird with tail feathers spread in ornamental splendor would add a touch of elegance to my environment, the perfect antidote to the endless mud and frustration served up each day by my more common animals. A must-have in my opinion!

"Neva, wouldn't peacock eggs be cool to get?" I called out.

She was lying on the floor working a puzzle. "I like ducks."

I was counting on my animal-crazed child begging for peacocks to provide a convenient excuse for further eBay shopping. Dang.

"Peacocks are so pretty."

"I like ducks."

"You will like peacocks, too," I said as I placed a bid on two blue peafowl eggs for incubation despite her lack of enthusiasm. (Blue being the common peacocks you so often see at zoos, which are actually green and turquoise in color.)

Within an hour, I'd won the bid for twenty eight dollars. Naturally, I felt compelled to browse more, just to establish what a good deal I was getting. Low and behold, another person was offering two pure white peafowl incubator eggs, and this seller was throwing in two of the more common blues too. The only thing more striking than a beautiful blue-green peacock would be a snow-white one! The white peacock bird eggs with the two bonus blue bird eggs were forty eight dollars. Shipping added about twenty dollars to each order, so all told, I had six peacock eggs for one hundred and sixteen bucks.

Whether or not I was going to end up with a viable baby peacock was anyone's guess, but I did the math and felt the project was a fair risk.

A fully-grown peacock costs about one to two hundred dollars depending on the bird's sex. Peacocks have a wild nature and when you acquire them as adults, they often fly the coop—literally. Two hundred dollars is a hefty price tag for an animal you may only own for a day or two, but baby peacocks bond to the place they are raised. I saw a pair of baby peafowl chicks at the feed store for a hundred dollars once. Fifty dollars for one little chick seemed expensive, considering young poultry don't always survive and the buyer had no clue what gender they were getting. Boys become the beautiful, striking peacocks that become the logo for a TV channel, but the girls grow up to be just big, grey birds. With my luck, I'd get two girls if I bought chicks.

All things considered, starting with peacock eggs seemed like a cost effective way to go, even though sellers won't guarantee eggs bought on the Internet because they can't control what happens after the product is shipped. If the eggs don't hatch, who's to say the failure is due to a bad egg? If the post office x-rays the package, the embryo dies. Too much jostling or cold might do damage as well. Assuming the eggs arrive intact and are put in an incubator, success still depends on diligence from the person caring for the egg and a heavy dose of luck.

Since we were now proud owners of six peacock eggs in transit, I couldn't help but speculate what the eggs would look like. Would they be blue like a pheasant's, or red like certain duck eggs? Maybe they'd be white like a goose egg, or green like a mallard's. Would they be as big as a fist? Bigger? Would I know the difference between the albino peafowl eggs and those of the more common blue peacocks? When hatched, would the white and blue chicks look different, or would they be impossible to tell apart until later, when they formed feathers? How long until the chicks lose their down and start getting feathers anyway? Would the feathers on a chick hint as to whether they would grow to be boys or girls, or would I have to wait two years to know what sex the birds were? Would male peacocks fight like roosters, so we could only keep one? My questions were endless.

Back to Amazon! I ordered more books, arming myself with as much information as possible. Once the eggs arrived, I would have to let them sit at room temperature, big end up, for 8 hours to settle. Then I'd have to put them in a preheated incubator at 100 degrees with light humidity and turn them four times a day for 39 days.

A hen of any bird breed only turns broody after she has laid a clutch of eggs, and when she begins sitting, she stops laying. Since the time required for eggs to gather are what trigger the bird's instinct, nature has arranged for eggs to stay "fresh" and hatchable for about six days while a clutch is being formed. This provides just enough time for an enterprising seller to list eggs on eBay and transport them to their new destination in time for a successful incubation.

Growing a peacock from an egg is like starting a garden from seed. I would have to spend a month or so tending the project just to get to the beginning stage – that place where everyone else was buying young plants (or chicks) as starters. But as many gardeners will tell you, growing your plants from seed is not so much about the money saved as the pleasure derived from refining one's gardening skills. I was convinced hatching a peacock from an egg would make my peacock experience more meaningful.

The duck eggs arrived a few days later, each nestled in a cut section of a foam tube. As I unpacked the last three, a slimy coating dripped from the shells. The very last egg had a hole in the bottom. Poor devil. My first casualty.

I didn't know whether I was supposed to clean the eggs or leave them with that slimy residue, so I again referred to my poultry book. No answer. I didn't want to invite bacteria into the incubator from spoiled egg slime, but I also didn't want to wash the eggs and remove the protective film that was so important during the 39 day incubation period. I decided to wipe the eggs off with a soft, dry towel and put a frowny face on these shells. If these eggs didn't hatch, I'd attribute the failure to my not cleaning them.

When Neva came home from school we carefully positioned the eggs in the incubator and discussed who would take each shift in the 39-day baby-sitting chore of turning the eggs three times a day. The robust eggs made our little lone chicken egg look like a cousin with stunted growth.

Concerned about starting off eggs at different intervals, I bought a second incubator for the peacocks. When the next package arrived, I carefully unwrapped the contents, eager to see how these exotic bird eggs would differ from the others. The white peacock eggs were brown; the blue peacock eggs a lighter colored beige. They were all the size of a closed fist. Weighty. Substantial, yet fragile. The seller had written a nice note, and thrown in a bonus egg of a black shouldered peacock. The surprise was like getting a diamond ring in a box of crackerjacks.

I took the eggs downstairs and placed them carefully on top of the packing peanuts to settle. I drew happy faces on one side and wrote a description of the breed lightly in pencil on the other, wanting to keep track so when the time came, I'd know what birds had hatched.

The phone rang, and I stepped out for perhaps three minutes. When I returned, my dog was standing in the room with a guilty look on her face.

"Maxine, what do you have?"

The dog lowered her head and ever so gently dropped a peacock egg at my feet, then slunk outside with her tail between her legs. I crouched down to inspect one of my special white peacock eggs that didn't seem to be damaged in any way other than dog slobber. I took the egg back to the box only to discover there, in the middle of the floor, sat another peacock egg. This one had a small crack in the bottom. As luck would have it, this was my special gift, the black shoulder egg. Granted, I didn't even know I was getting this egg a half hour earlier, but still, I mourned the loss. I considered putting tape on the crack, but knew once bacteria invades an egg, there was no chance of a successful hatching anyway. The bonus egg had to be tossed.

Fighting back the temper tantrum rising to a boil inside, I put the peacock eggs in my second, preheated incubator, turning down my internal heat by thinking things could have been worse. I could have walked into the room and seen my dog smacking her lips after consuming all five of the expensive globes.

The next morning, my other eBay peacock eggs arrived. I put the dog out and barred the door for the important egg-resting phase. Hours later, these eggs joined the others in the incubator. The peacock project was underway in earnest.

For several days, Neva turned the eggs, but the endless routine quickly lost appeal and she turned the job over to me. "Just call me when they hatch," she said, more interested in her Gameboy than the incubator. So much for the mother-daughter egg babysitting bonding.

For a month I hovered over the incubator, turning the eggs four times a day. I couldn't go to lunch or the movies. I had to plan my grocery shopping and equestrian chores carefully. Life went on, but no matter what, I had to turn the eggs.

One day, as I reached in for yet another turn, a duck egg exploded in my hand. Yucky blackish-green goo covered the incubator and the smell of rotten egg invaded the entire downstairs. Oops.

A few days later, another duck egg exploded. Several of the duck eggs were turning grayer each day. Were these eggs dead and just rotting? Perhaps the duck package had been x-rayed during delivery, thus killing the embryos. Then again, maybe I overheated the eggs on one bad day when the humidity dried up and the temperature spiked to 104. The eggs might not even have been fertilized from the beginning.

As I cleaned the incubator, I had visions of all eleven eggs going off like firecrackers, making my entire house smell rancid. Some looked healthy enough, but I decided to throw out the gray ones before they took out every last healthy egg in the incubator, like little duck landmines. I tossed the questionable eggs into the woods. One egg wasn't that gray, but was so messy due to the rotten gunk clinging to the sides that I didn't know what else to do with the thing. Not like you can rinse an egg under water this late in the process—or at least I didn't think so. The not-so-gray egg was weighty, and that bothered me, but still, I was pretty convinced that this egg hatching thing was going to be a complete failure anyway so I was ready to throw them all out. Thinning out the incubator seemed a prudent way to avoid the disgusting clean-up work later, if nothing else.

I moved the six better looking duck eggs into the clean (meaning uncontaminated) incubator with my peacock eggs and continued turning, turning, turning. I felt like the Dunkin' Donuts baker on the commercial who, looking exhausted, drags himself out of bed each day saying, "Time to make the peacocks…um, I mean donuts."

When I had just about enough, I reached in one morning to turn my donuts and there was a little bird staring up at me through the window. His feathers were wet and his body swayed to and fro as if gravity were too much for his weak little legs to handle. He rested his chin on his broken eggshell and closed his eyes. I called for Mark. Together, we stared through the tiny window attempting to figure out what had hatched.

"Is that a duckling or a peacock?" I whispered.

"It's probably Neva's little bantam."

"No way. You think he's a duck? He's yellow like a duck. I saw a baby peacock at the feed store once, and the chick was brown like Ameraucana chicks. Not like this."

"That doesn't look much like a duck to me."

I couldn't stand not knowing, so I reached in to get the shell. My copious notes written on the egg confirmed that this hatchling was one of the white peacocks, remarkably, the very egg my dog had carried around in her mouth. (I knew this because I had drawn a little frowny puppy face on the side of the shell.)

By the time Neva came home from school, we could hear peeping from inside the other eggs. Shortly thereafter, a duckling hatched. This bird had typical webbed feet, a bigger head, and a tell-tale round beak. The difference between the two baby birds was so obvious I had to laugh. A duck looks nothing like a peacock. Duh!

The two baby birds were still weak, so I let them stay in the warm incubator for a few hours to fluff out and get their sea legs. After dinner, we discovered another duck hatchling. Peeping was coming from eggs that were now moving on their own accord, rolling the slightest bit as the inhabitants struggled to greet the world. As my fascinated family stood by, all six of the duck eggs hatched.

All I could think about was the eggs I tossed into the woods. Had there been little baby ducks only one day from hatching curled inside as I hurled them to their demise? I felt awful.

The baby birds were now becoming more active, so I removed them from the incubator to a brooder cage heated by a light bulb. The young ducks behaved aggressively with the peacock, and since she was my most prized new chick, I put her in a cage of her own. She looked small and lonely in there, full of energy but anxious and uncomfortable in a cage all alone. She kept running back and forth, sticking her beak through the bars, acting frantic compared to the ducks who were all nestled together in a contented clump. I tapped on the incubator, trying to guilt the other peacock eggs into hatching, but the eggs lay there like dead rocks.

I named the peacock Early since she was the first bird to hatch, and by the next morning, I worried she might be the only egg to hatch because all the other eggs were quiet and still. Early obviously wasn't getting companions anytime soon, so I went to the feed store to ask for advice.

The proprietor, Linda, recommended I buy my peacock a chicken buddy just in case the other eggs didn't hatch at all.

"Will a chicken and a peacock get along?" I asked.

"If you raise the two birds together, the chicken will think she's a peacock. No problem."

Every Lone Ranger deserves a Tonto, I decided, so I picked out a cute chick. The moment I put them together, they became fast friends.

Eight days later, the remaining peacock eggs still sat lifeless in the incubator. This gave Early epic standing as a special bird. She was not just my only peacock, but tangible proof that I wasn't a complete idiot in the incubation arena. By now, Neva and I agreed to call it a day and clear out the incubator to make room for something else.

"I guess I'll just throw the eggs out," I said, thinking this had been a rather expensive experiment, considering Early had just become a $116.00 peacock chick.

"We have to open the eggs first," Neva said matter-of-factly.

"Oh, honey, I can't. What if there are birds inside that were almost ready to hatch, but died at the last minute? I don't want to see half-formed peacocks. That would be too sad."

"We *have* to open them," she insisted. "That's what the book tells you to do and the only way to determine if you did something wrong."

"Whatever you do, just handle those eggs far away from the house," Mark said, remembering the stench of exploding duck eggs.

In the end, Neva was insistent, so I agreed to open the eggs *far* away from the house. We hiked up a hill with the still warm peacock eggs in my infamous dead thing bowl. Neva brought a small garden shovel and dug a grave for a communal bird burial, which we agreed would be appropriate in case we found dead baby peacocks inside. If all we found was rotten undeveloped eggs, a nice deep hole would cover up the smell.

We crouched beside the hole and I picked up an egg.

"Couldn't we just bury the eggs whole?"

"No way, Mom. Crack it open. Aren't you dying to see what's inside?" she said with curious, bright eyes.

"Not a bit."

"Well, I am," she said, leaning closer.

I tapped the egg with the edge of the shovel. Out slipped a gooey yolk that looked like any egg you might open from the supermarket, except for the orange yolk, of course. The gooey mess didn't even smell.

Neva frowned and dug into the goo with a stick. "There isn't even a vein of blood. I bet this egg wasn't fertilized. Try another one."

Swallowing, I picked up a blue peacock egg and cracked this one open. Again, we found nothing but goo.

"What a gyp," Neva said.

I thought so, too, but not because we were being cheated out of viewing interesting bird embryos at different stages of development. I was thinking someone on eBay sold me the bird version of the Brooklyn Bridge.

We opened the last three eggs. The insides were thicker, like a dab of pudding was plopped in the middle, but there was no telling if the eggs had begun to develop or the yolks were just getting so old they were hardening.

"At least now we know we probably didn't do anything wrong," Neva announced, pushing dirt on top of the little scrambled egg grave. "We can try again someday."

After all that money and 48 days of sleep down the drain, my enthusiasm for homegrown peacocks had drastically dimmed, but I kept that opinion to myself. I thanked her for making me open the eggs, admitting that knowing is better than not knowing. She gave me a "told ya so" grin.

As we walked back to the house, Neva paused to pick some wild-flowers. Spying a cricket, she bent down to place the bug in the dead things bowl for a quick study. I could see my girl was growing up curious about the world, engaged with the core truths about life, and sensitive rather than sentimental. I had a single peacock now to add elegance to my world, but in that moment, I believed true elegance walked beside me in the form of a beautiful, inquisitive child with dirt under her fingernails, and a healthy love for nature.

"However mean your life is, meet and live it; do not shun it and call it hard names. It is not so bad as you are. It looks poorest when you are richest. The fault-finder will find faults even in paradise. Love your life, poor as it is. You may perhaps have some pleasant, thrilling, glorious hours, even in a poorhouse. The setting sun is reflected from the windows of the almshouse as brightly as from the rich man's abode; the snow melts before its doors as early in the spring."

—Henry David Thoreau

INSTINCT

"I can't believe you're living on a farm," my mother said when she came to visit.

"This is not a farm. We'll be living in a million dollar cabin in the Georgia mountains. I'm just raising some animals on the side for fun."

"You have a garden. Chickens. A peacock. A donkey. Horses. Rabbits. This is a farm."

"A real farm supports itself. It makes money. A real farm has pigs. I don't have pigs."

Her eyes slipped to mine. "Why not pigs?"

"Mark drew the line at pigs. I did, however, donate to a "save the pigs" campaign."

"See? You're living on a farm. Just not a successful farm," she said. "You two retired with all that money, and you could have gone anywhere or done anything. You chose a farm."

"Land's a good investment. We still plan to travel and do some lovely things with our retirement."

"When?"

"When Mark is done building his house. He's promised."

She lifted a skeptical eyebrow. "If anyone ever told me you'd end up here during those years you danced in New York City, I'd never have believed them."

"I admit moving to the country wasn't a part of my life plan when I was young, but living here has been a great adventure."

"I thought you sold the studio to have a less stressful life." She stepped over a pile of horse droppings and gave me a "do you see that?" stare.

"Me, too," I confessed.

Seeing our world through my mother's eyes made me feel foolish and very, very tired. I was the artsy girl who liked to wear long skirts, high heels and big earrings. I loved museums, Broadway shows and dance concerts. I preferred experimental theater to sporting events, and wine tastings to tailgate parties. I *fit* when I lived in the city. So, how was it, then, that I *fit* here in the middle of the country, too, with nothing but a donkey and some peacock experiments to stimulate my imagination?

You'd think I had a split personality, and perhaps I did. For years, the city girl had the upper hand, obscuring the quiet shadow of the country girl who, unbeknownst to us all, was buried in my bosom. Now, the country girl demanded her turn at bat, scratching her way to the surface with such aggression I couldn't help but wonder if my self-image as a dancer was only surface deep after all.

I wanted to blame this change on menopause. I prayed for hot flashes. Nothing. I was the same person I'd always been, only now my natural curiosity and my tendency to do everything 110 percent had wandered away from dance and towards sustainable living. I was still that girl with the middle-class American upbringing, a credit card-carrying member of the consumer class with all the expectations and sense of entitlement that came with the role. The difference was, now I had a donkey.

My husband of seventeen years was feeling the same pull towards this polar opposite world as I was, so there had to be something to our change of heart. Perhaps it was a fluke that two separate individuals were experiencing the same shifts in perspective at the exact same rate. Had one spouse not been on board, the entire experiment would have collapsed under the weight of uncertainty, for sure. But just as some couples start to look alike or begin finishing each other's sentences after many years together, we seemed to have developed a common vision that had us both balking at what was considered "the norm" for people of our background and potential. If living on a farm had taught me one undeniable thing, I'd discovered that instinct always prevailed over training. So it was with animals. So it was with us.

One day, as Chris, my burly cowboy-farrier friend carved away at my horse's hooves, he asked, "What's the donkey for?"

"Just a pet. I'm told they make good guard animals."

"What's he guarding?"

"Nothing yet, but someday I might get some sheep. We had a goat once, but I wasn't too keen on him. Sheep, however, might be interesting."

Chris's expression made clear he considered keeping sheep about as pleasant as rolling in poison ivy. "I'm a horse man myself. Had a buffalo once. Damn near killed anyone who came near the fence. I sold him."

I made a mental note to scratch buffaloes off my wish list. Not that I had a buffalo on my wish list, but after the donkey, I no longer trusted my whims to remain explainable. "I think a llama would be cool. They're exotic and otherworldly."

His expression made clear he considered my wanting an animal for anything other than practical use the height of self-indulgence.

I grew defensive. "I'm a writer, after all. I learn about things by experiencing them. If I had a llama, I'd write about the experience."

Being a writer had become my catchall explanation for anything I wanted to do that might come across as impractical to my new country acquaintances. No one ever asked what kind of books I wrote. Literature was something the locals admittedly didn't care much about, so whenever I professed my avocation, the words hung in the air like a fart people chose not to acknowledge.

"Well, I know a fellow who'll sell you a llama for cheap," Chris said. He wrote the man's name on the back of my bill.

I had only been speculating for fun, but thought I might pass the name on to Mark. My birthday was coming up and a llama would be a rather cool present.

"No way," Mark said when I handed him the llama trader's name with a brazen hint.

Six weeks later I was the surprised recipient of a huge black llama wearing a red birthday bow around his neck.

The llama was an odd, prehistoric-looking creature with a long neck, curved ears, and thick, feathery-looking fur. He had thin legs, two-toed hooves, and large soulful eyes fringed in long lashes. He moved as gracefully as a reincarnated ballerina, head held high as his feet treaded gingerly through the wildflowers in the pasture. One look at him and I wanted to burst out singing *A Whole New World*.

"You can name your llama whatever you want," Mark said.

"What was the llama's name before?"

Mark had decided that he wouldn't share that information unless I twisted his arm.

"You don't want to know. Trust me, you'll be changing his name."

"Well, now you *have* to tell me. How bad can his old name be?"

Mark paused a moment, then sheepishly said, "They called him Nigger, claiming the name fits because he is black and ornery."

"I wish you hadn't told me that."

"Tried not to."

Mark suggested I name the llama Dalai, just so I could say the Dalai llama lived at our house. Not very original, but I didn't care. In that moment, I was leaning toward calling him Martin Luther King, just for principle.

I thought Dalai was exotic and remarkably cool. I had seen llamas before, but never in my own backyard. While llamas are often aloof, this one was friendly enough, taking cookies from my hand and venturing to the feed bucket when the horses came for their meal. Most of the time, he paced the pasture from end to end, as if he were memorizing how many steps he must take to cross. After several weeks of diligent exploration, he picked out a favored spot in the pasture and plopped to the ground, rolling over and sticking his feet straight up into the air.

"Your llama is dead," Mark said every time he drove up and saw the animal laid out like a carcass cooking in the sun.

"Har, har," I'd say, but just in case I'd shout or take a few steps in the animal's direction, needing confirmation that the dang thing was indeed alive. I didn't know if this animal's nutritional needs differed from the horses, or if a llama should be wormed, or have his feet trimmed, or if his wooly coat needed to be treated for fleas. *Do they make a flea collar that big?* I wondered, thinking I really needed to learn more if I wanted to keep this pet alive and well.

Back to Amazon. I immediately ordered several books on llamas and joined the Llama Association of America. Apparently, country adventure had a cost beyond the original investment since each project required I stumble around trying to figure my way through the maze of new challenges.

I learned there are things you can do with a llama. They can be taught to pull a cart, and to haul packs when you go camping in rugged mountains. But I didn't need my new pet to be useful. Mostly, I just planned to stare at him, fascinated. The horses, however, were not as amused. They kept their distance, kicking up the dirt and whinnying. They scurried to get away every time the llama ventured close.

"They act like Dalai's a leper. Poor guy is all alone." I complained.

"Don't get any ideas. One fancy yard ornament is enough," Mark said, turning his attention back to another book on house building.

One llama was certainly enough to satisfy my curiosity for camelids, but I couldn't help but feel sorry for a herd animal forced to spend his days alone.

My horse, Dixie, finally gave birth two days later, and my concerns over Dalai's single status were put on hold.

The foal came on April 15th. We considered naming her "Taxes," but chose "April" instead. I'd been spending a great deal of time around the pasture in anticipation of the baby horse's arrival, but as luck would have it, I missed the delivery by only a few minutes. Mark called to tell me he stopped by the pasture to discover a newborn carbon copy of Dixie, still glistening wet, standing on wobbly legs under her mother. I was washing my car, but the minute I got his message, I raced out to the land, white suds flying off my vehicle like snow.

April was sturdier than expected, with long legs, a slim body, and a soft brown coat. She looked like a deer with a big head. Frisky and remarkably self-sufficient, she stuck close to her mother, but only a few hours later, she had enough confidence to bound a few yards away, exuberant and curious about the world.

The other horses accepted the newcomer with admirable tolerance, but Donkey seemed most pleased. Donkey and baby April became fast friends, kicking up their heels and instigating games to bring action and entertainment to the quiet pasture.

Our job now, according to the books, was to "desensitize" the new colt. Each day we tried to make contact. We would devote a half hour to catching the colt so we could put a halter on. I'd tug at the rope while Mark or one of the kids would push the colt's backside, a task not unlike attempting to get a parked car to move. Suddenly, the colt would dart forward, yanking us off our feet and we'd be running at the end of the rope as if we were attached to a speeding whirl-a-gig ride at the county fair.

"Imagine having to do this with a wild, frightened, adult-sized horse," I said when April had given us a particularly hard time.

Everyone nodded. Dabbling with animals and working the land certainly made us thankful to be living in an enlightened and cushy age where the definition of hard work was setting up a new computer rather than living off the land, literally.

Adding both a young horse and a llama to my ever-growing ark meant additional chores were suddenly piled onto my already task-ridden days. The feed bills escalated, now hovering around two hundred dollars a month, which is less than many women who retire with a million dollars might spend on a personal trainer or other hobby interests, but still I felt guilty about the costs, so I stopped nail and hair appointments to compensate.

Meanwhile, Dalai's hair had grown into Rastafarian dreadlocks that looked torturously hot, so I purchased a pair of wool shears and Mark and I spent three days trying our hand at wool shearing. We were left with blistered hands, an insatiable wool itch that hung on for days, and a llama which looked like a poodle run over by a lawn mower. Still, we felt a great sense of accomplishment. I put the wool aside thinking I could use the fiber for something, but I'd have to read up to figure out what.

In the meantime, April's skeletal system would not be well-formed enough to put weight on her back for two years. The cost of feed and maintenance for those twenty-four months of growing, not to mention the labor involved in preliminary training, meant we'd have to make a hefty investment in our baby horse long before we ever could ride her.

Caring for three horses, a llama, and a donkey was already more than I could handle alone. Adding a colt to the mix almost put me over the edge. Mark reminded me we could sell a six-month-old weaned colt for a modest sum, but April was a member of the family now, and I loved the romantic notion that she was born on our land and would live there for all her days.

To me this new pet was like the biggest dog in the world, with an appetite and vet bills that paralleled her massive size. I dreamt of the day I'd ride her all over our fifty acres, yet when she was eighteen months old, Ronnie offered to buy her, and damned if I didn't say yes. The time to begin training her was near and the fact was, I was too old, too inexperienced, and too much a beginning rider to do the job of a seasoned cowboy. I could go to Amazon and buy all the DVDs, books, and videos on the market for training a horse (and I certainly tried), but an academic understanding of the process wouldn't amount to a hill of beans when a powerful horse started flipping out while I was onboard for the first time. April was going to a good home and that was all that mattered.

Every time an animal is removed from the pasture, the dynamic of the herd changes. When April left, Dixie was agitated. Donkey was lonely. My other two horses started acting aggressively as they reestablished positions in the hierarchy. Dalai still kept to himself, all alone after 18 months. So, when I read an ad in the paper for a female llama, registered and going cheap, I couldn't resist. Days later, the second llama joined the herd, and Dalai's lonely days were history. Apparently within an hour of unloading her into the pasture, the new llama had not only become friends with Dalai, but she was pregnant. I now had an exciting new adventure to look forward to. A baby llama!

On the Internet I discovered llamas gestate for eleven months.

Did I mention time moves slowly in the country?

"To be a philosopher is not merely to have subtle thoughts, nor even to found a school, but so to love wisdom as to live according to its dictates, a life of simplicity, independence, magnanimity and trust."
—*Henry David Thoreau*

WHAT BLOOMS

Things bloom in the country. Flowers. People. Ideas. *Doubts.*

Some days, I felt myself atrophy, as if my heart and mind had been shot with Novocain. The lack of intellectual stimulus, beyond that gained from my reading and experimenting with animals and organic living, felt like I was slowly dying at a cellular level, leaving me so imbalanced internally I was crumbling from the inside out. Other days, the calm and serenity of the beautiful hillsides, the slow pace of living, and my newfound leisure felt as though I had discovered the missing element required for internal peace. I was discovering my best self, learning to live mindfully, and discovering reverence for a softer existence.

This dichotomy of joy and discouragement wouldn't have tortured me so much had I less time to ponder my singular existence. My husband was too distracted by his house project to pursue the plans and promises we had made to each other. I ached with a sense of loss, not for the life we left behind, but for the life I perceived as just beyond our fingertips. Everything I ever dreamed of for happiness seemed as right in front of me, only behind a window. I stood on my side of the glass with my hands draped around a donkey, waiting for my husband to slide the window open. The problem was despite a litany of heart-to-heart talks regarding love and money and our need to be together and explore a more expansive life as a couple, he refused to recognize the pane between us, much less what was on the other side. So, I clung to evidence of my children's contentment as validation that, despite our personal stress, our choices to move to the country had been for the greater good.

Kent had spent the first twelve years of his life in a dance school where male influence was in short supply. He now had friends who camped and swam and played sports. My son had become a modern version of Tom Sawyer, and I watched his masculinity explode to the surface like a geyser just breaking through the earth's hard crust. So delighted was I with him coming into his own that I wanted to fall to my knees and thank God each time he asked me to pack a basket of food for a campout with the guys.

Not having to work all the time meant I spent more time with Neva than I ever had with my other children during their tender prepubescent years. We cooked muffins together, chased chickens, collected eggs, and made gifts of jewelry or jam for her teachers. We puttered around in the garden, went to the feed store to gaze at or buy spring chicks, and spun honey off the bees' comb together. Before the family woke each morning, I'd crank up the four-wheeler to go to the barn to feed the horses, and almost every day she would come running out in her pajamas to beg a ride. I'd help her onto the seat behind me, relishing her little body pressed up against mine, the warmth of her hands and the soft pressure of her tiny arms clinging to my waist. We talked over the roar of the engine as we checked on the bees, zoomed by the garden to spy out what was growing today, and more often than not, stopped to pick blackberries.

Things were not as promising for Denver, however. As much as my younger children thrived among the country's lulling charms, my eldest still seemed tortured by the lack of stimulus and opportunity available for a young adult. She was unsure what she wanted to do with her life, but she knew she wanted more than what Blue Ridge offered. She continued to long for the opportunity to date more cultured boys, establish a career, and get a job that paid enough to support an apartment of her own. She yearned for the carefree, fun existence of the twenty-one year olds she'd gone to college with, to be back in the world where young people gathered in clubs and at parties and hung out with diverse friends arguing liberal philosophy because they had yet to be bogged down with a family, a mortgage, and responsibilities. She wanted to backpack across Europe. Join the Peace Corps. Find a career. Fall in love.

"I'm missing my youth," she reminded me, with no small touch of drama.

I might have made a joke about her youthful angst, except that I agreed she was missing out on the best years of her life. Everything about the country life that fed my soul and offered me opportunity for personal growth was different for her. I was retired and ready to rest and reflect. She hadn't yet lived, and I agreed with her that a dynamic woman on the cusp of life did not belong parked in a quiet corner of the world.

"We need to give Denver money to help her get out of here," I told Mark.

"She shouldn't have quit school. Her life is her problem now. We have financial limits, you know."

I wanted to point out that the house he was building was the cause of those financial limitations. Our child needed help, and I desperately wanted to allocate some of the money we'd spent a lifetime earning to her education, in whatever form her dreams took. As her parent, I wanted to give her a loving sendoff into the world.

"If she'd stayed in school we'd be paying for her food and dorm. Why don't we give her the money we would have spent, had she kept on course? She can also cash in the rest of her college plan. That will give her a nest egg to move someplace with more opportunity."

"You always make things too easy on the kids. Obstacles and hardship will teach her what real life is all about."

"Real life is also about families sticking together to make dreams come true for each other. We have more money than most families I know. Our resources shouldn't be allocated toward just *one* person's dream."

Mark bristled at the implied criticism. "I'll agree to give her money if she moves out. She's past twenty. It's time."

I bit my tongue to keep from reminding him that when we met, he was living with his mother at age twenty-three. He had accepted help from my family and his to get his start in life, and every phase of development we went through thereafter, such as buying our first house, growing our business, or funding life emergencies, required assistance from family. Wasn't it our turn to pay this kind of support forward?

Denver agreed that if we gave her a small nest egg of her own she could become independent. She took the money and enrolled at a folk art school called Penland to study silversmithing and jewelry design. I was delighted that my artsy daughter was exploring a new skill, but secretly wished she had gone further from home, where life's grand diversity would call to her louder than any country whisper. But when the six-week course was over, she returned to Blue Ridge, got a small apartment, and took up with a country boyfriend whose greatest talent seemed to be spitting chew.

"Please, let's allow Denver to live with us to save money so she can afford to get out of here," I implored.

"Daughter or no, I won't have anyone living in my house who won't follow my rules. I have made clear that food can only be eaten in the kitchen in my house, and yet she still eats in her room. I won't have it, I tell ya," Mark said.

"It's my house too," I argued. But we both knew that was no longer true. Somewhere along the line this expensive cabin monstrosity had become Mark's house. We lived on Mark's money. With Mark's rules. He was the man now, and as such, we were all subject to his choices. Denver was going to have to find her own way out of Blue Ridge, because my hands were tied. My resentment over not being allowed to invite my own daughter back home simmered inside and for the first time, I began questioning the fairness of our new dynamic. Mark felt entitled to control all the money that had been accumulated through our joint effort, but this money would never have existed had I not been the business person I was.

I shared my frustration with Kathy. Each time we met for lessons now, we spent the first few minutes gossiping about our lives. I marveled that two women with such unequal opportunity and resources could share what turned out to be the same stresses and concerns.

Kathy would talk about how hard she found paying the rent on her tiny shack could be, and I would think about how we couldn't afford the mortgage on our ever-expanding behemoth of a log home on 50 acres since Mark had taken out a mortgage for four times the amount we originally discussed.

"My eldest is dating someone that is all wrong for him," Kathy would fretfully say.

"So is mine."

"I worry about whether or not my son is learning enough in school."

"Me, too."

"Gas is getting crazy expensive, but still I like to drive my kids to school to be there for them. My youngest is late for school all the time."

"So is mine."

"My husband is so proud of me. He came home with flowers yesterday to surprise me. That man loves me like no other."

I sat quietly, shocked to realize I was actually envying this illiterate, destitute woman because she had hit upon a subject where I couldn't pipe in with "me, too."

One day, as I was setting up my notes and workbooks for Kathy's lesson, Carol, the director of the literacy program, stopped by to talk to me.

"You know, Kathy is the greatest example of success we've ever had as a beginning reader. Her test scores are amazing, and all you have to do is look at her to see what a difference you've made in her life."

"I can't take credit. She's just a wonderful student who works hard. She does what it takes. She keeps showing up."

"She keeps showing up because you make the lessons fun. You are never preachy or dry. You come to the table as a friend rather than acting like you're superior."

I smiled, thinking Kathy *was* my friend, the only person in my world I could talk to now. I didn't feel myself superior in any way.

"I was wondering if you would share your experiences and ideas and what you've learned from working with Kathy at a meeting next month for other potential tutors."

I wasn't convinced I had much to offer, really, but I agreed, and the next thing I knew, I was assigned a new role as trainer to all the new reading volunteers. I felt at home contributing something of value to my community like the old days.

"A woman at the high school has asked me to come talk to teenagers about the importance of staying in school, keeping clean, and resisting drugs," Kathy said weeks later. "She was wondering if you would come with me, so together, we could talk to them."

"Why do you need me?" I said.

Kathy's new teeth gleamed beneath a subtle smile. "Please? I can't do it alone."

So the next week I found myself waiting my turn to speak to the teens in the remedial high school classes. Kathy talked about the frustration of living as a non-reader. She talked about becoming a meth addict, losing her son, and going to jail. She talked about church, and how being involved in religion was central to her recovery. She took out her false teeth, showing the kids the mug shot taken on day she was arrested. Then she introduced me as the woman who helped her crawl out of darkness.

Kathy's honesty and real life experience was an impossible act to follow. I shared my theoretical opinions about education, but in the audience's eyes, I was just one of those transplants that the true residents of the area tolerated rather than respected. I was glad to meet the kids, however, mostly just for the chance to witness Kathy in a leadership role.

Overnight Kathy became the poster child in Blue Ridge for overcoming drugs and illiteracy. She began giving talks at the prison. She started volunteering at a woman's shelter. She was recognized at her AA meeting as the most inspirational participant.

"Will you come to my counseling group for drug offenders and meet my counselors?" Kathy asked as casually as if she were inviting me to lunch. "I've told everyone about you."

She seemed to be leading me deeper and deeper into the process

of healing our community, and I felt honored to have a karmic purpose at long last.

"Of course," I said.

Days later I was sitting with a dozen ex-meth addicts, half of
whom also couldn't read. I listened to story after story of struggles
with addiction and life upheaval tumbling out of the mouths of my
neighbors. The brother of my daughter's best friend was among the
group, as well as the father of my son's best friend. Three women in
the group talked about how they wanted to straighten out their lives
so they could get their kids back from foster care. These confessors
were not yet seventeen, my son's age.

The romance of living in the country—the charm and grace and
simplicity I associated to living among the trees— was now fading
in the harsh dawn of reality. Life in Blue Ridge was wonderful for a
retired visitor living in an upscale cabin for weekend visits. People
from a background like ours shopped in the area's antique stores and
rustic art galleries, took classes at the art center, boated on the lake,
and meandered through craft festivals thinking life in the mountains is sweet. But underneath the quaint charm of the neighborhood coffee shop, beyond the lilting accents of shopkeepers and the
cute smiles of friendly cowboys, lurked a wealth of sad stories and
threatening circumstances that I had no choice but to acknowledge
now. My new understanding of the sad, dark side of the fulltime
residents who were not transplants made me fear just how skewed
my children's perceptions were of what was a normal, opportunistic
existence for people of our socioeconomic class. I *did* want my children exposed to a less consumption-driven world, for I recognized
the value in their not growing up to believe a sugarcoated world
and a life of entitlement was the norm, but I hated that they were
totally removed from mainstream America where opportunity was
profoundly infinite and a greater emphasis on higher education and
liberal thinking prevailed.

To grow up balanced, secure, and whole, my kids needed the world
we left behind just as badly as they once needed exposure to a country existence. I no longer craved a trip to Paris for my own curiosity

about the bigger world. I now craved a trip, anywhere, for the whole family, a trip to remind us all that there was a vibrant life out there bigger than Blue Ridge, filled with life's marvels.

Things bloom in the city the same way they bloom in the country. Flowers. People. Ideas.

For me, now, *doubts* were in bloom.

"It is something to be able to paint a particular picture, or to carve a statue, and so to make a few objects beautiful; but it is far more glorious to carve and paint the very atmosphere and medium through which we look, which morally we can do. To affect the quality of the day, that is the highest of arts."

—Henry David Thoreau

MY MARTHA STEWART BARN

After months of my dropping blatant hints, Mark announced that he was going to build me a barn. This wasn't because he was disturbed by my toiling over animals in the sleet, rain, and mud (after all, I made that bed myself by assembling an animal entourage). No, he just wanted to provide additional work for the boys building our house so they wouldn't take a job elsewhere and become unavailable for the next building project he had in mind.

"Perhaps we should hold off. Money is tight and the payments we're supposed to be getting from the Smiths have been so irregular," I said. "I'm worried the school may be failing now."

"You've been whining about a barn for months, and now that I'm giving you one, you're complaining?"

"Of course not. I just think we should be a bit conservative under the circumstances."

He sighed, clearly exasperated with my endless lack of enthusiasm for his generosity. I should be overjoyed with his plans, considering how badly I wanted a barn.

Mark made clear that he was in charge of any and all building projects, but I'd been reading barn plans and studying horse stable designs in magazines for months with hope that someday our fifty acres would evolve to be more like those affordable turnkey farms I wished we'd settled for. I decided that, if we were really going to build a barn now to keep Ronnie employed, I might as well campaign for a few practical elements that would make my life easier.

Together, Mark and I designed a traditional two-story barn, with two roomy 12X12 stalls and covered paddocks the size of another stall connected to each as roaming space for the animals. If I closed the stall doors, I could use the outside paddocks as two open air stalls, sort of a convertible system to house four animals comfortably when necessary. I even made the interior fence rails removable so I could open up the space to create a bigger paddock or to make the stall area one duplex if I wanted.

Opposite the paddocks we planned a covered area for hay storage and on either end of the hallway were double doors big enough to drive a tractor through. We ran electricity to the barn for when winter hours stole the light early and to install a pump to bring water from the creek. Hallelujah!

Opposite the stalls were a feed and tack room, both with concrete floors; a workbench, and dozens of hooks on which to hang supplies. The upstairs of the barn featured a traditional hay door, but this was more for looks than for resale. Getting the heavy bales up was more trouble than I could handle on my own, so this area became designated space for storing beekeeping supplies, fiber, cages, incubators, and anything else animal or garden related. The second floor provided a dry place to keep newly hatched chicks or peacocks too, my very own clubhouse, welcoming messy projects with open arms. I even had a small concrete pad with a roof overhead in front of the feed room as a tiny patio to shelter a small bistro table and a rocking bench.

Thanks to the high quality of the leftover wood from our house and the innovative design that was both functional and attractive, we created a superb barn. Best of all, the barn was all mine, so I immediately set out to make the structure *look* like mine.

I bought life-size black plywood cutouts of rearing horses and had them affixed to the front of the barn, framing a wagon wheel that served as a base for an outdoor light fixture. I put a bigger-than-life cutout of a soaring eagle on the back side, and hung iron hooks made of western stars and horse shoes, for ropes and such. I found a huge horseshoe welcome sign for the front door and a rusty equestrian-decorated bell for the porch, and hung baskets of flowers and a wreath on the feed room door. Wooden cutouts of horses, painted with the words "feed" and "tack," labeled storage areas. I even had little street signs printed at the mall with the names of my horses to honor each of their stalls, and bought a stop sign that said "WHOA" instead of "STOP" to hang on the hitching post. Inspired, I picked up other gimmicky cowboy signs that I hung up with a bulletin board that proudly displayed a horse calendar.

To say my barn was cute would be an understatement.

"It's a barn, dear. Not a kid's theme bedroom. You've made a nice barn into something girly. Kinda embarrassing," Mark complained.

"You think this barn is girly?" I glanced at my horse paraphernalia. "Well, maybe so. But hey, I'm a girl. This is my barn. Naturally, I would have a girly barn."

"Don't you think the rearing horse cutouts are over the top?"

"You think I should have gotten the leaning cowboy cutout and put him up against the gate instead?"

"You're missing the point."

I leaned against my new horse dung shovel, complete with a cowboy hat engraved handle. "When we were planting daffodils, you told me the animal area was mine to make as pretty as I wanted."

"I was talking landscaping."

"You ain't seen nothin' yet. In another month my mixed-color flower bulbs will be erupting everywhere, putting the *pièce de résistance* on this beautiful barn."

He mumbled that other barns in the neighborhood were nothing more than barely-functioning buildings with slat walls and sections of roof missing.

"There is something endearing about an ancient building made of rough barn-wood, especially when covered in weeds and sporting cracks and bullet holes," Mark explained.

"Had we bought a turnkey homestead with a rundown barn and used the saved time and money for taking a trip or two, we'd have that kind, but you wanted to build our Shangri-La yourself. This is the result," I pointed out. "And for the record, most workshops around here are makeshift buildings too, and you instead built yourself two huge, decorative structures that could just as well be a second house.

He ignored that reality check. The next time we were out on a drive, he pointed to a weathered wreck of a barn that must have been fifty years old. "You have to admit a barn like this is quaint!"

"Whoever owns that place needs a plaque that says *'Every cowgirl deserves a great stud'* . . . and a horseshoe clock," I said with a sniff.

Since he now knew I was not about to remove my horseshoe coat rack in the interest of pretending my new barn was some kind of shabby-chic old wreck, Mark made clear to our country friends that he had nothing to do with what he now referred to as "my wife's Martha Stewart barn."

"Now, I'm not claiming to know everything, 'cause I only have 'bout a sixth grade education, but I think Ginny's barn is just fine. I'd have a barn like that if I could afford it," Ronnie said.

"See! Ronnie thinks my barn decorations are classy," I said to Mark. "Just because you're building a million dollar rustic log house doesn't mean you know squat about barns."

When my farrier came to shoe the horses, I took his visit as a perfect opportunity to get a second opinion.

"Nice barn, but where's the couch gonna go?" Chris said with a grin.

"Are you making fun of my barn?"

"Are you kidding? It's a great barn. Your barn is nicer than my house. I particularly like the horseshoe napkin holder on your bistro table."

"Considering all the time I spend with these animals, I figured I might as well make the environment inviting."

"I like the horse bell. The horseshoe sign is nice too. I'd like 'em more, had you bought those things from me, considering I have thousands of used horseshoes without purpose. Now, if you could just do something about that awful noise coming from the tack room…"

It took me a moment to comprehend what noise he was referring to. My boom box radio got reception from only three stations: a country station, a Christian rock station and a classical music station. Under the circumstances, I chose the classical station. I rather liked Beethoven serenading me as I shoveled horseshit or polished a leather saddle.

"I've been shoeing horses all my life, and I can honestly say I ain't never been to no barn with that kind of music playing. What's wrong with good old country music?"

"I'll stick to rhythm and blues or classical music," I said. "Listen with an open mind and you might develop an appreciation for the finer things in life."

"I'll just hammer louder," Chris mumbled.

"Some things can't be drowned out, even with a blacksmith's hammer," I said, "*class* being one."

Considering my boots were covered with horseshit and my nails were dirt encrusted, I got the response I deserved—good natured laughter.

"Men and boys are learning all kinds of trades but how to make men of themselves. They learn to make houses; but they are not so well housed, they are not so contented in their houses, as the woodchucks in their holes. What is the use of a house if you haven't got a tolerable planet to put it on? —Grade the ground first. If a man believes and expects great things of himself, it makes no odds where you put him, or what you show him ... he will be surrounded by grandeur."

—Henry David Thoreau

THE HOUSE FINALE

Mark had been working relentlessly on his dream house for over a year now. Each day, I'd drive to the land to take care of my animals, and then I would drive a four-wheeler up to the house site to see how things were coming along. Mark would be there, covered from head to toe in sawdust as he debarked and sanded over eighty trees to be a part of the stairway, a support column, archway, or roof beam. Slowly the home took shape, growing grander in proportion and stature each day. Clearly my husband was no longer building a dream house for his family, but the dream house of his imagination, a stately, sophisticated lodge that rivaled anything you might see on *Extreme Log Homes,* his favorite reality TV show.

"How big is this house going to be?" I said, awed by a 25-foot ceiling in the great room and the equally-high stone work around the fireplace, embedded with fossils and geodes.

"7,500 feet under roof," Mark said, not taking his eyes off the beauty-band of river rock a workman was cementing along the circumference of the room. He barked an order at two workers hanging solid oak cabinets in the kitchen and rolled his eyes and whispered, "Can you believe these guys, hanging cabinets without considering the inset space for lighting requirements?"

Considering our last home in Florida was only 1,700 feet and the cabin we had been staying in was half that (and both were simple abodes), I didn't know whether to panic or squeal with joy over the size and grandeur of his project. We had discussed simplifying our life and scaling down, but we also discussed a need for a home big enough for our family to enjoy before the last of our kids left for college. I suppose my dreaming about a family home with a big kitchen promoting family gatherings and space to play games or watch TV to promote togetherness sent a mixed message; nevertheless, I voiced my concern, thinking Mark had been confused about our agreed-upon life simplicity plan. This home was never a part of our joint vision. We talked of a simple log cabin home, and agreed we couldn't spend more than four hundred grand on the project. To me, that investment was plenty for a pretty fantastic cabin.

"Can we afford this?" I whispered, unable to imagine us living in anything so spectacular. "This house has become awfully big."

"You said you needed an office of your own. You wanted a good sized kitchen. When I told you we could finish off the basement and put in a workout room, you were thrilled. Most importantly, this house has big closets. I've manifested everything you asked for," he snapped.

I had three horses, a donkey, two llamas, chickens, other birds, and angora rabbits outdoors, and a laptop precariously balanced on a makeshift desk in a corner of our simple, uninsulated, 30 year old cabin. I already had everything I wanted. Everything, that is, except a husband to share all my newfound freedom with. An impressive house was not something I ever wanted or cared about. What I wanted and cared about was the man building it.

I stared at the antler chandelier Mark chose after weeks of perusing rustic galleries. My eyes slipped to the thick log fireplace mantle he'd spent days making to his satisfaction, and moved on to the oversized Jacuzzi tub perfectly sized for a man of his large stature. I observed the massive stairway leading to Mark's office, positioned in such a way that once he was up there, he could oversee the entire downstairs like a king gazing upon his kingdom.

One thing was obvious: this house was a not something a man seeking a stress-free life would build for his wife and children. Mark had built this house for himself, a place that embodied everything he considered impressive and fitting to his style and taste.

I wanted to be a devoted wife who supports her husband's dreams, but the escalating investment left me sick with worry. There was no stopping the trajectory of the project now, so rather than continue to complain of his opulence, I decided to at least make evidently clear certain elements I felt were important, such as extra light in my office and in the kitchen pantry for my 45-year-old eyes. I reminded him over and over how badly I wanted a double oven and a good cooktop in the kitchen since I was an avid cook with plans to make canning, storing, and processing food a part of our organic lifestyle. So much of my life had always been devoted to the drudgery of doing the family laundry, and with mud and saw-dust besieging our world now more than ever, I really did need a supersized washing machine. My fitness level declined every month, something that wreaked havoc on my self-image, so I pushed him to finish off the workout room, too, if he could do it inexpensively. A gorgeous house wasn't half as important as a functional house to me and I pointed out plenty of huge houses we'd seen cost a fraction of what Mark was spending now, but he responded by pointing out how cheap they were with their stock cabinetry or prefab stonework. He could do so much better. His house design would be a work of art. I began thinking that if I let him build something grand, we'd at least have something to sell later that would fetch a good price.

But more than anything, I wished he would stop building all to-gether. I wanted our *life* to be a work of art, while he wanted the building we hung our hats in to be his art.

He installed four fireplaces and stoned the back screened-in porch and the patio with expensive slate. He bought special order windows, awesome light fixtures, and an upscale generator so we'd never have to worry about blackouts. He spent a fortune on labor to get ev-ery detail perfect, preferring to supervise rather than do these tasks himself. Having overspent on fancy detail and materials, he had no choice but to cut corners in other places. Usually this meant forgoing the things *I* wanted most. He picked a stove smaller than the stove I formerly had in Florida and I was more than a little disappointed that hand hewn molding and fancy cabinetry took precedence over my desire for a down-to-earth welcoming kitchen made for cooking and gathering people together.

As the bills came rolling in, Mark would comment that the things I demanded, such as a few extra ceiling lights in my office, were the reason the house was costing far more than he anticipated. "I'm over budget because of everything you want me to do," he said.

I reminded him one more time that I had taken him to a builder and we had spent a day designing a beautiful home with as much space and functionality as we wanted and the price was one third of what he'd spent so far. When he had refused to sign the contract, his reasoning was he could build us a better house for less money. What happened?

"This house is my art," he said, as if that concept made the project worthy of every last cent of our family resources.

I tried to love his house, but the place was just so far removed from the quaint, comfy cabin we set out to buy or build, I couldn't help but feel disassociated. I had dreamed of close quarters to inspire togetherness, a home like all those cabins we had rented over the years that left us dreaming that someday we might actually own one. I desperately longed for freedom from financial strain and the liberties that would come with not having to chase a buck to get by. I would write. He would make art out of wood. No more absentee husband distracted and agitated by building blunders. No more spending, spending, spending, to set up this perfect life that I was starting to doubt would ever come about. I had hoped for green living. This was putting us in the red.

Eventually, inevitably, the house was completed. The new life that we had set out to live over two years ago was finally set to begin. Overnight we went from living in the total dishevel of a refurbished, ramshackle cabin to living in the grand quarters of a multi-million dollar home (if you counted the outbuildings and land).

The first night, our family stood in the grand foyer of our home with mouths agape. A sound like a gunshot rang out, causing us all to freeze.

"That was a log cracking," Mark explained.

With the heat turned on, the eighty logs he had harvested, sanded, and strategically placed were starting to dry and split. Our new home was talking to us, inviting us in like some uppity butler who seemed convinced we'd come to the wrong address.

"This will be like living in a bowl of Rice Krispies," I said. "I guess you're used to the sounds since you've spent so much time working here for over a year, but for us, just standing in such a fancy room feels weird."

"I'm not used to it either. I feel like I've just checked in to a resort I really can't afford," Mark said, humbled by his own creation.

"My tummy feels funny," said Neva, obviously nervous at the idea of setting her toys up in a room three times the size of her last one.

"Pepper likes the house," Kent pointed out as our city-raised cat leaped from log to log and walked along the high ledges, turning the rafters into his own indoor, forest-inspired amusement park.

The lack of furniture made the house feel a bit like a mausoleum. Our voices echoed in the cavernous great room. We had rolled out a rug from our former house, but the ten foot oriental looked like a postage stamp. Our dining room table was dwarfed by the open space, as if the furniture had shrunken to the size of an end table. Clearly, more shopping would be required as the simple life continued its ravenous appetite for every resource we had. I was afraid to ask what heating and cooling a home this size would cost us, especially now that we no longer had an income or the promise of one, but I seriously doubted Mark had given common sense expenses like that a thought.

"What this place needs is new furniture," Mark said.

"What this place needs is a Christmas tree," I pointed out, wanting to make the children feel more at home and to get us all focused on tradition rather than more consuming by buying furniture. "It *is* December, after all."

Everyone agreed a tree would be a good place to start. Mark didn't join me in bed to christen our new home or make me feel in any way comfortable. I went to bed alone. He stayed up to go online to buy a 15-foot artificial tree to fill out the empty spot in the great room, and shop around for potential furniture.

"I got a huge tree on sale so we actually saved money," he said after hours of online shopping.

I wondered how my husband, a true math whiz, continued to insist his spending money was a way of saving. He had spent over a million dollars so far, claiming all the while that he was "saving more money than anyone else could."

The tree arrived a week later and the entire family devoted three days to putting together the one thousand independent branches in the kit, but the finished tree was fittingly majestic. Now, even our Christmas tree looked as over the top as the one at Rockefeller Center.

So began our first Christmas in the new house. We had a tree two times the size of any we'd ever had before, in a house four times the size of any we'd ever lived in before. Boxes were unpacked, and family knickknacks were placed in corners to give a homey touch to the place. As we established a normal schedule I started to wonder if perhaps this house wouldn't come to fit us after all. Maybe I really did lack Mark's vision and I was a stick in the mud, constantly raining on the parade rather than just enjoying the party.

As we were putting up the last touches of holiday decorations, Mark got "the call." He looked at the number on the caller ID and took the phone up to his office, his muffled voice trailing down the balcony just loudly enough for me to deduce the severity of the conversation. When he came down he motioned for me to sit.

"The Smiths are going bankrupt," he said. "They aren't going to pay us the balance owed on the business. I'm calling our lawyer so we can begin the eviction process to get them out of our buildings. At least then we can sell the buildings and we'll have all that money to pay for our new life."

"Are we going to be able to keep this house?" I asked softly.

"We have a million dollar mortgage. Considering we are unemployed and have no prospects, and even if the Smiths did pay us everything, which they won't, we couldn't pay off the price of this house. I doubt it."

We hadn't been living in the house a month. The strain and sacrifice Mark had imposed on the family to get us here had been a nightmare. Now we were going to just move on before ever enjoying that ideal family time so long anticipated?

I could have been angry. But after 17 years of marriage, I knew my husband well enough that I should have assumed his house project would spin out of control before he even began. He made clear he wanted to show the world what he could do without me as a driving influence or as a factor in his success. He wanted to be a builder, and this house was his résumé. His need to feel important had always far outweighed the dull subject of his family's financial stability.

My shame was that I didn't stop him. I wanted him to have his dream, and I had been clinging to the hope that supporting him while he built his dream house would make him happy.

"This house has been so important to you. You must feel awful," I said.

He shrugged and ran a hand along a thick log support. "Leaving dance left this huge hole inside me. I poured all my artistic inspiration into this project instead." He gestured to the breathtaking room with a humble smile. "This house is the great recital of my building career. Performance art. But now that I've created something this cool, I'm done. I can let the place go."

And just like that, my husband severed his attachment to the grand house that had been his obsession for two years. He did so with the same ease he had changed hobbies or eating styles in the past. He'd had the thrill of spending himself sick, and enjoyed reveling in the warm wood tones and harmony created by his perfect juxtaposition of rock and tree. Since indulging his creativity had been what the project was all about from the beginning, he couldn't care about living here, and he certainly didn't want to become a slave, working to support an expensive home now. He started talking about the next house he wanted to build.

I was devastated by the simple truth that my husband felt indulging his creativity should take precedence over his family's welfare. But what was done was done.

"I really did intend to build us something practical, but every time I was faced with a choice, all that money in the bank made me think, 'why not'? So I kept inching forward on every decision, until I threw out the concept of limits altogether. Once I realized I'd gone too far, I figured I'd shoot the entire bundle. I knew when our money was all gone, we'd *have* to live simply. In the meantime, the house would be an icon to my potential. And because you kept harvesting homegrown eggs and veggies from the garden, it was easier for me to pretend we were still pursuing the simple life," he said in a moment of honesty.

"Hey, there's nothing simple about growing eggs at home," I said.

"So we'll move. Find a simple cabin in the woods like we talked about from the beginning."

I had no clue how he expected us to pull off another life reinvention with all our resources drained. "Do you think maybe we should consider leaving Blue Ridge?"

"I don't know. I'd sure miss my workshop. I still dream of creating art in the medium of wood."

I wondered how he could miss a workshop he had barely set foot in. Mark was in love with the *idea* of his workshop more than the reality. He still hadn't unpacked the glut of tools and wood he'd purchased despite our paying endless bills to set up electricity, water, shelves, and storage for a workshop that sat for years non-operable. He did make some lovely furniture in formal classes at the Campbell School, but only because the social element and other people were part of the process to witness and voice recognition of his talent. He had yet to make anything other than a rustic coffee table on his own. Mark had never been a man able to work independently, and I began to understand that to be his partner, I would have to embrace whatever art he was into at the time, rather than honor or commit to my own. When we were both dancers, life worked. Now, I'd have to be his crafting sidekick and channel all my efforts into his fleeting passions, or we were headed for trouble.

"I love my barn more than I ever loved this house." I said. "So I'm more than OK with selling and getting back on track with what we set out to do from the beginning."

Deep down, I still dreamed of following our original life plan. For

me, that meant exploring an organic lifestyle, having time to write
and reflect, and taking care of my family full time. Mark wanted to
work with wood and spend Sundays on his tractor, landscaping on a
supersized scale. He wanted to build houses and be recognized for
his unique talent and make a living as a builder.

Had we not had so much money to work with from the start, we
would have had no choice but to move slowly, cautiously, *practically*,
and we could have achieved the personal lifestyle we craved. Was it
too late to correct things now?

"I can still make this work," he said. "We can put the house up for
sale with twelve extra acres at this corner of the land. You've said
tending fifty acres is too much for you to handle anyway. We'll still
have thirty-seven acres, the barn and workshop paid off. I'll build us
a simple house on the other side of our property, the kind of house
we planned in the beginning."

My heart clung to the possibility.

The problem was America had just plummeted into the worst
housing and financial crisis in years. Houses were not selling anywhere, and property values had nosedived. The million dollars we
had in cash only two years ago was now buried in the land beneath
our feet, and the mortgage Mark took out had put everything at
risk. Luckily we had separated a few acres from our first mountain
property and we sold this lot, so we had a chunk of cash left to help
formulate and survive a back-up plan. Tallying up, we figured we
had enough money in the bank to hold on for a year or so as we
waited for someone to come along to bail us out of our oppressive
payments on the big house.

"We could go back to Florida," Mark said. "We could reopen the
dance school. We still own the buildings."

"I'd be fine with that, but how can we sell this house if we are not
here to keep up with the maintenance?" I said.

"I would much rather stay here forever and scrape by anyway," he
admitted.

Scrape by? Did we want to bury ourselves in a tiny town without
the security of a million dollars promising a comfortable retirement

and the ability to take care of our children's impending needs? Did we really want to raise our kids as country residents without opportunity and forego any hope of sending them to college or paying for weddings, braces, or anything else parents traditionally do for their children? More importantly, was *Mark* ready to downsize and live a more conservative life *for real*?

I sighed, thinking with tenderness of Donkey and how he would have to be left behind if we returned to our former lifestyle. "For richer or for poorer," I said. "But why is it we keep swinging between the two like a pendulum in overdrive?"

"Because wherever we go, we take ourselves along."

Always practical regarding business, I said, "Let's just sell the house for the mortgage amount and cut our losses. We are certain to unload the place quickly if we price it lower than others of its kind. We'll have learned an expensive lesson, but we'll still be left with half a million – which is more than we ever dreamed we'd have as two simple dancers."

Mark visibly bristled. "I'm not going to let us lose all that money because of my house project. You will likely throw that up at me for all time. I'm going to list this house for top dollar." He named a price five hundred thousand dollars over the most recent appraisal.

I thought he was kidding. No one would pay drastically more for a house than it was worth, especially in this economy. And we were in no position to play Russian roulette. I told him so.

"You only think that way because you don't value my house design the way others will," Mark said. "Trust me, rich people will write a check for any amount to get something they want, and they are going to want this house. Price won't be an object."

"Rich people are rich because they're careful with their money," I said. "In this economy, we'd be stupid to not just get out as quickly as possible."

Mark furrowed his brow. "I know what I'm doing."

I bit the inside of my cheek. I wanted him to be happy, but my parental instincts made me unwilling to gamble anymore. We still had children to raise and educate and a retirement to fund somehow. I didn't want to grow old and be a burden on my family or society. We had had our fun, but I could no longer play the little housewife who didn't contradict her husband's choices.

"Your plan just doesn't make good financial sense. Honey, we have no choice but to sell as cheaply as we can, and accept that we've made mistakes."

"What you mean is *I* made mistakes."

"I didn't say that."

"You don't have to."

"Selling the house for less than we spent on building doesn't negate your talent as a builder. You created a magnificent house. The horrid economy is responsible for spoiling our chance to escape without penalty."

Mark's jaw tensed. "You are so like your father. You have no vision. I have faith. If you build it, they will come…"

"Who will come? Bill collectors?"

A flicker of hatred flashed into his eyes and, taken aback, I let any further argument die on my lips.

"If we don't sell this house, it will be your fault," he said. "You are manifesting bad energy and I'm gonna pay the price for it."

I was always annoyed when he quoted new age philosophy as validation for avoiding common sense or conservative realities. "I just want us to think practically," I snapped.

"God, I hate that about you."

Apparently, there was lots he hated about me. But there wasn't one thing I could do about regaining his favor that wouldn't go against my best instincts or speed our downfall.

"Absolutely speaking, the more money, the less virtue; for money comes between a man and his objects, and obtains them for him; and it was certainly no great virtue to obtain it. It puts to rest many questions which he would otherwise be taxed to answer; while the only new question which it puts is the hard but superfluous one, how to spend it."
—Henry David Thoreau

FAMILY MATTERS

Mark's father, sadly, had passed away with cancer only months after Mark's parents moved to Georgia to be near us. His mother, Sonya, was now painfully alone, without her husband and the Sarasota community. She made clear to everyone that she hated the cold, hated the mountains, missed the malls and franchise restaurants, and felt vulnerable living anywhere other than in an active, suburban neighborhood. I felt badly for Sonya, and partly responsible for her unhappiness since the reason she moved was to be near us. She began slowing down, needing more care that we ever imagined she would. We helped her move into a small house near us and visited often to help with yard work or to share a meal. We encouraged her to get involved in church or to make friends, but as grief and loneliness took its toll, she seemed less and less inclined to fill the empty corners of her life with anything other than family. All she cared about was Mark, me, our children, and her daughter, Dianne. She pleaded with us daily to visit more, call more, to take her shopping, or to just make time to sit and talk.

I tried to be there for her, but she was Mark's mother, not mine, and I couldn't help but feel she craved *his* attention. I was a poor substitute. So, I implored Mark to let his mother move in with us as soon as we finished the house. His sister was in no position to take on the responsibility, and we certainly had built a large enough home. But just as Mark had refused to allow Denver to move back home when I wanted her to live with us, he wouldn't now entertain the thought of his mother's presence interrupting our new, free life either. He announced that since his sister had no children, she should be the one to take care of their mother.

"Dianne is fifty and single. You can't possibly want to burden her with an elderly mother."

"She's broke and could use a roommate to help pay her bills."

"Considering we have—well, *had*—a million dollars, and we have found our soul mates for life, we should take on this burden. Not like *we* have to be free to date."

"Sorry, but I don't agree. I'm like one of the three little pigs," he said. "My sister and my mother built their houses out of straw and sticks, and I was the only one who built a house out of bricks. Now that the big bad wolf is blowing their houses down, they are running to me to take care of them. But why should I?"

"Well, we did retire with a plan to devote time and resources to family," I pointed out. "And family doesn't just mean our kids."

"I didn't work hard for all those years to just give everything I have to others," he said. "Not like my family has ever been there for me in times of need."

I was dismayed by his selfishness. We'd turned to his family and mine numerous times over the years for help, and they never let us down. If he could so easily turn away from parents, friends, and our former students and employees, might he as easily turn away from his wife if I dared become a liability rather than an asset?

My knees shook as I recalled the many times in our life when Mark had seemed capable of leaving me on a selfish whim. When we first met, he begged me to walk away from my thriving business and comfy little home to drag my two-year-old back to New York City to resume the career I had left behind. He wanted me to return to New York, so I could help him forge *his* career in dance. I wasn't all that invested in our relationship then, so I told him to go alone. I had gone to great lengths to protect my child from that kind of instability and there was no way I'd ever go back. If he wanted a career in dance, he should take his shot, just as I did when I first moved to

New York with ambition and dreams. But Mark didn't go, claiming he loved me too much to leave.

A few years later, when our new son Kent was two, Mark became obsessed with Tony Robbins, the life coach. He announced his life's purpose was to join the road crew of the organization as a volunteer. He wrote letters obsessively every day for 30 days, begging for Tony's acceptance, thinking his determination would impress the powers that be. I remember waiting for a response daily, wondering what I would do or say when Mark packed his bags to run off with the Tony Robbins circus. I didn't know how I'd survive without his help if he left me with a toddler and a small baby to raise. The business had grown too large to manage on my own now, but I waited quietly with an odd sense of acceptance to see if he really would walk out on his family. So offended was I that he dared write those letters and his childish hope that they'd let him join the tour that a part of me wanted him to go. I was unnerved by his ability to put his own desires in front of the family's very vital needs; and wanted a good excuse to end a marriage with someone so lacking in responsibility. In the end, an acceptance was not forthcoming. Mark took one last shot at joining Tony Robbins by taking us to a "Walk on Fire" convention. Gripped by the excitement of hearing the inspirational speaker's empowerment lecture, Mark insisted we charge eight thousand dollars on my credit card for another convention in Tahiti a few months hence.

"We can't possibly afford that!" I said.

"Aren't you listening to what he's saying? There are no limits in life, if you just believe! The universe will provide us a way to fund the rest of the trip and pay off the credit card in thirty days when the bill comes due next month. Tony just explained how one couple won the lottery when they needed money. That could be us."

He expected us to win the lottery to solve our problems? All attendees at the convention were asked to write questions for Tony, to send forward on the break. I wrote, *What gives you the right to seduce people into spending money they don't have, Mr. Robbins? You say you want to inspire people to live a better life, but your lecture is destroying my marriage!*

I sent the note forward. To this day, I wonder if Tony Robbins ever saw the message amidst the pile of happy, soul-lifted questions.

"What did you write?" Mark asked, giddy with enthusiasm for the entire experience.

"I asked a question about the firewalk," I lied.

We never did attend the expensive Tahiti seminar. Instead, that $8000 charge was the final blow to our already stressed budget and I filed for personal bankruptcy. Mark had long since ruined his credit and had been using mine ever since we had gotten married. So now, instead of a trip to a glamorous retreat, I was treated to the experience of watching companies come to remove the furniture from my house and tow both our cars away. I drove a junker for the next three years and lived with laundry baskets in place of a dresser as we worked our way out of that crash.

After the Tony Robbins incident and the bankruptcy, I took over the family finances. My dad loaned us money to save the business from going under, but only if we allowed him to take control of the studio accounts. I started doing things like opening college savings plans for the kids in my name only, planning quietly for the needs of the family. I paid extra on our mortgage payments to take our thirty year mortgage down to seven years. I made the mistake of sharing how quickly our equity grew, and Mark took a second mortgage to remodel the kitchen and build a cabin-style porch and garden.

I just had to accept that Mark's commitment to family took a different form than mine in regards to honoring our children, our parents, or our marriage.

We'd recently had a huge falling out with my parents. My father had long played the role of financial counselor since that early fiasco, so naturally he voiced concerns now about Mark's mismanagement of our funds, feeling that our life was spinning out of control again. Mark had absolutely no intention of turning over his financial freedom ever again, and the truth is painful to hear, so my parents became the enemy in his estimation.

Mark convinced me that my father's criticism was unfair and unfounded, and his conservative attitude about money was limiting for

artistic people like us. Not wanting to admit we were making foolish mistakes any more than Mark did, I found it remarkably easy to
align myself with his attitude. Delusion is a large part of love, and I
would do anything to avoid facing truths that shed my marriage or
my husband's financial savvy in an unflattering light. So, defending
Mark, I wrote letters to my folks trying to justify our losses and to
explain my feelings about Blue Ridge hoping to soften arguments
and misunderstandings. This only made matters worse between us.

My father helped us plan and negotiate the sale of our business,
with the understanding that we would compensate him for the risk
he had taken way back when he had put his entire retirement's savings into our school. After a great show of self-congratulations and
recapping our brilliance for pulling off this financial miracle, we gave
Dad his promised bonus. But instead of writing the check with a
sense of gratitude, Mark deeply resented sharing even a fraction of
our windfall. He insisted only an unloving parent would take money
from his kid. Eventually, his twisting of facts and constant reminders that our dreams were being hindered by those dipping into our
resources—especially my parents—penetrated my own psyche. I
found myself criticizing my family too, forgetting that love begins
with gratitude and appreciation for the faith your loved ones display
when they take risks with their own savings to support your personal
dreams or help you in times of crisis.

Mark's insistence that everyone was trying to rob him of the fruits
of his labors continued to expand until I became suspect, too. One
day, finding myself without a cent in my purse and with no money
at all left in the only account I had access to, I slipped some change
from the enormous quarter jar in our bedroom to give my son so he
could buy lunch at school. The jar was teeming with thousands of
dollars of change that Mark had dumped into the container over the
years we owned and operated our family business.

I told Mark I had handled the need for lunch money by taking a
few quarters, assuming he'd be as embarrassed as I was that we were
so broke we were scraping change, but he became furious, claiming I
had no right to steal his money. He may have been the one to emp-

ty his pockets into the jar each night, but the money nevertheless came from our joint earned income, so naturally I thought he was being silly. I wasn't taking his quarters to pay my bookie; our son just needed lunch money! Certainly he was willing to crack open the jar to support the cause.

Mark felt differently and the next day he took the jar to his real estate office so I wouldn't have access to its contents. I pointed out that if we were so broke that we couldn't buy lunch for our children, perhaps we should put the contents of that jar into our family bank account anyway. Mark was adamant that the jar was his private savings and for something special he might want for himself someday. Only three days later, the entire jar was stolen. I thought the theft an appropriate end to the whole episode, dripping with karma.

Pondering this new turn of events, I now stood at the window of our grand house looking out at Donkey in the pasture below, taking count of the things that mattered most to me, and how many of them were broken. My husband was disconnected from me, physically and emotionally. I had lost the friendships and meaningful connections I had forged with students and fellow workers. My parents had been cut from our lives and I was ashamed because I knew deep down that they deserved better. My oldest daughter was destitute and needed direction, and despite what I felt was a mother's right to nurture and protect her children and give them an edge in life, Mark would not permit her to live with us. His mother was lonely and unhappy and his sister was broke. I had lost the power to influence the welfare of those I loved most in any real way. I had allowed myself to be systematically removed from doing or saying anything that affected my own financial life, too. But the most distressing thing was being expected to accept things as they were and to stop complaining or crying about it. Mark insisted I was going through a midlife crisis, when in truth it was a *life* crisis I was facing. I was fearful of what would happen to everyone I loved who had been counting on me for years to keep the status quo because I was systematically un-empowered.

What can a woman do when she needs grounding? What can she

do when she feels inadequate, unappreciated, and undervalued? What does she do when she sees the answers, but is not allowed to ask the questions, much less offer the solutions?

She can cook.

After years of working nights and weekends, I now found opportunity to celebrate family in the old fashioned way: the traditional sit-down dinner. I didn't take this gift lightly, and made a noteworthy occasion of dinner each Tuesday. Mark may have been distracted by his building aspirations and the kids by their friends, but by God, one night a week they would arrive home by six to break bread as a family or there would be hell to pay. Life was falling apart, and things were going to get worse. I needed this connection badly, and so did they, I told myself.

My weekly family dinner was a means to fill Grandmother's empty days. Cooking was a way to lend a small hand to Mark's sister, who was running ragged trying to fulfill her mother's endless need for company while struggling to making ends meet. My family dinners became a means to seduce my husband at least once a week to stop shopping and attend to his domestic role. The weekly meal was an attempt to keep my kids connected to each other and their relatives and to create feelings of family normalcy, even if I knew, deep down, Hendry family harmony was smoke and mirrors. Tuesday dinner was a way to catch up with my oldest child and get to know who she was dating and keep abreast of her plans for escaping Blue Ridge. Cooking was a way to feel useful. And preparing a meal for those I loved took my mind off of our financial nightmare.

I took those dinners to heart, striving to prepare elaborate menus filled with country goodness. I used veggies from my garden, eggs from my chickens, and served homemade wine. I prepared apple cobbler from apples I picked at the local orchard. I cooked twice as much food as necessary so there would be ample leftovers to send off with everyone. Feeding my family was my way of loving them, so I drowned them in casseroles, side dishes, and muffins. Even if their bills weren't paid, their stomachs would at least be full. Even if my family no longer saw me as a dynamic, efficient woman who had the respect of an entire community, at least they would see me as a worthy homemaker.

After each dinner, I'd clean up while everyone gathered downstairs with dessert and coffee to watch American Idol. I loved knowing they were all cuddled up before a fire together, even if I was upstairs alone washing dishes. I'd spent 40 minutes with my hands sunk in suds, happy to know that I had connected my family and nourished them. But I'd also be thinking of my own mother, of how she would have loved to spend one meal a week with her grandkids and been a casual part of their everyday lives. For years we lived right by my parents, yet we were too busy running a business and juggling kids and work to spend any quality time with them. Now that we did have the time, these moments were entirely devoted to Mark's family. I imagined my own daughters growing up and having families of their own, showing consideration and care to their in-laws while pushing me away. I didn't know how I could bear losing my own daughter's trust and respect, and as a result I suffered guilt over my own mother's pain.

I had always been kind to Mark's family, always gone out of my way to help financially and emotionally. I made them a part of every holiday and family celebration. I bought them gifts, and went to great lengths to build positive associations to them in my childrens' viewpoints. I encouraged Mark to help his sister out even when he didn't feel so inclined, and insisted she be included in family vacations and special occasions because she didn't have a family of her own. I did this not because I loved my in-laws (although as the years passed I truly did) but because I loved Mark.

To me, one way of honoring and respecting your partner is to honor and respect their family. Promoting harmony eases the personal torture that can come with complex family dynamics. I desperately wanted Mark to help me repair the damage that had erupted with my folks—as an act of love for me, if not from his own sense of obligation for all they had done for him over the years. And I wanted him to note the effort I made to create positive family relationships on his side and act accordingly.

"I moved to Georgia to get away from your family," he said. "Sorry, but you can't make me like them."

"Can't you do this for me? I've always been good to your family."

"I never asked you to be nice to my family. I think you're a fool to do as much for them as you do," he said.

I wasn't someone who would change her behavior out of tit-for-tat frustration. Besides which, I thought his mother was sweet and his sister a soulful, kind friend. After seventeen years of marriage, I felt protective of them both. They were *my* family now too, and deserving of the same devotion I felt for my own family of origin.

Mark's mother was hard of hearing. He thought it was funny to playfully insult her when she was only a few feet away. The insensitivity always disturbed me and I was forever reprimanding his boorish behavior like some kind of uptight prig. Even if Mark wasn't hurting his mother's feelings, I believed he should have been more mindful of the message he was sending our own children. He was teaching them that mothers don't deserve respect, and I didn't want to grow old and ever experience my children speaking to me with such discourtesy. Belittling one's mother lacked class and seemed unforgivably rude.

"We're just having fun. Everyone knows I love my mother. Get over yourself. You have no sense of humor," Mark said.

I couldn't defend myself because he was right. I *had* lost my sense of humor. Lately, fewer and fewer of the things he said and did seemed funny.

"If we will be quiet and ready enough, we shall find compensation in every disappointment."
—Henry David Thoreau

SPIT

Death converged on our hobby farm, starting with the animals, and moving on to our dreams, our hopes, and finally, our love...

An opossum, or perhaps a weasel, got into the henhouse and ate the heads off of thirteen chickens in a single night. Trying my best to maintain a stalwart composure, I bagged up the headless birds. Shortly afterwards, four of my six ducks were attacked, leaving me with partial carcasses and a pile of feathers floating on the lake like dandelion wisps blown in from the overgrown weeds.

"Why not leave?" The trees seemed to whisper as I passed by bloody carcasses. *"You're too smart, too sophisticated, and too worldly to spend your days picking up dead poultry. Face it, you don't fit in here."*

I started imagining my return to the dance world, older, out of shape and slightly bitter, which drove me back to the barnyard with determination to get a handle on my life. A neighbor's dog killed off a few more chickens, so I took to keeping poultry in their pens unless I was working around the barn. Now that my birds were no longer in the pasture eating fly larvae, I was battling a siege of flying pests along with my depression.

One day, I went to let Early out of her cage to roam freely around the barnyard. She seemed oddly quiet, so I stroked her and placed her in a comfortable position by the food bowl. Later, she lay peacefully but lifeless in the very same position. I was grateful she hadn't died by dog attack or opossum raid, leaving me with a gruesome last view of my beloved peacock's remains, but that didn't lessen my feelings of loss. Did I feed her too much, too little, or the wrong combination of nutrients? Was the water bowl tainted? Was the floor of her cage so dirty it created a hothouse for bacteria? Who was I to think I could raise a peacock?

"Maybe it was the heat," Mark said.

"Early usually spends her time in the shade, not to mention that peacocks are tropical by nature. She just died...like everything else around here seems to be doing."

"I'll buy you some healthy, grown peacocks. No more guessing or disappointment that way."

"We are unlikely to be living here next spring. Can't take them with us after all."

"Don't say that. Someone is going to buy my house for top dollar, and you'll see I was right all along."

How desperately he needed to be "right" all along. The people who bought our business crashed and burned due to self-indulgence and an unwillingness to make conservative choices in a field they really didn't know anything about. Mark was quick to point out their stupidity, yet he had been doing the very same thing as he moved along with far more self-confidence than reasonable considering he had no real experience in the construction field. Perhaps karma was at hand, and Mark and I deserved to lose everything. Perhaps life was giving us our much-needed lesson in humility. Perhaps the universe was testing our love, as is the case for many couples who live together for years and years and forget why they came together in the first place. Might we come out wiser and stronger for our mistakes? Might our love grow stronger from this adversity? I prayed this would be the case.

The next day, I went to the barn and found my rabbit cage had been ripped open and an angora killed. I buried the remains in the base of the fire pit, then spent the afternoon putting together new cages and hanging them high on the side of the chicken house to protect the other rabbits.

"Unless coyotes can fly, you'll be safe here," I told the angoras, but in the morning I discovered the side of my new metal cages had been peeled back like a banana. Another rabbit lay dead on the ground.

"I don't see how a coyote can do this," I said.

"I'll ask Ronnie to look at the carnage. He'll know what we're dealing with," Mark said.

Ronnie came out later and shook his head. "That's a bear for sure," he said. "They don't usually attack rabbits, but they'd tear open the cage for the food, and if a bunny is easy pickin's, he might just get scooped up, too. I'd be happy to camp out here and shoot a bear for ya, but it's not bear season, so you can't tell nobody if I clip one."

"Thanks, but no thanks."

I still had two other angoras to worry about, so I repaired the cage and wound extra wire around the joints. Mark had bought me three young peacocks a week prior, a gift of good faith to convince me things were going to be fine. I heightened the security of their pen, but extra wire didn't protect the poor things when an unexpected cold snap rolled in later that week. One bitterly cold morning, I found them huddled together, dead from exposure.

Mark said, "These things happen."

"After all I've read about raising poultry, I should have known better. I should have set up a warming bulb in a nesting box or something."

My little peacocks joined Early and the others in the fire pit, my designated cremation center now.

"Let's go to the flea market," Mark said as he and Ronnie piled into his pickup the next Saturday.

While the boys were looking over used tools, I wandered to the livestock area, my eyes caught by what appeared to be a bag of peacock feathers. A closer look showed that they were attached to a fully-grown peacock trussed up in a sling like a broken arm.

"You like peacocks?" the woman selling the birds asked.

"Oh, yes. Lost one I loved dearly just recently." I didn't mention the other young birds I'd lost through stupidity.

She gestured to the back of her truck. "These two gotta go to someone who will really appreciate them," she said with a wink. "They're beauties, and for some reason I like you so I'll make you a special deal. A hundred dollars for the pair."

The last thing I needed was to spend money on birds, but buying them somehow established my faith in a Georgia future in some way, so I turned over my small stash of mad money and within minutes the birds were inside our truck wedged under the back seats.

Once home, I cut the binding off their bodies and let the peacocks run free in my big chicken run. I named them Prism and Palate and kept them in the pen for a full six weeks so they wouldn't run off.

Each morning I stared in awe as the male displayed his tail in colorful splendor, the symbol of elegance I sorely needed in my mud-filled world. I imagined baby peacocks following in their wake, and in time, a barnyard filled with graceful birds in a home saved by our trust in the universe. But the first time I opened the pen, the male peacock flew up over the trees and without so much as a backward glance over his shoulder, left forevermore. I had, with good intention, tried to create a world of colorful, dramatic poultry, but in the end all I had to show for my trust was one gray, unremarkable bird. The peacocks were a living metaphor of our entire country adventure. Colorful dreams. Drab reality.

For weeks, the bear continued to return on a reliable seven-day schedule, tearing apart rabbit cages and defecating on the ground around the chicken house no matter what I did to thwart further destruction. One morning, I spied the backside of a bear going into the woods. I chased the beast, with no idea what I might do had I come face to face with a testy bear. I just felt compelled to face down anything and everything that was killing off the things I loved. I hiked several yards into the thicket, but there was no sign of him, so I returned to the barn to inspect the damage.

The peacock was lazily taking a dust bath in the sun and my rabbits were nestled in their wooden privacy boxes. When I went to feed the bigger animals, Dalai was missing. I assumed my llama was just hiding in the trees to escape the heat. When Dalai didn't show up for a second feeding, I turned to Ronnie for a dash of country advice.

"Now, I'm not claiming to know everything, 'cause I only have 'bout a sixth grade education, but it seems to me a bear wouldn't be a threat to a llama 'cause bears really don't eat meat. Dalai probably just escaped. Have you checked with the neighbors?"

I asked around, but no one had seen a loose llama. I walked the perimeter of the fence in case he was hiding in the trees, but Dalai wasn't inside. No llama. No llama remains either. I spent two days searching, then put posters around town and an ad in the paper offering a reward for my lost llama. People hinted that the animal might have been stolen. Llamas are territorial, so even if he did slip out of the pasture, he'd stick nearby unless foul play was at hand. Everyone I saw driving down the road with a livestock trailer became suspect. The very thought that someone might steal my beloved llama made me crazy.

Two weeks later, Mark noticed a horrible smell. He followed his nose to discover Dalai's remains in the overgrown weeds near the creek. Losing a chicken or a rabbit is one thing, but losing a llama is quite another. I cried all afternoon, unable to get the vision of my mangled pet out of my mind. Then I called the Georgia game warden and made arrangements for him to come out to give me advice.

I said, "Joe, look at this poop. What do you think?"

Joe spat. Joe had to spit every third sentence due to the chew in his mouth. He inspected the damaged cages, kicked at the pile of poop left by the renegade attacker and made an assessment.

"You have a bear. He seems to be appearing every seven days or so, which means he is making regular rounds." (Spit.)

"How long will he keep coming?"

"As long as he finds good things to eat. You need to stop leaving food in your rabbit cages. Your bear thinks this a grocery stop now. I can set a trap, but traps are dangerous for dogs and kids, often more trouble than the bear." (Spit.) "Bear season is around the corner. You can always just shoot the bear then, if'n you want."

As mad as I was at the animal, I couldn't imagine killing something as majestic as a bear. "What if I feed the bear? If I leave a bucket of food he likes, perhaps he won't bother my animals."

Joe just about choked on his tobacco. "Feeding a wild bear is a really bad idea."

I led him to the remains of my beloved llama. "Do you think the bear did this, too?"

He narrowed his eyes and spat, inspecting Dalai's remains. "Looks to me like this animal was taken down by coyotes. You can tell because they gnaw at the flanks but leave the rest for other creatures to polish off. They do this with deer, too."

"Llamas are supposed to be guard animals. I thought they chased coyotes away."

"One llama can't fight off an entire pack."

"Can a donkey?"

"They're better at keeping predators away, but even so…" (Spit.)

My arms broke out in goose bumps as I imagined my donkey being the next prey. "How do I get rid of coyotes?"

"They're not indigenous to the area so there's no law against killing 'em. But, even if you're a crack shot, you won't get rid of them 'cause coyotes repopulate faster than you can reload a gun."

Gritting my teeth, I described the thirteen headless chickens I found previously and asked if I should assign blame to the coyotes or the bear.

"Probably a possum, weasel, fox, or something else."

"So, what you're telling me is nature is going to keep coming at me over and over again, despite my best efforts to thwart her."

"'Fraid so." (Spit.) "Don't feel too bad. You know what they say; anyone raising livestock is raising dead stock." He chuckled at his joke and got into his truck.

After he left, I stood staring at my barnyard, mad enough to spit, myself.

We may have had one foot firmly planted in the country now, but the other shoe still hadn't dropped. *Where do we belong?* I kept wondering. For all that I was frustrated with the country, I couldn't imagine our returning to the rat race either. My farm experiments and reading had turned me into a passionate environmentalist with a serious commitment to lower my carbon footprint. If we lived in some metropolis, we could do without a car and walk or take public transportation to work or the grocery store, a choice that is more earth-friendly than growing your own chicken eggs ever could be. Cities have a decent library and all the other intellectual pursuits I missed too, but is a culture fix worth living where noise and pollution assail the senses and people have long since forgotten to pause to say "how do?" to a neighbor? Could I ever again live where houses were so crowded together you could hear neighbors' conversations from your back porch? Could I return to a life without a donkey? Then again, if everything I ever cared about and loved was dying in the country, would I even have a choice?

"Thus we kept on like true idealists, rejecting the evidence of our senses"
—Henry David Thoreau

LLAMA TRAUMA

The possibility of the coyotes returning to pick off my pregnant llama haunted my thoughts. Pulani might be safe enough in the pasture now that Donkey was close by, but her soon-to-be born fragile baby would make a perfect appetizer for hungry predators. Unless I wanted to spend my nights standing guard like a sentry, I had to put her in the barn, at least until she gave birth.

For all that Dalai had been a dear and lovely creature, his female companion, Pulani, was a very evasive, impersonal bitch. Pulani spit great wads of slimy grain at Donkey. Every time I picked projectile goo from my darling donkey's face, I vowed I'd sell that nasty llama someday. I just hadn't gotten around to doing so because she was Dalai's only company, and now that he was gone I was enamored with the idea of watching a baby llama come into the world.

In all fairness, I hadn't bothered with the female llama for a full year, so I was guilty of indulging her bad habits and perpetuating them. Ignoring an animal won't make her any less ornery, just harder to catch…which happened to be my current challenge.

Kent and I had a system for llama entrapment that involved holding a long rope between us. We would maneuver the animal into a corner and in trying to escape, she would run into the rope. We would hightail it to opposite sides to wrap the rope around the animal's neck. The force usually caused burns on our sweating palms, but lassoing served up a great cowboy high as we moved in to get a halter on. A llama will follow your lead, docile as a lamb, once the halter is on.

For an hour and a half, Kent and I chased Pulani. We had the rope around her neck a few times, but she went wild, flinging her head in circles, ducking and escaping with Houdini-like efficiency. Exhausted and frustrated, we eventually admitted that we needed a third party to chase this llama into the rope.

"I'll call Dad and ask him to come home early to help," I said.

"Let's just try one more time," Kent said.

So, we quietly stepped into the woods again, a few feet away from the llama. "I'll sneak up from the back," he said, "You distract her here." But before we could implement our diabolical plan, Kent started screaming. He ran out into the open pasture, flapping his arms and dancing about.

Now, my son has a propensity for physical humor, so at first I thought he was just being his crazy self, trying to make me laugh. But then, I realized he was under attack from an underground wasp nest he'd stepped on.

I charged after him, brushing off the violent insects, all the while cursing the llama rather than the wasps. My son was stung 15 times, on the face, legs, and arms. Pulani watched from the woods, smug as always.

I took Kent to the house to attend to his stings.

"I'm so sorry," I kept saying, feeling guilty that my kids had to deal with things like wasps and mean llamas in this stupid life we had thrust them into.

He shrugged. "These kinds of things are bound to happen once in a while. It's OK."

When Mark came home we went out to catch the llama again. We chased her for another hour, all humor from the situation long since replaced with resentful complaining. No luck. Eventually a car came sputtering down the road with our neighbor's kid at the wheel.

"Hey, want to help us catch this llama?" I asked.

How many sixteen-year-olds do you know who would say no to a question like that? None, in the country, I assure you. We now had two more hands joining in the pursuit. Nevertheless, with three hundred pounds of bad disposition fueling her, Pulani proved impossible to catch as she continued pulling the rope out of the hands of whoever was holding it.

"Maybe you should just leave her out here for the coyote's next meal." Kent said.

Giving up was tempting, but I was determined to save the baby, if not her. "Give me that rope. I'm getting her. This time I WON'T LET GO UNDER ANY CIRCUMSTANCES!"

Mark handed me the rope. "Go for it, cowgirl."

The next time I caught Pulani, I didn't let go. Unfortunately, this meant she dragged me about 15 feet over rocks and weeds like I was a stuntman in a western movie. When I stood, the skin was scraped off of the entire right side of my body. I had a bruise the size of an open hand on my right hip and my knuckles were bleeding. There was a scrape on my chin and another under my eye. Worst of all, I had dropped the rope in the end, so the llama was still at large.

The boys laughed nervously. Who could blame them? Here I was, a middle-aged woman cussing at llamas, letting myself get dragged in the dirt to prove I was master of the beast after bragging about how I wouldn't let go. Boy, didn't I show everybody how tough I was?

I sat in the dirt, dabbed at the blood and said, "Well, I didn't let go."

"And we admire you for that," Mark said.

"Stop smiling." I marched after the llama with bloodthirsty determination, ready to punch her lights out, a la *Blazing Saddles*.

By now, a horrible growl-like gurgling was coming out of the llama's throat. She stood her ground as we closed in, too tired to run one more time. This made possible our winding the rope around her neck to put the halter on, all the while dodging spit and a few lackluster kicks.

"Your days are numbered," I snapped, yanking on the lead rope as I led her to the barn. But once inside the stall, she behaved sweet as pie, peering over the gate and begging for food. Fool that I am, I gave a treat to her.

Each day thereafter, I went down to the barn to visit my nasty llama, hoping to desensitize her with handling to avoid ever having to go through such an ordeal again. My scars were healing, but the distrust on both of our parts was still raw.

Our interaction typically went something like this:

I'd enter the stall. We'd stare at each other. She'd pin her ears back. I'd squint like Clint Eastwood and say, "Go ahead, make my day."

She would then lift her head as high as she could, her nose straight up in the air to establish her superiority. I'd hold my eyes downcast in hopes of alleviating her aggression even though I felt in no way contrite.

I'd slowly walk around the stall. She'd side step away. I'd corner her and pat her back, feeling her skin nervously shake under my fingers. When I could, I let my hand slide down to her belly, hoping to feel the baby, but this always made her kick so I'd pull away. Pulani's due date came and went. She didn't even look all that pregnant. Was it possible to keep two llamas together for a year and not have the female end up pregnant? I recruited the vet for a house call, and he confirmed that she was indeed pregnant, but she had another two months to go. Since catching her was almost impossible, Pulani would have to stay in the barn for some time.

The vet gave me some nasty paste to squirt into her mouth to help her produce milk when the time came, but left me no clue how to actually accomplish that. I decided to hook a lead to her halter and tie her head up against the wood fence so I could force the applicator between her pressed lips. One more lovely bonding experience for me and my barbaric pet...

The poor animal grew bored, hormonal, and lonely locked up in the barn so long. Each day, we did our love-hate dance. I forced the medicine in her mouth, then followed the unwanted cream with a carrot treat. Eventually, she acted glad to see me, moaning whenever I showed up and following me with her eyes as I did my barn chores. She still wouldn't take a cookie out of my hand, but I'd drop a treat into her bin or hold her grain in a scoop over the fence and she would take the first few bites despite how close I was.

One day, she tentatively took a piece of carrot from my fingers. Within a week, she was leaning her head over the fence begging for cookies or carrots every time she saw me. In time, she started sticking her nose into my empty hands too, as if I were a magician who could make cookies appear with a mere flick of my fingers. Over time, we had come to terms with each other and developed an odd relationship built on respect, curiosity, and cookies.

One morning I arrived at the barn to find Pulani humming frantically and pacing the stall. I noticed her stomach quivering. *This is it! She's finally in labor!* I thought.

I turned to run up to the house to get Neva so together we could watch a baby llama come into the world, but as I stepped around the corner into the outer corral, I stopped short. Staring at me with wide curious eyes, wobbly legs, and a sweet shyness was a baby llama with a bit of membrane hanging from its head. My baby llama had arrived and just as with the baby horse, I had missed the delivery by moments. Life can be cruel.

"Hello," I said softly, marveling at the newborn's tiny size and independence. "What are you doing out here? I think your mommy is missing you."

I picked him up and carried him back to his mother. His head was the size of my fist, his ears perky, and his lashes as long as a showgirl's.

I closed the door to the outer corral and watched mother and baby snuggle.

Mark joined me and we both noticed Pulani didn't seem interested in feeding her baby.

I was told Pulani hadn't cared for her last baby, which was one of the reasons the previous owner sold her, so I had done enough research to know what I was supposed to do if such a thing happened again.

"Here I go," I whispered as I slowly climbed into the stall to intervene. Pulani folded her ears back and lifted her chin in warning. I gulped, my mind spinning with thoughts of motherhood turning my new friend back into a raging protector. Slowly I tied a lead rope to her halter and handed one end to Mark so he could pull her face to the wall like we'd done so many times when I fed her medicine. Once she was secure, I caught the baby, turned him onto his back (no easy feat) to lay him down on a towel to cauterize the umbilical cord by dipping the gooey string hanging off his belly button into a cup of iodine. This was one of those "you've come a long way, baby" moments for me, let me tell you.

"I think we have a boy, don'tcha agree? Doesn't that little thing look like a baby llama penis?" I said, pointing between the little llama's legs.

Mark peered over the fence. "Yeah, maybe. I don't know. Could be. It's small."

I stared at the little nugget, the size of a marble. "What else could that thing be? This baby has gotta be a boy. Llamas don't have balls, ya know."

"Pulani sure seems to have balls some days."

"I'm convinced this is a boy."

Mark pulled on the lead rope to wedge Pulani closer up to the wall. "Careful. She's getting antsy."

"She needs to feed him. I'm going to try to move things along," I said. I started massaging her udders. She kicked a bit and made a mean growling sound so ominous Mark and I both laughed, albeit nervously. I pulled, massaged, and tweaked under her belly, but nothing like milk came out.

"She's totally dry," I said, worried.

"Are you milking her right?"

"How would I know? I've never even milked a cow, let alone a llama. You want to try?"

Mark's eyebrows shot up to his hairline, "Not on your life."

I grabbed the baby and tried to force his head under the mother's belly, but Pulani kept moving away, kicking and growling.

Since all the speculating in the world wasn't going to make me a llama midwife, I went back to the house and called the only person I knew who might give me answers, a woman I heard about who owned a llama breeding farm. She was generous with her advice, giving me encouragement and urging me to buy a baby bottle and give the baby cow's milk.

"That is, as long as the baby isn't a boy," she said. "You can't bottle-feed males. They develop what's called *crazy llama syndrome*. Too much handling will make a young male imprint on humans, and when they grow, they get aggressive. Sometimes they have such behavior problems they need to be put down," she said.

I got off the phone to return to my llama trauma, feeling damned if I did, damned if I didn't.

The baby was licking the walls and acting hungry. No time to waste. I drove to the feed store and bought a lamb nipple and some starter colostrum for newborn livestock. I also picked up a tub of dry goat's milk, just in case.

When I got home, I prepared a bottle. I was alone this time, and far more worried about the baby dying than Pulani kicking my brains in. She stomped and put her nose on my head, but she didn't spit or act more aggressively than that. Deep down, after all our months of togetherness, I think she knew I had good intentions.

I pried the baby's mouth open and forced the bottle on his tongue. He didn't know how to suck, so he just chewed the tip, his tongue darting out as he tried to figure out what this eating thing was all about.

The taste of that milk seemed to trigger the baby's instincts. Suddenly, he broke away from me and poked his nose into his mother's neck and thighs like someone groping in the dark to find a light switch. Pulani understood what he was trying to do and pushed his head with her neck towards her hindquarters. After about five minutes the baby finally found his way under her belly, and soon began suckling. I quietly crept out to give them time alone.

Throughout the day, I continued to visit the baby, delighted to find him eating every hour or so, just as he was supposed to. I named him Pauli, a combination of both his mother and father's name.

I stapled mesh around the outer corral so his willowy body wouldn't slip out again, and the barn was given over completely to the llamas. Each day I mucked their manure and kept the water fresh and the hay trough filled. More work, but with a tiny llama shyly greeting me and giving me kisses every day, I couldn't complain.

Pulani's prolonged confinement and my determination to make her more civil made me feel more connected now. We'd been through an ordeal together, and come out with mutual respect and trust. Things began working the moment she surrendered her pride and allowed me to help.

Contemplating it all, I thought that if Mark and I were to survive our own threatening problems, we would have to do the same.

"I too had woven a kind of basket of a delicate texture, but I had not made it worth anyone's while to buy them. Yet not the less, in my case, did I think it worth my while to weave them, and instead of studying how to make it worth men's while to buy my baskets, I studied rather how to avoid the necessity of selling them."

—*Henry David Thoreau*

BUILDING A MASTERPIECE ON A WEAK FOUNDATION

Building a million dollar house hadn't totally satisfied my husband's newfound passion for wood. As we took long walks, he'd point out the difference between oak and walnut, pine and cherry. He would gasp and swoon over twisted branches filled with burls and knots the way other men would gasp and swoon over a Playboy bunny centerfold. He'd slam on the brakes when he saw a felled tree in someone's yard, speculating on whether or not they'd let him drag home huge chunks of the tree trunk, then spend half an hour pondering how to get the heavy wood into his truck without a tractor. Plenty of days he arrived home with his truck bed laden with gnarled tree trunks he picked up, bought, or cut down himself. Lord knows how he finagled them into his vehicle because it always took three of us to get them out.

He would arrive home late for dinner, explaining he'd seen some wild laurel growing by the road, so of course he had to pull over and cut the branches down. Sure enough, his truck would be overflowing with sticks that he'd show off like another man might display his prize tickets to the Super Bowl. The metal building next to his workshop became filled to the rafters with wood for future projects. He continued enrolling in classes to learn how to make things with his new glut of tools and materials. He still didn't venture into his workshop to work independently ever, but the vacation-like ambience of courses that gave him opportunity to craft with friends meant he had company to share the experience with, and that seemed to be the key to his productivity. Mark never could work alone.

Wood became Mark's favorite topic of conversation and like a good, dutiful wife, I nodded, responding with supportive comments like, "Yeah, that gnarly tree, split down the center by a bolt of lightning, is definitely something I wish I had in the living room," or "Yeah, it sure would be great if you could chainsaw the neighbor's tree down in the middle of the night...but, um, in the interest of remaining friends, perhaps you could make do with the other three hundred tree stumps you have piling up at the workshop?"

He had formed a friendship with a local woman wood turner and taken up wood turning; he now spent his free time with her, making a few huge wooden bowls from tree trunks and stumps, sometimes leaving bark edge on the rims so the vessels looked as primitive and artful as pieces from an otherworldly table in a fantasy movie. My husband liked to do things in a big way, and his wood turning projects, like his house, were no exception. Oiled to bring out the streaks of color and subtle shades in the wood, I was offered one huge bowl after another for popcorn, apples, or anything else I might want to pile into a bowl bigger than a kitchen sink.

"How about you make some smaller bowls, for salad and such?" I'd suggest, only to be handed a bigger bowl the next day, something that could easily serve as a fishpond if wood were designed to hold water (wood bowls are not, unfortunately).

Showcasing bowls became a high priority in our decorating scheme, that is, until the bowls gave way to rustic furniture and the house began to fill with homemade chairs sporting legs made of twisted branches with the bark still clinging on the edges, and coffee tables that looked like they belonged in Fred Flintstone's house, with huge slab tops resting on a base of woven sticks, deer antlers, and logs. The furniture was all beautiful, looking like a cross between something you'd see in the Museum of Natural History and simple items under a tent at a craft fair. Each addition brought us further away from our former Rooms to Go world and closer to a Thoreau-inspired lifestyle where nature rested not just at our fingertips, but under our butts when we sat down to dinner.

When there wasn't a surface left on his rustic tables that wasn't buckling under the weight of an oversized bowl, he moved on to making antler baskets, a tightly woven basket that is anchored to a deer antler serving as a handle. Antler baskets became the container of choice for washcloths, knickknacks, and as a center piece on tables and mantles. He next began creating baskets from other natural materials, his deft hands mastering a variety of complex patterns to braid reed, rope, and vine into homemade country crafts he deemed 'art.' I loved his talented projects, but his obsession with crafting felt threatening. There were dozens of people, mostly retirees enjoying crafts as a hobby or uneducated county residents who threw together stick furniture because it brought the family some money on the side as vacation cabin owners gobbled them up, all kicking out folk crafts for festivals and to fill the little county shops, but few of them called themselves artists, or acted as though every project belonged in a museum as my husband seemed to feel about his pursuits.

Baskets, while more versatile than huge bowls, can fill a house quickly, too, so Mark moved on to brooms. Of course, my husband wasn't one to make the standard broom on a stick that comes to mind when you think of a broom. His brooms were fastened to antlers, twisted branches, metal rods hand-hammered in a blacksmith shop, or found objects. The broom corn heads whisked and swirled, joined together with more creativity than the most elaborate of hairstyle seen at a high school prom.

The walls were now dripping in art brooms, and I crossed my fingers in hopes that he'd move on to something new, perhaps an obsession for making something less crafty and more utilitarian. Handcrafting was great for the soul and tons of fun for an individual, but I was still waiting for a suitable dining room table, and for all that I was impressed by and adored his talent, country crafts were not going to support a family driven to the brink of bankruptcy.

"I wish I could make this stuff for a living," he said wistfully.

Mark's obsession with building had slowly but surely emptied our coffers. His unwillingness to deny himself any artistic indulgence made each exciting new dream he pursued a fresh nightmare of fi-

nancial strain. Throughout our marriage, he had stretched our resources beyond comfort or toleration with endless hobby art projects, crafting, and fanciful remodeling of our Florida home and
studios. In Georgia his obsession with design began with a small
cabin, then a monster log home, my barn, and two workshops for
himself, each and every undertaking coming in way over budget and
beyond our means. At the close of each project, he fell into depression with his heart aching to begin something new.

"Well, this sucks," Mark said one day as we stood together on our
porch overlooking the ducks gently swimming on the pond, their
path making ripples in the vibrant reflection of autumn that graced
the water.

"I really believe the house will sell if we lower the price," I ventured.

"We can't afford to retire with less."

"We no longer can afford to retire at all."

His jaw tightened. "I have faith my house will sell, even at my
price. The thing is, we're going to need a place to live then. I'm going
to have to build a house on the other side of the land, one we can
afford."

"If this house sells…"

"Actually, I've been working on some house plans. I'm going to
start building a new house for us next week so we'll have a place to
move to when the time comes."

I looked out at the ducks thoughtfully. Had we built a reasonable
home from the start, we'd enjoy this striking view forever. This life
forever. Happiness forever. Impracticality was tearing our dreams
down piece by piece. The madness had to stop.

"We need to conserve every cent we have to survive until this
house sells. We can't get a mortgage for a second house since we
don't own the land separately from our current mortgage."

"Actually, I *have* worked out a mortgage, a temporary solution. We
can pay the debt off when the house sells. The bank is going to
release everything outside of the twelve acres listed with the main
house. Ronnie and I are going to build a new house for us on the

other side of the land, which we will own outright. We've decided to start the project this week."

"Why would the bank release property if they already have it to secure our debt? That doesn't make sense."

"A new loan is all arranged and in a few weeks we will sign the papers. In the meantime, I'll use what's left of our cash to get the project started."

"Oh, Mark, you can't."

He didn't take his eyes off the ducks swimming in the lake. "I've got a guy coming to grade the lot tomorrow."

My eyes swelled with tears.

Disgusted, he left the porch.

Within days, my husband was again lost in his next building project, happily purchasing doors, bathtubs, fireplaces, and beams. In the evenings, he invited me to take a walk to the new house site to admire his work. He talked animatedly of his brilliant creative plans to finish off the house 'someday' while I listened, mute.

Of course, just as I expected, the bank refused to give us a loan for a home on land they already had as security for our original loan. Mark reported the news like a child who had just been told he couldn't go to his best friend's party.

"It isn't fair," he claimed.

"You told me the loan was assured. A done deal."

"Well, I *thought* they'd give it to me."

"You have to stop this project," I implored. "We have to put a freeze on all the spending and hunker down with our last resources to hold out for as long as we can. Maybe the house will sell before we are totally broke."

"I can't stop now. We will lose the thirty grand I've invested in grading the lot."

"The foundation won't be lost. The concrete is there, and the materials will save. Things will be fine until we can afford to continue building. We will only lose a little on the wood frame, which you've only just started. But we will lose more if we continue! Perhaps everything!" *Perhaps each other*, I thought.

"You have no vision and no faith," he snarled.

In the next month Mark spent two hundred thousand dollars more on half a house situated on land belonging to the bank. The last of our money had been wiped out in one last thrill ride on the building merry-go-round.

With only a small reserve for mortgage payments or living expenses, the months clicked by in an unbearable limbo of stress. We discussed opening a rustic art gallery or a coffee shop with rustic home décor in a showroom out front. This way Mark could make crafts for a living, while I was expected to get up at 5 AM to work the coffee bar and register. The problem was a new business requires investment capital, and we no longer had cash for a life reinvention.

Mark told me not to worry. He had arranged a bank loan to finance our new business. A sure thing. In good faith I spent days once again putting my bachelor's degree in business management to work, creating a business plan for the loan he assured me was already approved. We had always been successful working together as a team, so I believed this project, *any* new project, was key to saving our marriage and getting life back on track. I was excited and ready to dig in and working on a project as a couple.

Since Mark adamantly insisted we had a foolproof loan from a bank, we decided to pay what was left of our cash to purchase outright the commercial lot he wanted to build on.

"Doesn't that have to be a part of the loan for cash flow purposes?" I asked, consider all I learned from our previous business financial experiences. "They don't give out business loans if you are not investing some cash of your own."

"It's covered," he said. "The bank assured me they will refund what we spend in advance for the project."

"I've never heard of that being done."

"Trust me."

He began enthusiastically making plans to build his next project, a log cabin art gallery. His new rustic coffee shop included striking details and would be unlike anything else in the area. Mark's coffee shop had a projected price tag of over a million dollars.

"You want us to take out another million dollar loan?" I asked. "For a coffee shop with a storefront to sell homemade crafts in a little run-down town?"

"A building like this will be an investment that will make us rich years from now." He showed me his plans, which included a 20 foot tree rising through the center and out the ceiling in Disney-esque magnificence as the central focus of the decor. His vision included balconies, stained glass windows, and rustic details worthy of a million dollar cup of coffee should someone in the middle of a repressed, tiny town have a taste for one. His gorgeous coffee shop was going to regenerate the town and put Macaysville on the map, he explained.

I couldn't deny the plan was magnificent in theory. The problem was, the scale was impractical. And the bank thought so, too.

After spending the last of our cash on the lot, our bank account now had less than three months of living expenses to cover the family. Mark sat me down to confess the coffee shop loan was not forthcoming. We were now stuck with a useless lot and more debt than ever before. He blamed our predicament on the bank, of course.

Perhaps Mark could still do what he loved for a living, I thought, fighting ever-growing panic, yet still believing our saving grace would be to make him happy once and for all. I researched the cost of booths at art festivals and considered what would be involved in putting his crafts in local rustic furniture stores, but no matter how we crunched the numbers, creating crafts was a labor of love that, in the end, wouldn't provide much more than minimum wage to the artist, if that.

A meager, art-driven income would have been enough if we were an older, retired couple who just needed a little extra to pad their social security checks and lifetime savings, but wouldn't cut the mustard for our family, facing the financial responsibilities of college tuitions, childrens' weddings, and saving for our own retirement. Had Mark wanted to make handcrafts for a living, the choice would have had to have been made when we first moved here with enough money to make long term investments and to purchase a home outright.

But Mark had built a house rather than a life. Our perfect plan for financial independence had been sunk by the weight of sanded logs and expensive rock. Like it or not, we had to get practical and take care of our family now. Our indulgence towards personal dreams would have to stop.

Mark enrolled in a course to get a real-estate license.

"I will just need a few things to set myself up to make money," he said. "I'll be great at this, you know. I love houses and staging homes. I see potential where others don't, and I will really enjoy a job that allows me to share my vision for a home."

Delighted that my husband was thinking along practical lines, I joined him for a trip to the mall to buy a computer for his new job—a celebration that we were now on the same page. We had half a dozen computers already, but Mark felt he needed a higher quality machine to give him an edge in the business. But at the store, Mark didn't settle for one high-end computer. He insisted he needed *three* state-of-the-art Macs: one for his office at work, one for his office at home, and a new laptop for his car, too, to be efficient. My body went numb as I watched him write a check for eight grand.

The next week he bought not one, but two used cars for himself, one a lovely fuel-efficient car for distance driving and the other a heavier vehicle with 4 wheel drive. He paid cash for both. All I could see was a double insurance payment, and more cash we couldn't afford to spend, gone… He went on to rent billboards. Not one, but three. His smiling face was all over our small town now, five feet high, along with real estate signs and costly ads in the local chamber magazine.

Our three months of living expenses was now gone too, and I learned his plan to fund his new career was to stop paying our mortgage and other bills totally.

"I thought you were going into business because we need to make money, but all you are doing is spending more," I said, my wave of panic cresting as I wondered how I was expected to feed the kids.

He gave me a sideways glance, his resentful stare more and more commonplace nowadays. "I promised you when you let me take over our finances that if I did anything to lose our money I'd take care of you. Getting into real estate is how I plan to do that."

"Maybe I should go back to work, too," I said softly. "Just until the house sells."

"You don't have faith in my ability to support this family?"

"It's not a lack of faith in you. I'm just not convinced anyone can support a family properly in a small town where opportunity is so limited. The economy is bleak for everyone, not just the people in the country. And most people in real estate are getting out of the field the way the economy is."

To him, my every comment was evidence of me balking at our newly assigned roles once again. He was the man now, and I was supposed to be the good wife who trusted his decisions and quietly accepted the outcome of his choices. What was wrong with me that I couldn't trust fate and the universe to provide? He talked of books like *The Secret,* complaining that my negative energy was standing in the way of his manifesting a solution to our problems.

I loved him, couldn't seem to stop even though I saw less and less to love the man for, but my practical nature couldn't be curtailed. Certainly this beautiful land had value for something other than putting a barrier between the people who lived here and the world at large. People have made an honest living off the land for centuries. Why not us?

I again began crunching numbers. Could we farm? Might we plant the pasture with corn or grapes and open a grist mill or winery? Could we raise goats or horses, cows or chickens for a living? Plenty of people in our area did these things successfully, but in every case they were working at a farm business that had been in the family for years so they were working land with a very low or non-existent mortgage, which kept overhead to a minimum. The income derived from farming was modest at best, and hobby farming had taught me that growing food or raising livestock from scratch required a hefty investment of time and money for set up, after which the owner was subject to all manner of catastrophes that might be set off by weather, pests, or sheer bad luck. Forming an agricultural business would be a huge risk under the best of circumstances. And even if we came up with a plan that had the potential for success, we still wouldn't earn the income necessary to support Mark's million dollar mortgage debt. We had to get rid of that house, but no one was going to buy our house with a hugely puffed-up price tag.

My sad fingers punched away at the calculator as a magazine with an article on America's foreclosure epidemic smirked up at me. We weren't upside down on our mortgage like other people who had gotten in over their heads with loans they didn't really qualify for. The value of our initial investment was declining but we still had over a million dollars of equity in the property with less owed, and I'm not talking about theoretical equity that can be attributed to estimated property values, but hard cash we had plunked down only two years earlier while the rest of the world was taking unsecured loans on their holdings. The appraisal of our property still hovered high above what we owed. Ours was still just a cash flow problem.

"We have to lower the price of the house," I implored again.

Mark would not budge on the issue. Lowering the cost of the house would be making a statement that his creation had less value artistically. His house was a masterpiece, and he was willing to lose everything to prove so.

I stood on our porch watching the babbling brook that ran through our fifty acres, thinking I was looking into shit's creek, and we were up it.

Mark was counting on a miracle. At night he was still poring over building magazines and fantasizing about the next magnificent home he would create.

"I won't go crazy next time," he said. "I am done spending, done consuming, done trying to live a life straight from the pages of a posh cabin living magazine. I'm ready to be like the case examples in all those books you've given me to read, *Your Money or Your Life*, *Affluenza*, and *Simple Prosperity*."

"You finally read them?"

"Well, no. I'm too stressed to read. But you told me enough to understand what's in them. And believe me, I am all for living the simple life now."

I thought of the new home he had started for us. The final price of that structure would land in the half million dollar vicinity, still more than we had agreed to spend on a home when we started out this adventure as millionaires.

I kept mulling over our choices. Did we really want to continue living in this small town, two isolated city folk, raising kids in a repressed area, if being a resident of Blue Ridge meant living without security and some level of comfort? Did we really want to stay in a place where every pair of shoes we owned was dirt encrusted and there wasn't a single radio station that didn't play country or Christian music? Nature was wonderful, refreshing for the soul, but perhaps the people keeping secure jobs in the real world, the ones who spent weekends in the country for fun, had it right. The truth was, full-time residency in the country is not unlike waking up in the morning to your perfect-model date and finding out that, without makeup, she looks much the same as every average person. In fact, she looks worse because you anticipated something far more special, and in reality, your lover is plain as toast.

As I voiced my concerns about our future, Mark grew ever more distant. Clearly, I was too focused on money; a sellout if I thought returning to the commercial world we left behind was any kind of solution to our problems.

I listened to his postulating about how he alone understood what counted in life, my eyes wandering to the beams lofting 25 feet overhead in our 7500 square foot 'simple' cabin. His sentiments sounded wise and true, spoken with such passion as they were. But his words, despite the most convincing sincerity imaginable, simply didn't match his acts. Not now. Not ever.

We jointly agreed we couldn't and shouldn't cast blame for our predicament on others, ourselves, and especially each other. The truth was, we had grasped for a brass ring and missed. Mark could have made more reserved choices, but we also could have avoided the merry-go-round all together and missed the ride and we had learned important lessons on this journey.

At least our adventure, while a failure, had taught us about our own strengths and weaknesses. I was ready to embrace whatever mindset was necessary to start fresh. My family was irreplaceable, and I could always make more money. I just needed Mark to untie my hands and allow me back into the decision-making role so I could begin.

I ventured to the barn to consider what I was going to do with Donkey, since all things pointed to our losing all our property now. We hadn't paid a mortgage payment in a year, and fewer and fewer people bothered to look at a house so overpriced, so even the silly hope for a miracle was wearing thin. I had begun selling my animals the month before, sending my llama off to a llama rescue organization, unloading some chickens, and putting feelers out for the horses. Now, I walked myself through the scenario of finding a home for my donkey.

Sniffling back tears always had a way of making Donkey appear by my side, as if he could sense my need. I stood, scratching between his ears, watching leaves flitter to the earth around me like an ominous sign that a harsh winter was soon to come. I imagined saying goodbye to the labor, the mud, the ignorance, and the frustration that hung on the skirts of country life. Next year, my family could well be back in the world where sophisticated conversation, paved roads, and decent employment opportunities were commonplace, a land where I'd ask new friends *what* they were reading rather than *if* they could read.

Perhaps leaving the country was for the best for a family like ours, after all. We were too educated and too worldly to ever be happy in a town with so few opportunities. Perhaps rejoining urban society was the only way to meet our potential and contribute to the world in a real way. Perhaps fate was correcting a mistake by forcing us out of the country. If we truly had the mentality and attitude of simplifying life, Mark would have built us a simple cabin and a sustainable life, not a lodge fit for a celebrity family designed only to impress others.

Donkey nuzzled my side. I imagined him saying, "Forgive me, I was the catalyst. I'm sorry I ended up a disappointment to you."

"It's not your fault," I said aloud. "You taught me to breathe again, to pause and enjoy the quiet moments. You reminded me to laugh and learn and wonder at life. You were my best entertainment, my best education, and my best friend. Knowing you was worth the risk, the failure, the fear and discomfort. I'd do everything again, even knowing the outcome. Living in the country was fun. Fascinating. *Real.* My children bloomed here. And I had had the gift of being attentive and present to witness their growth. I've never felt so amazed by the world. Thank you."

As my fingers ran through the donkey's dusty fur, I knew just how true my admission was. Mark and I had stretched our horizons, rebalanced our souls, and tested our moral center as we reached for a dream despite the impractical implications to our balance sheet.

Most importantly, our journey wasn't over yet. We might still sell our home and be left with enough money to rebuild our lives. That monstrosity of a house might even springboard a new building career for Mark someday. Mostly, I prayed my husband would at long last learn from his mistakes, and accept and admit his weaknesses so we didn't have to replay this painful drama of financial irresponsibility again and again.

"It isn't fair. We've changed too much to go back now," I announced to the trees.

Donkey blinked in acquiescence.

"Our chairs are now made of sticks and antlers, so they won't fit in a neat suburban living room. Our wine isn't liquor store imports, but fruitful flavors gurgling and fermenting in a five-gallon carboy in the basement, every batch possessing a better kick and far better body than mass-produced lofty labels. We've lost our taste for imported greenhouse tomatoes and pale store-bought eggs, preferring homegrown tomatoes with a touch of dirt still clinging to the stem. Our dogs are too big, our cars too dirty. Mark's wardrobe is too Paul Bunyan-esque for suburbia. Kathy is reading at the third grade reading level and there's still a lot more she can teach me... um, I mean that I can teach her."

The trees smiled as I poured out my confession.

"Most importantly, this family still has a donkey to raise, and he has a good 30 years of living left that require wide open spaces and fresh, clean air for health and happiness…and so do we."

The donkey brayed endearingly, but not to me. Mark was standing on the gravel road watching me. He wasn't driving his tractor, holding a chainsaw, or even covered with sawdust, but framed as he was by trees and the open sky, he looked perfectly at home. He flashed me a distant smile, and my heart constricted. God, I loved him. Just once I wished he would walk up and put an arm around me. I wanted him to make love to me in the barn or lay with me in the field as I had dreamed since we first bought this land. I wanted him to squeeze my hand with shared confidence that we were in this together. Just once.

"What's up?" I asked.

"A realtor just called. Someone wants to see the house tomorrow. No promises, but it's a chance…Who were you talking to?"

"Donkey. I know that sounds silly,"

He didn't comment.

"Can we please lower the cost of the house to be in line with the appraisal? That might give us a fighting chance to sell it tomorrow."

I had made the request so many times Mark probably heard it in his sleep.

He turned to leave and I sighed. I had once again spoiled the moment. My husband had not bothered to visit me at the barn to talk for months. He had not bothered to be alone with me for months. We hadn't stood this close for months.

I followed him. "I don't want you to feel I don't trust your judgment. We simply must take affirmative action to handle our problems. The bank will take this property if we don't."

"Well, you always know the right path to take," he said, his voice dripping with sarcasm as he quickened his step.

I stopped following him. I knew better than to say anything more. There was no winning. Not with nature, and not with my husband who had long since left me in heart, mind, and body. The truth was, I had lost my husband the day we sold our business and he was instantly empowered by a million dollars and free rein to spend as he wished. Until then, he needed me. Someone had to be there, working tirelessly to provide him a certain lifestyle. My life had been an endless treadmill of effort to out-earn his spending and support his artistic whimsy. But I became expendable the moment he became financially free from having to answer to me, or my family, or anyone else.

"You're not selling much real estate, so can't you stop spending so much time at the office and come home for a while? We really need to spend some time together. I feel like we've been nothing but glorified roommates for ages, and I miss you," I said, feeling pitiful that I had to beg for my husband's affections.

"You want me to come home so I can listen to your concerns and fears? Your endless crying and begging me to talk about things is disgusting. No, thank you."

I turned away to hide the wellspring of tears that had surfaced in my eyes. To the top of that salty spring floated a memory, unbidden and unwelcome, but all too clear. The memory was so overwhelmingly pain-filled that I must have tried to drown it forever, but a moment in time came back to me now with a harsh message I was at last ready to hear:

A month prior, as I had walked down the path to the barn, I got a strange sensation that something was amiss. I instantly did a spot check for chicken or peacock carcasses littering the barnyard, but no evidence of night marauders seemed apparent. Still, Pulani was pacing the fence nervously with her ears bowed forward, humming in an agitated, nervous way. The dogs were barking and Donkey stood at the fence staring at me with his usual wise gaze, as if to advise me, "Take a breath." Instantly, my eyes darted over the pasture checking for my baby llama. He was never far from his mother, so his absence now instilled an even stronger sense of foreboding. Where was Pauli?

My feet sunk into the boggy mud as I went through the pasture gate. Perhaps if I hiked the perimeter I'd find him munching on grass in his first show of independence. Just two steps in, my hope died. A huddled heap of wet, bloody llama fur was lying in the creek. At first, the mound was still, and a sinking sadness crept over me, but the body suddenly jerked, followed by a painful wail. That cry for help was a sound unlike anything I've ever heard from one of my graceful, quiet llamas. His haunting moan was like heaven crying.

I raced to where the animal lay, almost retching because Pauli's side had been torn open and half of his internal organs were now in plain view. The coyotes had apparently attacked again, intent on making a meal of my beloved pet, but something must have scared them away before the deed was done. Pauli now was lying half in and half out of the creek, flinching in agonizing pain. I felt the vibration of his desolate hopelessness in my own gut. Since coyotes attack at night and it was now late in the morning, I imagined he'd been suffering for hours. I didn't know how this wretched creature was still alive, but clearly, he wouldn't be for long. I sank to my knees, stroking his head with shaking hands. My poor, innocent, beautiful llama! I had done so much to care for him and keep him safe, but despite every effort, this harsh country existence had again found a way to ravage and destroy something I wanted to protect and love.

Pauli struggled to stand, desperately trying to lift himself from the water, but his legs buckled and he collapsed again, his body landing in an even more contorted position. A trickle of red flowed downstream, the loss of blood draining his life in a slow, relentless weakening of his constitution.

I hated to leave, but I needed to get help, so I ran back to where I'd dropped my belongings, grabbed my cell phone, and raced to the only corner of our land that got reception so I could call Mark. I needed my husband. I needed to hear his voice assuring me that everything would be okay. I was falling apart, overwhelmed with grief and worry and fear, and all I wanted was him. I needed him the way a woman needs a man for his strength and leadership. I needed him the way a woman needs her husband when she feels small and helpless and overwhelmed, and she desperately wants to fold herself into her partner's arms to feel protected from a world that suddenly seems threatening and frightening.

I was sobbing on the phone, almost incoherent as I poured out the situation and my panic about it.

"I'll call Ronnie. He'll come out and shoot the poor thing and put him out of his misery." The practical and probably necessary solution was still painful to hear. I sobbed harder, holding the phone to my mute mouth because I had only tears and no words.

"Can you come home?" I finally managed to whisper.

"I'm really busy. Ronnie can take care of this. Let's hang up so I can call him."

"Please…" I wasn't sure what I was begging him for. I just knew I couldn't handle this alone. I had handled too much alone these last years, and witnessing the suffering of this innocent pet, seeing his guts spilled out over the grass and looking down at the blood on my sleeve had put me over the edge. I am not someone who falls apart, but I was falling apart now. I needed my husband more in that moment than I had ever needed anyone.

"Please," I whispered, moaning out loud as another piercing cry from my young llama filled the air. The dogs were barking, circling the beast excitedly, their behavior enhancing Pauli's fear and making everything seem even more chaotic and out of control.

"Oh, God, Mark, the dogs are attacking him, too. Please!"

"So get off the phone so I can make some calls. Christ…I know you love that llama, but pull yourself together."

I was embarrassed by my uncontrolled emotions, mortified that I was begging him to come home to me, destroyed that the man I loved considered me a nuisance because I had the gall to turn to him for comfort. Things die in the country. I knew that. I wanted to be tough and take farming life in stride, but I simply couldn't. All the stress and sadness I'd been battling for the last two years had come together to break me in one final heart-splitting earthquake.

Mark hung up and I rushed back to Pauli, kicking at the dogs, and panicking because as he struggled to stand he kept slipping deeper into the creek. I was afraid that moving him would cause more pain, but also afraid that if I didn't try to move him he might hurt more. So I just sat beside him, yelling and kicking at the dogs one minute, then turning a tender voice to the llama the next.

"Ronnie is coming, honey. You are not alone. I'm here." I whispered to my dying llama.

But Ronnie didn't come "soon." I sat with that suffering llama over half an hour, each minute intensifying my distress until my own body shook with such heart-wrenching pain it was as if the llama and I were one.

When I heard a truck finally coming down our road, I left Pauli, and ran back to the barn. It was Mark! He had come! Instantly I felt that things would be fine after all. My husband had rushed home, and this made me feel safe and cared for.

"Ronnie is on his way. I told him I'd meet him here." Mark leaned against his car with his arms crossed, making no move to come towards me. "Damn coyotes."

My steps slowed. Mark had come to meet Ronnie so they could take care of the business of killing my llama, not because his wife was experiencing an emotional crisis. Still, I kept coming towards him, hoping he would give me a hug and let me cry against his broad chest. I wanted him to fold me in his arms as proof that no matter how harsh the world was, I had a place of tenderness where I could turn. Him.

A splash sounded behind me and I spun around. Pauli had grown too weak to hold his head up now, and he had collapsed into the water of the creek. His body started convulsing and thrashing about. He was drowning. I watched my dying llama fight for life despite his pain and suffering, and all I wanted to do was run to him and hold his head up and save him from suffocating. But I'd only be saving him to be shot a few minutes later. Death was at his heels, and the sooner it arrived, the better, considering his incredible pain. So all I could do now was stand there and ache for him, watching a pet I loved drown in water filled with his own blood. As his convulsing body finally succumbed to the stillness of death, I collapsed to the ground, curled up, and sobbed.

Mark watched but he didn't move. When I finally looked up, he shrugged sadly, a polite gesture as if to say, "It sucks that your llama died."

I reached my hand out to him, but he didn't move to comfort me.

A moment later, Ronnie drove up and hopped out of his truck with a gun. Mark shook his hand and explained that they had both come needlessly. The animal had died. They talked a few minutes about coyotes and what I should do with the mother llama, and Mark said he'd get the tractor and bury Pauli out in the pasture so his body wouldn't draw more predators or spoil the creek water.

Ronnie looked at my tear-streaked face with concern. "You okay?" he asked compassionately.

I stood up, doing what I could to pull myself together. "Not my best day," I said.

Mark never did touch me that afternoon—not a hug or a hand held out to help me stand from my knees after I had collapsed in misery. He turned and left, saying he wanted to get back to work, and he drove off, leaving me to walk home slowly, one last look over my shoulder at my beloved dead llama half floating in the creek.

I had that horrible wrung-out feeling that comes after you've cried yourself out, a feeling of emptiness and loss that I recognized now was coming more from the fact that Mark couldn't—or wouldn't—put his arms around me than from Pauli's sad death.

The entire episode was a perfect metaphor for my life over the past five years. I had done everything I could to minimize the pain and suffering our new life in the country had unexpectedly doled out. I had desperately wanted to do whatever was necessary to hold our heads above water, even knowing we were bleeding to death financially. I had sat on the sidelines, filled with empathy and sadness, waiting for Mark to do something to make the pain stop. I had waited for him, alone, lonely, scared, and incapable of doing anything to lessen the overwhelming pain, my sadness and fears perceived as an annoyance rather than a cry for help.

Meanwhile, Mark wanted me to just buck up and be strong. It never occurred to him that my strength, ample in the past, had been used up and depleted, or that my strength came from loving him and feeling that he loved me and that whatever happened, we would face life's trials together. I had been falling apart in a myriad of ways because clearly, my husband had no intention or interest in being there for me. His lack of consideration or care had broken my heart in ways I never knew a heart could be broken.

I opened the impressive teak door to the albatross house, and stepped into what Mark still believed was the most beautiful log cabin in the world. To me, that stately log home, with all the hand-hewn logs and geode-encrusted stone work, was a monster that had swallowed security, safety, and hope, not just for me, but for my children. The walls vibrated with my husband's ego and arrogance, his creativity dripping from every detail as evidence that nurturing and celebrating his artistic ambitions took precedence over any call to be a provider or lover or man who wanted to protect his loved ones from hardship. Building that house was his dream come true, but his dream came at the price of stripping others of everything they needed and deserved.

He was okay with that. But after today, I no longer was.

We had bought a donkey, and lost the world.

"In what concerns you much, do not think that you have companions: know that you are alone in the world."
—*Henry David Thoreau*

WHY I LEFT THE WOODS

As foreclosure loomed, Mark seemed to do anything and everything he could to avoid me. He worked 14 hour days at the real estate office, and when I begged him to come home for meals or to spend time together, he had a plethora of excuses why he couldn't. He made new friends and began eating his lunches out, eventually going to parties to hang out with real estate buddies in the evenings, too. I was left alone on the 50 acres with nothing but my growing panic to dwell on. I had the kids, of course, and laundry and cleaning and endless upkeep so the house would look presentable if a buyer stopped by, but despite all the wide open space around me, I felt the narrow confines of my isolation and my bottomless loneliness slowly suffocating me.

I talked about returning to Florida to open a small dance studio to generate some much needed income. Mark responded by finding a small space to rent locally, negotiating a lease, and encouraging me to begin a business in Blue Ridge. This is where he wanted to stay, and my running a new business would take some of the pressure off him to earn money. I assumed his efforts to help organize a studio meant he was ready for us to work as a team again, but after setting me up with the responsibility, Mark chose not to be involved, further evidence of his disinterest in rebuilding our life as a united front. We'd always approached dance as a couple before, but I was a solo act now, one more disappointment poured into a heart overflowing with sadness.

My grief spilled out to fill the cracks and corners of the house. Hard as I tried, I couldn't pretend things were normal around the kids. They would catch me crying on the couch or gripping my coffee cup with a sad stare as I gazed at the pasture. I didn't cry because

I was losing my home, my million dollar retirement nest egg, or my dreams. I cried because Mark had railroaded us into losing all of the above, blindly and erratically, steaming our marriage down the tracks in spite of obvious signs the bridge was out ahead, and I felt almost as though he had done it on purpose, one final way to act out his resentment towards me. Worse, I felt responsible for not pulling his hand away from the throttle and putting on the brakes myself. My love for him, my willingness to agree to anything he wanted in a last ditch effort to make him happy, had taken us both down, and I hated myself for my weakness. I hated myself for loving someone who simply had no clue what love really means.

I still longed for what seemed impossible now: to feel my husband's arm around my shoulders and to hear his voice whisper words of hope for a different future once this mess was over. But I knew no apology or tenderness would ever come. I was a witness to his failure, and even though I never voiced blame, he projected ceaseless silent accusations from me. Perhaps he couldn't forgive himself, and therefore couldn't imagine how I could ever forgive him either. Living with guilt and regret is far harder for the spouse who *made* the mistakes than for the one who stoically pays the price for them.

One night, Mark came out of the bedroom dressed in a fine silk shirt and gold chains and asked me to make him a late dinner. He'd been working out obsessively at a new gym and had lost a hundred pounds in the last four months, another fanatical move towards becoming a new man. Each day now, he took a long time dressing to show off his new physique. He had spent hours that afternoon pulling out boxes of clothing he hadn't donned since we lived in Florida. He shaved, too and had taken to wearing sunglasses, his rugged natural look shifting to something more GQ than he had emulated in years. This was a different Mark than the dancer in sweats and a baseball cap who had been my partner in the past. He was no longer the mountain man who had spent the last few years in jeans and faded flannel shirts, either. Long gone was the Mark who only months before had blended with the country boys like a decoy duck on a pond of mallards. Despite all that had happened to us, conceit seemed to swirl about his every move, a sure sign he was gearing up for yet another change in persona.

He asked me to make spaghetti, and when I set the plate before him, he took off his shirt to hang on the back of his chair to avoid potential stains. He ate his meal hungrily, then put his silk shirt back on and told me he was going to work. *What work was there to do at ten o'clock at night?* I silently watched him leave, not able to bring myself to question his obvious lie. Neither of us wanted to speak aloud the words that would forever put the truth on the table before us.

Hours later, he returned. I wondered who he'd been with. I had called the office and someone stopping by to collect a contract told me he was out at a party with some male agents whom Mark had previously told me crossed the lines of sexual and ethical propriety. For once, embittered by another night of disappointment and hurt, I decided to ask him outright where he'd been.

"Work," he lied.

"From ten at night until one in the morning? I was worried about you having to work so late so I called the office. Someone answered and told me you were at a party. Why lie to me, Mark? Are you seeing someone?"

He sighed, collecting his things to move out of our bedroom. "I just wanted to go to the party alone. I can't stand to be around you anymore. I'm sick of your logic, your crying, your endless heart-to-hearts. You bring me down."

He had brought us both down. There was nothing left to say.

"Do you want a divorce?"

"Yes, I do."

There they were. Three simple words with the power to change the trajectory of my life again. With the Smiths , the three words were, "I'll take it." Now it was "Yes, I do"—an affirmative statement that really meant 'No.'

No, I won't accept counseling to work out our problems.

No, I don't want to stay if staying married means I have to actually take care of you.

No, I won't be there to hold your hand when we grow older as I once promised.

No, I don't believe that after twenty years we should talk openly about what went wrong to bring us to this point.

No, I won't ever admit I have made mistakes at your cost, and I would rather start over with someone else than live with someone who knows the truth about who I am and what I've done.

No, I don't love you.

I was reminded of a lesson I learned with Kathy: that most all of our communications, even the most complex of messages, are nothing but basic, simple words linked to create potency or poignancy. I felt the impact of his words now with an odd combination of dread and acceptance.

We had moved to the country with a mutually agreed-upon plan, but Mark and I had had different agendas from the very beginning. I had moved to the country for a fresh beginning with the man I loved. Mark had moved to the country for a fresh beginning. Period. At last, we could stop pretending otherwise.

Every autumn in the country, gardens that have flourished and produced throughout their season of growth are torn down. The wilted vegetation and the unfinished produce are tossed on a compost heap or burned in a fire pit. The gardener often takes a moment to contemplate, at this point, what could have gone better. Perhaps different varieties or a different arrangement of plots, a more beneficial companion planting, more of something and less of something else—all these might have made for a better season and a richer harvest. Autumn was a fitting time for my marriage to be torn down, the season for endings and the precursor of a cold time to come. I contemplated, now, the twenty-year season of my time with Mark.

I could have begged him to join me for counseling. I could have once again taken responsibility for all our problems and fed his ego to keep the status quo as I'd done for years and years. I could have had yet another heart-to-heart with him in one more gentle attempt to turn this moment around because loving him was a habit like smoking: not good for you, but still hard to break. I could have once again embraced delusion to protect the romantic story I harbored within about the amazing Mark and Ginny, dug in to find inner reserves no matter how frayed, and done whatever had to be done to climb us out of this mess - and later, give him credit for everything.

The problem was, twenty years of emotional exhaustion kept my mouth clamped shut. I had seen too much shadow in our garden, even when I tried to view shadows as proof of sunlight. I was forced mute now by having lived with a partner who invited drama and crisis into our life like a junkie for the adrenalin created by senseless risk. If total freedom from work responsibilities, two million dollars' worth of resources, and a wife encouraging him to follow his heart no matter where it aimed was not enough to make a man happy, this man of mine would never be happy. And I just didn't want to live with someone whom I could never make happy. Just once, I wanted to wake to someone who considered my contributions to our life a gift rather than a dreadful bore.

The question now was: what would I do for the cold winter of my life after Mark?

Living in the country was a dream we had both shared, but for me this dream was designed for a couple. I couldn't imagine living in that quiet village without land to tend and animals to care for. I couldn't imagine being stuck in a small town without financial security to keep my children safe from the downward spiral of classless ignorance and mental atrophy. I couldn't imagine living where everyone knew everyone else's business as I tried to go gracefully through the painful process of severing two lives so intricately entangled from twenty years of raising kids, building a business, making money and going bankrupt, building homes, and sharing dreams. I couldn't even imagine finding someone else with whom to pursue this dream as a new couple, because moving to the country had been our dream, Mark's and mine, together. This life was a dream designed through years of joint experiences as a couple, joint experiences that formed our attitudes and desires. Living in Blue Ridge was the end result of all we had learned. The life I had so long imagined with him, a life of creativity and art and discovery, a life of simplicity and connection in the place we dreamed of moving to for years, would never feel the same with anyone new because the rewards of forging that free, artistic life in this time and place would not have been earned authentically.

Blue Ridge once represented love to me–my love for nature and my love for Mark. If he wanted a divorce, I had just lost both. Blue Ridge now represented nothing more than loss, loneliness, failed dreams, and gross self-indulgence on the part of a husband who, in the end, not only had broken every promise ever spoken to me, but clearly made those promises knowing all along that he was going to do what he wanted rather than what we agreed. I stared at the garden of my life and could see nothing at the moment but complete crop failure.

I took stock of our situation. Mark didn't want us living in the same home another day. He offered to leave and get his own apartment, but I couldn't possibly handle the upkeep of that monstrosity of a house alone, and since he had control of our money, I couldn't afford to move out myself. I also knew, just as he thought nothing of leaving me with babies to feed while he went on a grand chase after Tony Robbins, Mark would spend any and all of our last resources to set himself up in a new place with no consideration for his children's or my survival. It would be every man out for himself. I just couldn't trust him to not make matters worse for everyone.

Mark had spent the last two years building his real estate business and, despite the challenges of the real estate market, made six figures that year, thanks to a lucrative listing received from a friend. Not enough to support a million dollar mortgage, but certainly enough to live comfortably on his own. I had a fledgling dance studio that, at best, might make a few hundred dollars weekly a year hence, *if* I could manage the impossible and hold out without income long enough for the business to turn around. To survive, I would have to fire my older daughter who was working with me. Denver was counting on this job as her one means to live independently and she still hoped to escape Blue Ridge someday. I couldn't bear to let her down, and even if I did, the business would never make enough to support someone my age with retirement and other pending life demands looming, such as the responsibility of raising my younger daughter, sending her to college, helping my son in college, saving for retirement, and so forth.

I was up against a wall. I knew that only one of us who would listen to the wisdom of logic. At fifty-one, how many working years did I have left that I could dare waste in a dead-end proposition simply because I refused to accept the futility of the situation? Even loving nature and animals and the gentle soul-stroking of the country as I did, I had no choice but to move back to a place where I had a fighting chance to reclaim a purposeful life, parent effectively, and not become a financial burden on others. And if Mark felt we couldn't share one home (and we couldn't afford two), I had no choice but to live someplace free, which in this case, meant moving home to my parents at the ripe old age of fifty-one. The humiliation of admitting how far I'd fallen now made every choice painful, but I couldn't see any other solution. I called my parents, expecting an "I told you so" speech. What I received instead was compassion, love, and sincere sorrow over all that I'd lost. Of course they offered to help, without judgment and with a generosity of spirit I didn't deserve. Their support was the truest example of love I'd witnessed in years as they reminded me, once again, of the kind of parent I hoped to be myself.

I carefully explained my plans to Mark for my future "garden," going through my thought processes, sharing my fears, and offering my practical contemplations. I still believed our mutual survival was a problem we had to solve together. I got nothing from Mark but agreement that leaving Blue Ridge was best for me, and an offer to help me pack.

So it was that I found myself driving down the highway, back to Florida to get assistance from my parents so I could survive the short term and plant whatever crop I could on my own. I was all alone, driving a big cargo truck, larger than any I'd ever handled. Mark and Kent had packed it with my books, my clothes, a leftover couch from our basement, a chair, and a TV. I had a new cellphone with twenty-five dollars' worth of minutes that Mark had purchased as a concession when he took my cell phone from me so he wouldn't have to pay my bills. I had enough cash, borrowed from my sister, to pay for fuel at the truck stops when I wrestled the big rig into them. As I drove down the lonesome highway, my belly churned around the pizza that had been our last shared meal together as a family. I thought over the sad arrangements we'd made.

Mark claimed he didn't have the means to support me anymore and it wasn't his problem to help me find a place to live or a way to support myself, so he would not be sharing any money he made from this point on.

"You're tough. You'll land on your feet. You always do," he said, almost as though he hated me for my strength when, in fact, that had been the trait that had kept our heads above water for twenty years.

He promised to send Neva to me when school was out because by then, surely, I would have a place to live. Kent was going off to college, and Denver, at twenty-five, was ready to be self-sufficient.

Together, we decided to offer Denver ownership of the dance studio. Mark felt he could cancel the lease if she didn't want to take over, in which case I'd take the teaching materials with me to begin anew. I could have sorely used the resources, but Denver liked the idea of being her own boss and picking up a turnkey business, so along with her boyfriend, she decided to try to make a go of the school. I believed offering her the business was a way of showing her my faith in her potential and I liked that we were giving her an opportunity to claim some direction in life.

She would later blame me for her choice to take over when the reality of just how hard running a business can be came to light. I had hoped her experiences might give her insight into just how hard I'd worked in my life to build a dance school business. Perhaps that would help her to better understand my commitment to supporting the family, but instead, giving her the studio created a wedge of resentment that would take years to chip away. We didn't speak for over three years.

The loss of my daughter's love and her lack of empathy hurt much more than the loss of my marriage, because I just didn't see it coming. Every adult knows marriages are fragile and can deteriorate, but I never dreamed the bond between me and my children could be broken, even temporarily. Denver, more than the other two, always seemed most connected to me. As Mark's stepchild, and a young woman with a bit more innate practicality in her worldview than the others, she'd always been less inclined to excuse Mark's less-than-admirable qualities and she saw things as they really are. But she aligned with him now, adding more weight to the burden on my broken heart.

I drove through the night by myself in that big truck, shaking with sadness and blinded by tears. The temptation to just ease that big wheel to the left and end all my troubles came and made itself at home for a moment before leaving. I knew deep inside that I had no other course than to keep moving boldly towards a new life, even if I didn't *want* a new life.

Middle-aged, with no home and less than a hundred dollars to my name, I didn't even know where to start to rebuild. I had no car, no credit, no savings, no retirement, and no career to fall back on. Mark had changed all the credit cards to his name when he took over finances, so he alone had access to credit to help survive the coming months. He had put my car in his name, too, so I had to leave it behind along with the two cash-purchased cars he claimed were his alone and that he needed for work. Mark kept most all of the money we had in the bank claiming he needed every cent we had to keep afloat while the house was for sale. There was an additional five grand in debt still owed for the new studio, but Denver agreed to pay that bill in exchange for the business. But the business didn't have much promise in my estimation, and every family member was destitute now. Which of us would make the payments if she couldn't?

Too sad to argue any point, I slipped away quietly, demanding nothing, in a state of stupor as I focused hazily on what my children were now going to live without. The last thing Mark did as I left, was ask for my wedding ring.

"I want to sell it for the gold. I could use the cash," he said, with a callousness that made my heart shatter in ways it would never be put together quite as whole again.

I looked at the solid gold chain hanging around his neck, worth three times what he paid for my ring, and for the first time in my marriage I said a flat out *"No"* to the man I loved. He had taken enough, and I decided that one last shred of dignity was mine to retain.

Months later, I was still struggling with my attempt at my new garden, digging out rocks that were sharp, ugly, and painful to handle. Divorce is never easy, and the pain of a life ripped apart creeps into every fiber of your being, coloring behaviors and actions in the worst of ways. Mark and I had twenty years of resentment and history to wade through. Just as Mark had claimed he wanted to live a simple life in a simple log cabin while he spent over two million dollars on one complex building project, he now claimed he wanted a mutual friendship while secretly planning a surprise lawsuit that would damage both of our chances for financial and emotional recovery. My naïve dream that we could part as friends crumbled further with every act of cruelty he committed.

With help from my family in Florida, I opened another small dance and yoga studio and began the arduous process of building a new business from scratch with zero resources. I expected my former reputation to give me a fair head start in the process, but despite my strong reputation and massive experience, not a single dancer from the past enrolled. My fresh-start studio was laden with bills and debt from the beginning, and I had no students to lighten the load. Life with Mark clearly had not humbled me enough. Fate decided I needed the experience of feeling obsolete and unworthy in the dance world to learn the lessons of humility, too.

Still, I did everything I could to set up a life so that when Neva joined me as Mark had promised, I'd be prepared to care for her in the way she deserved. I kept telling myself there was no place to go but up. I didn't have the fortitude to wake up and carve a new life for myself in my depressed state, but you could bet I'd do whatever I had to do for my children.

Then Mark broadsided me with the custody case. I was accused variously of abandonment, being an unfit mother, an adulteress, and emotionally unstable. These unfair accusations had a way of shocking me out of my grief, but since I was in Florida, he had the home court advantage, and in his zeal to create a scenario where he was the victim and I was the enemy, my children were given a distorted perception about what had happened and why. Suddenly they stopped speaking to me. They stopped calling. Resentment poured out of them in words and deeds.

I couldn't afford the legal battle, financially or emotionally, and losing intimate contact with my children ripped every last ounce of fight in me away. We had finally sold that monstrosity of a house, and also the second half-house, both at pathetic prices, but this last stroke of luck did leave us with a modest sum in an escrow account awaiting the final divorce decree. I proposed the money be divided equally. Mark wanted more. He sued for alimony, too.

Financial desperation was crippling everyone in the family, and just as Mark had been willing to lose everything we had in order to retain his self-perception as a magnificent designer, he now seemed willing to risk everything we had to prove another point: that he was somehow the wronged spouse and the better person. The legal bills were escalating, eating up the cash so quickly that soon we would be in debt beyond the escrow amount. Weak from my wounded heart, and having just discovered Neva was living on food stamps and was now showing extreme signs of emotional instability, I finally cracked.

In my ultimate act of exhausted love, I gave in and let the last vestige of life in our erstwhile relationship slip underwater and drown. I was simply too tired to face one more Mark-induced crisis. Twenty years of watching him burn through our resources in the pursuit of personal aggrandizement made it all too clear that if I didn't stop the madness, we would have nothing left at the end of the battle to divide. My youngest child needed more than either of us was providing at this time, and something had to be done to instigate change. The only way I could be a responsible parent now was to minimize the emotional and financial damage this divorce was causing so my child at least could have food and shelter and a chance to balance her emotional upheaval. And I needed to buck up and get life back on track so I could be someone my kids could count on, and fast.

I had one last heart-to-heart with Mark, swallowing all the pride my gut could stomach, as I apologized for any and all offenses he perceived from me. I offered to give up alimony, any earned settlement to balance the investment we'd made in his new career or tools, and custody of my daughter—all things my lawyer insisted were a mistake to forego—if he would just lay down his sword and quit spending the money on a lawsuit.

Mark was so used to getting his way through petulant behavior that he wasn't the least bit surprised by my surrender.

"I sure miss having money," he said with a charismatic grin, cheerfully signing the papers my lawyer had drawn up and acting as if we were best friends again. "I hope this goes through quickly."

I drove home from the signing, feeling a strange, sickly combination of relief and grief. Sometimes when you win, you lose, and for me, breaking the gridlock was both. I needed my share of the settlement to start paying back my family for the help they had offered during those first miserable months. Mark said he needed his in order to follow the plan laid out by his debt manager to get life back on track. Certainly his plan would create better, more stable circumstances for our daughter, which was my primary concern.

I had dearly wanted to fight to the end no matter the cost, tempted to just let him ruin us both to prove he was his own worst enemy, and certainly mine. But my job had always been to lessen the damage Mark innocently created and to wait out the pendulum swings of his personality with gritted teeth and dogged determination. We were simply living true to the dynamic of our relationship from the beginning. Ruminating about the injustice of the situation, I thought of how Mark had asked me for my ring back. Of course, it never occurred to me to ask him to return his. Didn't that say it all?

On the day our divorce was final, Mark was at the lawyer's office within the hour, anxiously demanding his settlement check even before I had been notified the marriage was officially over. Apparently, he had jumped the gun on his next remodeling project, a cabin on four acres that his new girlfriend had bought, and he was already deep in the throes of debt. From the moment he knew money was forthcoming, he enthusiastically allocated all he could into remodeling that house (for Neva's sake, he insisted) and the small workshop on the property (for *his* sake; to house the thousands of dollars' worth of tools he had insisted on keeping).

His veering from the practical plan to pay off debt and stabilize life didn't surprise me, but his sudden alliance with the new woman did. Being the first and only woman he had ever dated in his life, I found it odd he didn't feel a need to shop around or gain more relationship experience before settling. She also happened to be a student of mine whom, while we were married, he had adamantly claimed was not at all his type physically. Weeks before we came to our compromise, I had voiced concerns about his new alliance and he promised me that under no circumstance would he move in with her if I gave him custody. I'd agreed to let him raise Neva because I trusted him to live true to this agreement.

His breaking yet another promise to me was frustrating, but the fact that he had offered Neva no voice in the matter nor given her advance notice that they would be moving in with another woman showed such a lack of sensitivity to our children's need for time and patience to adapt to our family's devastation that I almost had an anxiety attack. For the first time in my life, I actually sought counseling to cope. Had I really turned over the care of our children to a man who put his wants over everyone else's needs, no matter how serious the circumstances?

I thought again of the inscription I had put in his ring, *You Are All Men*, feeling ultimately stupid because obviously this collection of "all men" had included one man so devoid of responsibility that after twenty years of marriage he felt entitled to leave his former wife without resources, support, and most importantly, without her beloved children. And his demand of custody when he had no intention to put the child's needs at the forefront of his own seemed inexcusable.

I hated myself for being practical. Just once I wanted to be the petulant, demanding one who created havoc and twisted reality until I got my way. I just wasn't strong enough to be that weak.

I was at long last removed from the potential risk and stress of Mark's choices, but the distance didn't alleviate my sadness to see the same patterns that brought so much loss and misery to our family continue as the backdrop of my daughter's life, and now others, too. I watched, once removed, as a person might stand at an airport window and watch a plane crash after missing the flight by mere minutes. I couldn't help but feel thankful for having avoided the tragedy, but I felt guilty, too, as though I was meant to go down in flames with him, and had sidestepped my destiny unfairly.

Mark had received the same settlement as I, but ignoring any lessons he may have learned from the past, he was broke again in only ninety days. Creditors and his work crew were swiftly demanding their share of his new funds for a remodel that was costing far more than he originally planned. My children and I learned after the fact that he had actually secretly married his new girlfriend the very week we got divorced, reasoning he needed to pool their resources to survive.

Meanwhile, I paid all my bills from the settlement, including the studio debt because Denver, now filled with anger, claimed she had done me a favor by taking over and the associated debt was mine to address. What I wanted most was to perhaps purchase a little home for myself as Mark had done, or take a vacation and meet an exciting new man, but instead I choose to buckle down and clean the slate. I was slowly reclaiming the dignity of respect that comes with making responsible choices, something I had long since lost and deeply needed. Life was joyless during this period, but not embarrassing.

Mark then announced that now, after years of making excuses about why he could not pause to attend to his bad hips, he would be using his new wife's health insurance to get hip replacements. I felt circumstances were critical enough that we both had no choice but to dig in to support the kids and undo the damage our experiment had caused financially as well as emotionally. I understood more than anyone that his operation was long overdue, but his timing seemed one more act of aggression and a way to skirt taking responsibility for the mess he had created. If he had waited this long, might he not wait one more season and get the family stable first before turning his attentions and resources to his personal welfare yet again?

Mark's surgery provided him an excuse to avoid work or responsibilities for eighteen months, during which time he could not pay his own bills much less contribute a single dollar to his children's welfare. A few months later, he and his new wife bankrupted both their debt and all the escalating bills they'd built up excitedly pouring cash into their new home and attending to their health. For once, I wasn't the one facing the calls and discomfort of angry creditors because of gratification spending—a small consolation. But still, Mark's irresponsible decisions depressed me for reasons I couldn't explain.

Later, when he finally recuperated and was fit to work, he announced he was going to devote his life to his own dreams and aspirations. He'd decided to become a full-time basket weaver for a living. As a self-proclaimed "artist" he would not be able to devote any of his resources to school tuition, clothes, or any of the typical expenditures that come with raising kids. His new wife, on the cusp of turning sixty, emptied her retirement savings to fund a craft shop so Mark could make baskets and brooms for a living. In a letter to the kids he explained he no longer believed in Christmas gifts, nor did he feel obligated to spend money raising them just because society claimed a man should. At long last he had a life partner who supported him and loved him for who he was, so he was going to focus on himself at this stage in life. He asked the kids to understand and joyfully support his right to do what he loved and to view his decision as an example of bravery.

Being once removed from the crisis *du jour* should have softened my sadness, but the grief I felt over Mark's choices and the convenient way he rewrote our history clouded my brow and made me stare off into the distance, lost in thought, more often than not. Most painful was his proclaiming that he had finally found someone to love him for whom he was. Love was the motivation that made me willingly shelve my own artistic, dreamer traits to create a solid foundation for his to flourish for the last twenty years. He didn't recognize it then, or now.

People said to me, "There but for the grace of God ..." as if to remind me that escaping that downward spiral was a cause for celebration. But as each month put more distance between us—not time and space, but the clarity that comes with removing yourself from patterns long enough to see them clearly—I couldn't help but view the story of our past with raw honesty rather than through marital blinders. I had been infatuated with my husband's good looks, his charisma, and his childlike humor. I've always been a helpless romantic, so no wonder I had created a storybook tale of two dynamic, creative people on a life journey that defied traditional paths and chose to dismiss any signs to the contrary. For years I justified my husband's selfishness and the inequality between us out of blind loyalty, convincing myself I had married an *artiste*, which for some reason made him exempt from adult responsibilities or expectations.

When I told my best friend, someone who had witnessed all twenty years of my marriage, that Mark and I were getting a divorce, I expected her to be shocked. She shrugged and said she was sorry to hear the news, but not surprised.

"How can you not be surprised? I'm surprised. I never dreamed we could fall apart and things could get so ugly."

"That's because the problem with your marriage was obvious to everyone but you. Ginny loved Mark, and Mark loved Mark, but no one loved Ginny."

Hearing the words spoken out loud was devastating.

From that point on, I mourned my marriage, not because of what I lost, but what I now understood I never really had. Most of all, I mourned my lost innocence. Some days, when my heart felt empty and family memories made me ache for happier times, I sorely wished I'd been just stupid enough to preserve my blind delusions until death did us part. That certainly would have been easier in some ways.

But "easy" has never been what I want from life. I want substance.

"Nothing makes the earth seem so spacious as to have friends at a distance; they make the latitudes and longitudes."
—Henry David Thoreau

THERE ARE NO MISTAKES

Months later, I sat at a Starbucks sipping a cup of coffee before heading in to work. My new business was painfully, slowly, but surely beginning to build and I felt the first stirrings of contentment that accompanies being engaged in authentic work. My future looked promising, at least in a meager way, and I felt secure because for the first time in twenty years I didn't have to fear someone I loved exploiting or abusing my love or the resources I worked hard to establish. I was sending Kent money to help him get through college, and funding most of Neva's needs. Denver had gotten engaged, and though she and I still were not speaking, I sent her what money I could scratch together to help with the wedding, deeply dismayed at the fact that my daughter had no choice but to fund a budget ceremony all on her own. I made every sacrifice I could to assure my kids didn't feel destitute and vulnerable, all the time hiding my ever present fears of what was to become of us if I couldn't keep up with the financial demands.

When I learned my mother in law had passed away, I sobbed for days over the fact that I wasn't invited to the funeral. I also was not invited to the family celebration of my son's graduation, nor were Christmas cards responded to from my former sister in law as twenty years of friendship was shelved. I received searing hate mail from Mark's new wife, my former friend, and when I dared take exception to the rude correspondence, Mark claimed her offensive letter was "his proudest moment." After twenty years of sharing a warm, intimate connection with the Hendrys, the ease with which I was dismissed and made to feel grossly unwelcome broke my heart.

As was often the case in a quiet moment, my mind slipped away to the world I so dearly missed. I imagined Donkey chewing slowly on a carrot as I ran my hand along his back, my children laughing as they picked blueberries and watching the antics of our dogs. I remembered the rumbling sound of Mark's tractor in the field as he plowed over daffodils and tree trunks and how handsome and romantic I thought he was when covered in sweat and sawdust. I wondered where his orange hard hat was now, and if this too had gone the way of all the other personal items that held such meaning for me, items I had witnessed him insensitively selling on Craigslist, in garage sales, and at the local thrift stores without my approval. I wondered about Denver, if she was happy and healthy. I pined to be a part of her life and worried that her anger towards me would leave lasting damage on us both. I thought of my sister-in-law every single day, deeply concerned about how she was handling the loss of her mother, and feeling badly that the divorce would rob her of holiday traditions and family activities we had all come to know and love. I was feeling sad, missing my children, drowning in that familiar ache of motherhood-interrupted, a sadness I seemed to carry with me all the time now.

I had long since come to the conclusion that the five years I spent in the country had been a mistake, the great millstone of my life, an unworthy and unproductive garden. I, the formidable woman whom everyone considered so accomplished, talented, intelligent, and caring, had failed. I'd worked diligently, made a fortune, given heart and soul to my family, and yet ended up with nothing whatsoever to show for my life. I wasn't missing the money. I was missing the things that count most—the love and respect of my children and the family closeness. I missed being in love with a man whom I blindly assumed cared just as much for me in return. I even missed Mark's endless issues because they were all associated to my purpose. Without a self-inflicted crisis to troubleshoot, I didn't know what I was meant to do each day. I missed being the unrecognized factor that kept our family functioning, because I understood the importance of my sacrifices even if no one else did.

A daily mantra ran through my head. *If only I'd never moved. Never taken a risk. Never trusted Mark to take the reins of our life. Never dared pursue a life that put his devotion to family to the test.*

My meanderings were interrupted by the trill of my cell phone announcing a text. I put my coffee cup on the table to grab the phone, hoping to discover a message from one of my kids, but this message came from a number I didn't recognize. I put on my glasses to read the text.

Hey Ginny, I just got a new phone and they are showing me how to use it. Guess what? I can text now, thanks to you. I wanted you to be the first to see. Thank you. Thank you. I miss you. I love you. You are the best friend I ever had. Kathy.

Kathy was still reading! She was *texting!* And she was texting me. I glanced around at the well-dressed Floridians milling about, people reading the paper, working on a laptop or playing with their cellphones, and was hit with the realization that in a town far away lived one woman who understood something as commonplace as reading and texting was, in truth, an amazing gift. Because of Kathy and all I had endured, I understood the miracle of life's simple gifts, too.

I wanted to whoop right out loud. I placed the phone on the table so the message would stay illuminated, unwilling to let the words fade to black on my phone or in my mind.

Was moving truly a mistake? Can I honestly say I didn't have anything to show for my life just because I loved a man blindly and grabbed at a brass ring and missed?

I kept Kathy's message on my phone for many months, the inspiration I needed to live again. The origami project of my life had come unfolded, and the time had come to take that flat, overworked piece of paper and begin folding in the edges to create new angles and creases until something beautiful and interesting took shape once again. I needed to stop crying and start creating with the seasoned fingers of an artist who understands that starting from scratch reveals infinite possibilities.

So I set to the work of reinventing my life again: older, wiser, and armed with the lessons of the birds, the bees, and a million dollar donkey to guide the way.

From Thoreau's Journal: 22-Jan-1852

"I left the woods for as good a reason as I went there. Perhaps it seemed to me that I had several more lives to live, and could not spare any more time for that one... But why I changed? Why I left the woods? I do not think that I can tell. I have often wished myself back. I do not know any better how I ever came to go there. About 2 o'clock in the afternoon the world's axle creaked as if it needed greasing, as if the oxen labored with the wain and could hardly get their load over the ridge of the day. Perhaps if I lived there much longer, I might live there forever. One would think twice before he accepted heaven on such terms."

"Make the most of your regrets — never smother your sorrow but end and cherish it till it comes to have a separate and integral interest."
—*Henry David Thoreau*

EPILOGUE

So what did I do after the season of my life with Mark passed, other than suffer for a long, long time that unexplainable phantom pain that lingers after an infected limb is amputated to save a life?

I planted a new garden. Literally.

Six years later, I live on 7 beautiful acres and run a holistic yoga retreat center. I work harder than ever, but have been rewarded with a business that is successful, monetarily, as well as in regard to personal fulfillment and contribution to the community. My relationships with my children, parents and friends has not only healed over time, but grown stronger than ever before. Kathy and I communicate regularly over Facebook.

I visit my eldest daughter, still in Blue Ridge, from time to time. The town finally passed the liquor law and, as codes loosened, a Starbucks and several other franchises moved in, filling the town with so much traffic and tourist friendly attractions that Blue Ridge today barely resembles the scene of this story. Timing is everything, I suppose, because I'm quite sure the new improved Blue Ridge is not a place I'd choose for my grand life reinvention, had I a chance to do it all again.

The first few years of my recovery I worked diligently to grow my business while living in a small apartment that looked over a concrete parking lot. My longing for deeper connections, nature and space was almost unbearable, and while I was left with some deeply negative associations to country living, I didn't hesitate when the opportunity to move back to a more rural environment presented itself. I now dabble with hobby farming on a smaller level, enjoying the pleasures of canning, winemaking, animal husbandry, and nature crafts for pleasure, rather than combating with the natural world as my lifestyle model.

The first thing I did on my 7 acres was plant a large Chakra meditation garden. I took great joy in putting whatever color or type of plant I wanted in any place that suited my whim. Each day, before attending to life's endless tasks and responsibilities, I pull a few weeds, prune, plant new flowers, and pause to see what needs to be nurtured to keep the garden thriving. Afterwards, I wander amongst the plants with a cup of coffee to savor the poignancy of nature's remarkable ability to renew itself in the constant cycle of death and rebirth.

Everything I loved and lost has come back to me in a natural restructuring of life. The lessons gained from my adventure, however hard, fuel my happiness today. Even so, I still miss my donkey.